el

15X

10

THE "LUSITANIA" STEAMING 25½ KNOTS ON THE MEASURED MILE

THE

CUNARD TURBINE-DRIVEN QUADRUPLE-SCREW

ATLANTIC LINER

"LUSITANIA"

CONSTRUCTED AND ENGINED BY

MESSRS. JOHN BROWN AND CO., LTD.,

SHEFFIELD AND CLYDEBANK.

Reprinted from "ENGINEERING."

Patrick Stephens, Wellingborough

For my father

© New material in this edition 1986 Mark D. Warren

Originally published 1907
PSL edition first published 1986

4 6 8 10 9 7 5 3

British Library Cataloguing in Publication Data

"Lusitania".
The Cunard turbine-driven quadruple-screw
Atlantic liner
1. Lusitania (*Ship*)   2. Ocean liners —
Design and construction
623.8'2432   VM383.L/

ISBN 0-85059-847-8

*Patrick Stephens Limited is part of the
Thorsons Publishing Group*

Reproduced from the original. Additional material
photoset in 8 on 8½pt Century Old Style by
Harper Phototypesetters Limited, Northants.

Printed in Great Britain by
Butler & Tanner Ltd, Frome and London

INTRODUCTION

THIS book is primarily a facsimile reprint of a rare, limited-circulation volume, originally compiled in August 1907 from a series of five articles that had appeared in the magazine *Engineering*,* and published as a commemorative souvenir to mark the launch and forthcoming maiden voyage of the RMS *Lusitania*. To date, it has remained the most comprehensive published record of the construction and launch of the *Lusitania*. However, the measurements given in the section entitled 'The Saloons of the Ship' do not coincide with those found in the original master blueprints. In addition, photographs of many important interior views were lacking. For these reasons, a supplementary photograph and blueprint section has been added to this reprint, starting with Plate XLII on page 112. This section incorporates new material without undermining the integrity of the original publication.

The year 1907 was remarkable in the history of trans-oceanic navigation. Not only was it the centenary of the development by Robert Fulton of the steam-powered boat, but it also marked the maiden voyages of four of the largest ships in the world. On 8 May 1907, the White Star Line's *Adriatic*, then the largest British ship ever built, made her first voyage from Liverpool to New York. Norddeutscher Lloyd's *Kronprinzessin Cecilie* followed on 6 August, completing their fleet of four 23-knot express liners, and on 16 November the RMS *Mauretania* made her maiden voyage to New York. The most important date, however, was 7 September 1907, when Cunard's RMS *Lusitania* began her maiden voyage from Liverpool to New York. With great excitement, over 200,000 people waited until after dark to see the largest, fastest and most luxurious ship in the world sail off into history.

The *Lusitania* is best known today for her tragic sinking by a German submarine on 7 May 1915, with the loss of 1,201 lives, and her subsequent pivotal part in Twentieth Century world history by influencing America to ally herself with Great Britain. However, the *Lusitania* was also a pioneer — a ship of many 'firsts', which incorporated the most advanced marine engineering technology then known with a magnificent interior of unprecedented size. She was the first of many four-funneled British liners, the first ship over 700 ft in length to be powered by turbine engines, and the first ocean liner to be propelled by quadruple screws, which established a tradition in the design of the largest ships which followed.

Upon completing her second west-bound voyage to New York on 11 October 1907 the *Lusitania* became the first ship to cross the Atlantic in less than five days. Her record time was 4 days 19 hours and 52 minutes, at an average speed of 23.993 knots, a record she was later to break again and again. In July 1908 the *Lusitania* was the first ship to cross the Atlantic at an average speed of more than 25 knots, and in August 1911 was also the first ship to make two complete round trips to New York in less than one month.

The origin of the *Lusitania* dates back to 1897, when Germany's Norddeutscher Lloyd snatched the Blue Riband from England with the third voyage performance of the first four-funneled ocean liner, *Kaiser Wilhelm der Grosse*, which crossed from New York to Southampton in 5 days 17 hours and 8 minutes, averaging 22.35 knots. This record was to be broken by the Hamburg-American Line's four-funneled *Deutschland*, whose maiden voyage in July 1900 was 0.13 of a knot faster than the *Kaiser Wilhelm der Grosse's* previous record time. The next contender was the four-funneled Norddeutscher Lloyd's *Kronprinz Wilhelm*, built in 1901 to recapture the Blue Riband. This was achieved on 16 September 1902, when the *Kronprinz Wilhelm* shaved 26 minutes from the *Deutschland's* fastest west-bound crossing. The *Deutschland's* east-bound record was captured on 20 June 1906 by the third four-funneled Norddeutscher Lloyd ship, the *Kaiser Wilhelm II*, which had sailed on her maiden voyage some three years earlier.

All these speed records were more than disconcerting to the British, who were already demoralized by the fact that they no longer 'ruled the waves'. Worse still, the American financier, J. P. Morgan, had been buying up most of the Atlantic steamship firms, incorporating them into his own International Mercantile Marine Company. Cunard's largest British rival, the White Star Line, had succumbed to Morgan in 1902. As a result, fear spread that Cunard, the last major independent shipping firm, would be next.

In order to protect Cunard from falling under foreign control, an agreement was reached in 1902 whereby the British government loaned Cunard the money, at a nominal interest rate, to build two super-liners that would recapture the Blue Riband and restore British pride. Cunard was required to build the ships to exact Admiralty specifications, so that they could be used in the event of war. The government agreed to provide Cunard with an annual operating subsidy and guaranteed mail contracts. In these circumstances, then, the twin express liners, *Lusitania* and *Mauretania* were built.

The Admiralty specified that both ships would have all their vital machinery, boilers, steering mechanisms and rudder below the waterline, as added protection against attack. Each ship would have to be capable of maintaining an average ocean speed of 24½ knots in moderate weather, and if the average speed fell below that, a penalty would be levied in the form of a reduction in the annual subsidy. In addition to being at the disposal of the government, should war be declared, both ships had to be large enough to carry substantial six-inch deck guns.

In 1905 Cunard had experimented with various power plants by installing Parsons Turbine engines in the *Carmania*, and at the same time fitting her sister ship, the *Caronia*, with standard four-cylinder quadruple-expansion engines. The tests showed that the turbines in the *Carmania* increased the average speed by a full knot, so it was decided that they would be installed in the new express liners. The Admiralty, however, demanded an increase of two full knots, which required 68,000 horsepower, a 79 per cent increase over the most powerful engines then known.

Various proposals for the design of these two great ships had been submitted to Cunard by all the major British shipbuilders. The earliest of these dates from 1902, and shows the *Lusitania* with only three screws and three funnels. Eventually it was decided that, since the German express liners all had four funnels, Cunard could not have less. This proved a wise decision because passengers equated the number of funnels with the speed and safety of the ship, and therefore booked passage in great numbers on the 'four-stackers'. The main difference in the ships' appearance, however, was that the German liners had positioned their funnels in two pairs, whereas Cunard's funnels were evenly spaced.

The architect of the *Lusitania*, Leonard Peskett, had an overwhelming task to fulfil all the Admiralty's demands, and at the same time meet Cunard's requirements for the 2,165 expected passengers and the crew of 850.

Forced to locate all the ship's vital machinery below the waterline, Peskett built the ship high to accommodate the large numbers of passengers and crew. Six decks were built 56 feet above the waterline, a plan which would allow an unprecedented amount of space for many public rooms to be decorated by the Scottish architect, James Millar. Their dimensions, given in the following paragraphs, were taken directly from the original large-scale blueprints of the *Lusitania*.

The largest room on board was the three-deck high First Class Dining Saloon, the perimeter of which was 85 ft long and 81 ft wide on the Upper Deck. It came equipped with a 17 ft long mahogany sideboard with brass fittings, and seating for 323 passengers at one time. The Dining Saloon's second floor on the Shelter Deck measured 65 ft square, and could seat 147 passengers. It, too, had a 16 ft 6 in mahogany and brass sideboard. Both floors were capped with an enormous 29 ft by 23 ft 6 in eliptical plaster dome, rising 27 ft 6 in above the Upper Deck floor. The Dining Saloon was decorated in Louis XVI style, with highly ornate carved mahogany walls which were enamelled white and embellished in gold. The plaster dome had four oval panels painted after Boucher. The fancy oak parquet floors and rose-coloured upholstery of the seats completed the picture.

On the Boat Deck, directly above the First Class Dining Saloon dome, was the First Class Lounge and Music Room, which measured 68 ft by 55 ft and was enclosed by walls of inlaid mahogany panelling in the late Georgian style. A 51 ft 6 in by 23 ft 6 in barrel-vaulted plaster and stained glass ceiling rose to a height of 18 ft. The furnishings in this room included a grand piano, green carpeting and two enormous green marble fireplaces, each 14 ft high.

The Grand Entrance on the Boat Deck was found just forward of the Lounge and Music Room. This spacious H-shaped room with white enamelled mahogany walls measured 49 ft square. Its central attraction was the exquisite wrought iron and gilded bronze elevator cage and railings, surrounded on three sides by wide staircases, and crowned with a 21 ft 6 in by 18 ft skylight. Carved white Corinthian columns, 9 ft 6 in high, supported the ceiling. At one point, the white walls around the first landing reached a height of 18 ft 6 in.

The Grand Entrance led directly forward into the First Class Writing Room and Library. This measured 53 ft by 41 ft, was decorated in the late 18th Century Brothers Adam style, with etched glass windows and panels of grey silk brocade on cream-coloured walls. The aft end of the room was fitted with a large mahogany bookcase of 18th Century style, which measured 23 ft long and 9 ft high. Across the room, facing the bookcase, was a black and white marble fireplace surmounted by a mirror. The delicately moulded 10 ft 6 in high plaster ceiling had an elegant circular leaded glass skylight, 9 ft 6 in in diameter, which raised the ceiling height to 14 ft. All this was supported by carved white Corinthian columns 9 ft 6 in high.

At the other end of the Boat Deck was the First Class Verandah Café, measuring 49 ft 3 in by 23 ft 6 in, and including potted trees under a 17 ft by 13 ft 6 in skylight.

From the Verandah Café, the Boat Deck gangway extended to the Second Class area of the ship, which was not as grand as First Class, but was still impressive by 1907 standards. The first room one encountered from the gangway was the octagonal Second Class Lounge, which measured 43 ft 6in by 39 ft, and had a 21 ft by 17 ft skylight over the staircase, rising to a height of 15 ft. This staircase led down to the Second Class Ladies Drawing Room, whose tapered perimeter measured 42 ft by 28 ft. A large leaded glass dome 13 ft in diameter brought the height of the room to 12 ft 3 in. Around the entire perimeter were comfortable rose-coloured banquettes that matched the colour of the carpeting. An upright piano provided the means of entertainment.

Abaft the Ladies Drawing Room was the Second Class Smoking Room, tapered in shape and measuring 38 ft by 52 ft, with walls of highly polished mahogany. This room also had a high barrel-vaulted ceiling with a 14 ft by 18 ft skylight, which rose to a height of 13 ft. The large, rectangular, bluish milk glass windows and the banquettes that surrounded the room added to the effect of total comfort.

On the Upper Deck, located two decks below the Second Class Smoking Room, was the Second Class Dining Saloon, which measured 61 ft by 74 ft, could accommodate 259 passengers at one sitting, and included an upright piano and a mahogany sideboard 24 ft 6 in long, 9 ft 9 in high, and 3 ft deep. A striking feature of the room was a circular balustraded opening 19 ft in diameter, and rising 19 ft to the Shelter Deck above, whose ceiling was supported by a single centre column.

The largest Third Class public room was the Dining Saloon on the Upper Deck, which measured 79 ft 6 in by 58 ft, could seat 332 passengers at one time, and also included an upright piano.

Many views of the public rooms described above have been included in the supplementary section of photographs and blueprints in this book. The original page design has

**Engineering: An Illustrated Weekly Journal*. Published in London 1 and 8 June 1906, 12 and 19 July and 2 August 1907.

been adhered to so that these new photographs blend with the original material. In order to maintain the book's former style of short captions, the following notes were omitted from the captions to the new photographs:

In Plate XLIII, figure 236, showing *The First Class Writing Room and Library*, teacups have been cleared from the tables for the photographer, and placed temporarily inside the bookcase. The photographer's tripod and camera appears in the reflection of the mirrors in Plate XLVII, figure 244, Plate XLIX, figure 249 and is just visible in Plate LIII, figure 257. The photograph of the *First Class Barber's Shop*, Plate XLIX, figure 249, was made from the original glass negative which, along with many others, subsequently became cracked. This fracture is now visible in the form of a jagged line in the upper left-hand corner. *The Third Class General Room*, Plate LII, figure 255, is set for dining, although the Dining Saloon is actually located on the deck below.

The Deck Plan of the Bridge is a new addition inserted on page 101, where previously there was a blank page.

It should be noted that illustration plates I—XLI appear after page 62, as they did in the original volume, and not in the order inexplicably given in the list of illustrations on pages 6 and 7, which is also reproduced in its 1907 form and to which details of the additional illustrations in this reprint have been added.

MARK D. WARREN
NEW YORK, APRIL 1986

ACKNOWLEDGEMENTS

I WOULD like to acknowledge the assistance of those people who helped me in compiling the photographs in the new section, as well as in the production of the book. They include: in Newport News, Virginia, Mr Ardie Kelly of the Mariners' Museum; in Baltimore, Maryland, Ms Laura Brown at the Steamship Historical Society of America; in Liverpool, England, Dr Alan Scarth at the Merseyside Maritime Museum and Mr Rowland Brown at the Cunard Archives, University of Liverpool; in London, Messrs Martin Taylor and Terry Charman of the Imperial War Museum, and Messrs James Vaudrey and David Slough; in Edinburgh, Scotland, Messrs George Balbour, Peter G. Vasey, Bruno Longmore and J. D. Galbraith of the Scottish Record Office, as well as Messrs Richard Bacon and John Bain; in New York, Ms Terry Ariano at the Museum of the City of New York, Mr Dennis Hudson, Mr Jim Mairs of W. W. Norton & Company and Mr Herbert Gstalder of the Bettmann Archives.

Special thanks for most generous assistance go to Mr Allan Lang of International Book Marketing Ltd, and Mr Thomas Coffey, both of New York; Mrs Alma Topen and the staff·at the University of Glasgow Archives; Mrs Catherine Stecchini of Princeton, New Jersey; and Mr Darryl Reach, Editorial Director of Patrick Stephens Ltd.

PHOTOGRAPHIC SOURCES

Page 6: Scottish Record Office, Edinburgh; Plate XLII: Museum of the City of New York, New York City (both); Plate XLIII: Museum of the City of New York (both); Plate XLIV: Museum of the City of New York (both); Plate XLV: Museum of the City of New York (both); Plate XLVI: Scottish Record Office (both); Plate XLVII: Scottish Record Office (both); Plate XLVIII: Scottish Record Office (both); Plate XLIX: Museum of the City of New York (top), Scottish Record Office (bottom); Plate L: Museum of the City of New York (both); Plate LI: Cunard booklet, 'Lusitania — Mauretania and some notes concerning them' ca 1910 (both); Plate LII: 'Lusitania — Mauretania and some notes concerning them' (top), Scottish Record Office (bottom); Plate LIII: Scottish Record Office (both); Plate LIV: Museum of the City of New York (both); Plate LV: Scottish Record Office (top), Culver Pictures, New York (bottom); Plate on page 101, and Plates LVI, LVII and LVIII: Keeper of the Records of Scotland, Upper Clyde Shipbuilders' collection, John Brown Shipbuilding and Engineering Company.

BIBLIOGRAPHY

The Shipbuilder, *The Cunard Express Liners Lusitania and Mauretania*: Reprinted by Patrick Stephens Ltd, London, 1970. Simpson, Colin, *The Lusitania*: Little, Brown and Company, Boston, 1972. Shaum, John H. Jr, and Flayhart, William H., III, *Majesty at Sea*: Patrick Stephens Ltd, Wellingborough, 1984 and W. W. Norton & Company, New York, 1984. Miller, William H. Jr, *The First Great Ocean Liners in Photographs, 193 Views 1897-1927*: Dover Publications, Inc, New York, 1984.

EARLY THREE-FUNNEL PROTOTYPE SHIPBUILDER'S MODEL OF THE *LUSITANIA.*

GENERAL INDEX.

LIST OF ILLUSTRATIONS.

LIST OF ADDITIONAL ILLUSTRATIONS

THE CUNARD TURBINE-DRIVEN QUADRUPLE-SCREW ATLANTIC LINER "LUSITANIA."

THE Lusitania is a most encouraging success. It is not so much that her official trials, reported later, promise the realisation of the contract condition that she shall make a double voyage on the Atlantic between Liverpool and New York at an average speed of 24½ knots within a year of her entering the service—this is gratifying in the highest degree—but the success carries a greater significance. Although the vessel certainly marks the progress so far in marine construction, she must, further, be regarded as a pioneer—as beginning a new era. This is because of the adoption and success on a huge scale of the steam-turbine as a ship-propelling engine. Other vessels, it is true, are now run by turbine-driven screws; but when the system was decided upon for the Lusitania, the experience with this type of engine on a large scale was limited, and particularly so as regards durability. The confidence of the owners and builders of this ship, now justified by trials, gives promise that the future will see greater developments. In writing thus we do not disparage in the slightest degree the great work of the constructors. The Lusitania marks a step—great, but still only a step—beyond which Messrs. John Brown and Co., Limited, will probably be among the first to advance, because any review of the past, as well as of the achievements of the Lusitania, offers abundant encouragement for the future. We find that each successive generation has had at command almost equal mental activity and mechanical ingenuity, with the important addition, that lapse of time brings accumulated experience, to enable higher results to be achieved. The problems are now greater, if more clearly defined by reason of our more exact scientific knowledge; but the encouragement afforded by past successes is also greater; and thus there is no reason to suppose that the Lusitania will be other than a stimulant to greater effort to surmount new difficulties and sweep away new obstacles which beset the path of progress in the most fascinating of all branches of applied mechanics—the rapid, comfortable, and safe transportation of passengers across the seas, often turbulent and ever resistant, which separate the increasingly friendly nations of different continents.

Conscious that any study of the past, as well as any contemplation of the achievement of the present, is useful as an incentive to renewed activity, we may premise our description of the great Cunard liner with a brief review of the progress of marine construction as applied to Atlantic steamships. Such a review will serve to support our contention that the development of the full-speed liner has not yet reached finality. The stories extant of the Savannah, Royal William, Sirius, Great Western, and other early Victorian vessels which essayed ocean voyages with the assistance of steam, have often been told. Then, however, sails were the main propelling agent, and even in Brunel's leviathan of 1843—the Great Britain—which was little more than one-third the length and less than one-tenth the tonnage of the Lusitania, the great spread of canvas bulked largely in the hopes of the captain in reaching his destination. The question of steam economy had not then been tackled with full knowledge of thermodynamics. When the Cunard Company started their regular service in 1840 the steam pressures available were 9 lb. to 12 lb. per square inch, and the coal consumption was at the rate of 5 lb. per unit of power per hour. Our knowledge of hull form in relation to resistance was but meagre. The splendid high-tensile steel of to-day, equal to the withstanding of a strain of 40 tons per square inch, was not then available. One must, therefore, grant as great a mede of praise to Mr. (afterwards Sir) Samuel Cunard, Mr. (afterwards Sir) George Burns, and Mr. David McIver,

for their courage in commencing a regular steamship service with our then indefinite knowledge of marine machinery, as to their successors at Liverpool in ordering two ships of nearly double the displacement of some of their competitors on the Atlantic, and with an engine-power 50 per cent. greater than that of any existing steamship.

Progress in speed was necessarily slow. By 1850 12 knots had been attained, by 1862 13 knots. The time of the trans-Atlantic passage had thus been reduced from about fourteen days to eight days twenty-two hours, the latter the performance of the Scotia, the last of the Cunard paddle-steamers. In this ship there was an increase of nearly 90 per cent. in the displacement, and of 440 per cent. in the horse-power, as compared with the first Cunard liner, in order to ensure a gain of about 50 per cent. in the speed. John Elder had, in the interval, introduced his compound vertical inverted-cylinder engine. His first application in 1854, but progress even here was slow, largely because of the difficulty of securing reliable metal for the boilers working at higher steam pressures. By this time also the screw-propeller had proved efficient, and the Great Britain, of 1843, with chain-geared engines, was the first of the Atlantic liners to be driven by the screw-propeller. The Cunard Company adopted the screw for the first time in fast liners in the China, completed in 1862; but in the slower Cunard liners the screw was applied in 1852. Meanwhile we had, in 1854, Brunel's great triumph in the Great Eastern, built by Scott Russell. It was a triumph, because subsequent experience has enabled the naval architect, if not the general public, to realise that in this work he foreshadowed, if he did not point the way to, great developments.

An important step was made by the Cunard Company when they ordered the Russia from the Clydebank Works in the 'sixties. She was, in a measure, the forerunner of the modern high-speed steamer. With a tonnage of 2960 tons gross and engines of 3000 horse-power, she had a speed on the Atlantic of 14½ knots, and her consumption of coal was only 90 tons per day, as compared with 159 tons in the side-paddle-steamer Scotia, of similar capacity, alike for passengers and cargo. There followed a succession of six or seven Cunarders from the Clydebank Works, each larger than its predecessor—the Abyssinia, the Algeria, the Bothnia, the Gallia, and the Servia.

No record of progress would be possible without some reference to the great work of the late Sir Edward Harland and the late Sir William Pearce, both of whom exercised far-reaching influence, particularly on the form of hull, as well as on the enterprise associated with the Atlantic steamship competition. The former began with the White Star liner Oceanic in 1871, followed by the Britannic and Germanic in 1874; the latter with the Arizona in 1879. The City of Rome, constructed by the old Barrow company in 1881, also contributed, although in some measure in a negative form, to the problem of Atlantic steam navigation. We do not propose to analyse the dimensions of the several successive steamers. The list of dimensions given on the next page, along with a diagram of results, the comparative cross-sections on page 11, and the profiles of successive notable ships published on pages 12 and 13 will, we hope, create a desire on the part of the student to investigate this subject more closely than we can do here.

The Servia maintained a speed of 17 knots on a daily consumption of coal of 190 tons, so we find that in forty years from the institution of the Cunard line the speed had doubled — from 8½ to 17 knots—but the power had gone up to 10,000 indicated horse-power, or from 0.36 indi-

cated horse-power per ton displacement to nearly one indicated horse-power per ton displacement. Owing to the increased steam pressure, however, the coal consumption per unit of power was greatly reduced, and thus, although power had increased more than fourteen-fold, the coal consumption on the voyage had only gone up barely three times. An effort was next made to reduce the size and displacement of ships. The cargo carried by these middle Victorian era high-speed ships was in some cases equal to 15 to 20 per cent. of the displacement, and the outlay for power, alike in first cost, fuel consumption, working expenses, and depreciation, became so steadily greater that the carrying of cargo was beginning to be unprofitable. This movement for the elimination of cargo then begun has continued, and to-day the proportion of cargo to the total displacement in high-speed liners is less than 5 per cent.

The beginning of the movement towards the purely passenger liner was probably inaugurated with the Aurania, built at Clydebank in 1882. Just as the Gallia, in 1879, had been opposed by the Arizona, and the Servia in 1881 by the Alaska and the City of Rome, so the Aurania found a keen competitor, in 1883, in the Oregon, and the consequence was a series of great contests on the Atlantic. The Aurania, as is shown in our table on page 10, was not only a deep ship, but a broad ship for her length; and one may almost date from this period the advance in these proportions.

The America, which was built at Clydebank in 1884, was a great step forward; and one may trace from the model of this ship the subsequent stages in trans-Atlantic steamship-design. The America, on her first voyage home, broke the record—a performance never before achieved by a new vessel—attaining a speed of well over 18 knots, which at that period was a remarkable performance. The net result of the competition during the five years between 1879 and 1884 was an increase from about 16 to just over 18 knots. The vessels of this quinquennial period gave rise to the term "greyhounds of the Atlantic," and opinion seems still to give the steamers of those years credit for great advance in speed; but the addition of the 2 miles per hour to speed throws into brilliant contrast the great step taken in the Lusitania, where, at one bound, the speed is to be increased by an equal amount, notwithstanding that the augmentation involves such a great increment to power.

In 1884 the Cunard Company had built the Umbria and Etruria, and these vessels succeeded in reducing the Atlantic record between Queenstown and New York to 6 days 1 hour 44 minutes, and between New York and Queenstown to 6 days 3 hours 12 minutes, the mean speed on the runs being about 19.2 knots. In fifty years from the first advent of the Cunard liners in the Atlantic we thus find an advance in speed from 8½ to 19 knots; while, at the same time, the size, passenger accommodation, and cargo capacity very considerably increased. The improvement in boiler and engine efficiency made an increase in the coal consumption only four times, although the power was twenty times greater. The results are briefly set out in Table II., on page 11.

From Clydebank there came, in 1888, the Paris and New York, two of the most remarkable ships of that period, and as competitors they had the Majestic and Teutonic of the White Star Line, built by Harland and Wolff at Belfast. Again we had keen competition, with the result that the Clydebank ships asserted their superiority, and reduced the time on the outward voyage by nearly twelve hours, and on the homeward run by 7¼ hours, the mean speed attained being in the former case nearly 20¾ knots. This was the per-

DIMENSIONS AND PERFORMANCES OF NOTABLE ATLANTIC STEAMERS.

TABLE I.—DIMENSIONS, &c., OF NOTABLE ATLANTIC STEAMERS.

Steamer's Name.	Builders.	Date.	Moulded Dimensions. Length.	Moulded Dimensions. Breadth.	Moulded Dimensions. Depth.	Proportion of Length To Beam.	Proportion of Length To Depth.	Draught.	Displacement.	Gross Tonnage.	Cylinders. Diameter in Inches.	Cylinders. Stroke.	Boilers. Heating Surface.	Boilers. Grate Area.	Boilers. Working Pressure.	Indicated Horse-Power.	Speed on Trial.
			ft.	ft. in.	ft. in.			ft. in.	tons			in.	sq. ft.	sq. ft.	lb.		knots
Great Eastern	Scott Russell ..	1858	680	83 0	57 6	8.192	11.826	25 6	27,000	24,360	Screw, four 84-in.; paddle, four 74-in.	S., 48; P., 174	..	..	30	7,650	14.5
Britannic .	Harland & Wolff	1874	455	45 0	36 0	10.111	12.640	23 6	8,500	5,004	Two 48-in., two 83-in.	60	..	..	70	5,500	16
Arizona ..	Fairfield Co. ..	1879	450	45 2	37 6	9.955	12.000	22 0	..	5,147	One 62-in., two 90-in.	66	..	..	90	6,300	17
Servia.. .	Clydebank Works ..	1881	515	52 0	40 6	9.903	12.716	23 3	9,900	7,392	One 72-in., two 100-in.	78	27,483	1014	90	10,300	17
Alaska ..	Fairfield Co. ..	1881	500	50 0	39 8	10.00	12.607	22 0	..	6,932	One 68-in., two 100-in.	72	..	..	100	10,500	18
City of Rome	Barrow Co. ..	1881	543	52 0	38 9	10.432	14.000	22 0	11,230	8,141	Three 46-in., three 86-in.	72	29,286	1398	90	11,900	18.23
Aurania ..	Clydebank Works ..	1882	470	57 0	39 0	8.245	12.051	20 9	8,800	7,269	One 68-in., two 91-in.	72	23,284	1001	90	8,500	17.5
Oregon ..	Fairfield Co. ..	1883	500	54 0	40 0	9.259	12.500	23 0	10,500	7,375	One 70-in., two 104-in.	72	38,047	1428	110	13,300	18.3
America ..	Clydebank Works ..	1884	432	51 0	38 0	8.470	11.520	23 0	9,300	6,500	One 63-in., two 91-in.	66	22,750	882	95	7,354	17.8
Umbria ..	Fairfield Co. ..	1884	500	57 0	40 0	8.772	12.500	22 6	10,500	7,718	One 71-in., two 105-in.	72	38,817	1606	110	14,321	20.18
Lahn	Ditto	1887	448	48 10	36 6	9.174	12.247	23 0	7,700	5,661	Two $32\frac{1}{2}$-in., one 68-in., and two 85-in.	72	..	..	150	8,900	17.78
Paris*.. ..	Clydebank Works .	1888	528	63 0	41 10*	8.373	12.610	23 0	13,000	10,499	Two 45-in., two 71-in., and two 113-in.	60	50,265	1293	150	20,600	21.8
Augusta Victoria	Vulcan Company, Stettin	1889	460	55 6	39 0	8.288	11.795	22 9	9,500	7,661	Two $41\frac{5}{16}$-in., two $66\frac{15}{16}$-in., and two $106\frac{5}{16}$-in.	63	36,000	1120	150	14,110	18.31
Columbia ..	Laird Brothers	1889	463	55 6	39 0	8.333	11.860	22 9	9,500	7,578	Two 41-in., two 66-in., and two 101-in.	66	34,916	1226	150	13,680	19.15
Teutonic ..	Harland and Wolff	1890	565	57 6	42 2	9.826	13.425	22 0	12,000	9,686	Two 43-in., two 68-in., and two 110-in.	60	40,072	1154	180	19,500	21
Normannia ..	Fairfield Co. ..	1890	500	57 3	38 0	8.730	13.150	22 0	10,500	8,716	Two 40-in., two 67-in., and two 106-in.	66	46,490	1452	160	16,352	20.78
Spree	Vulcan Company, Stettin	1890	463	51 6	37 6	9.00	12.346	22 0	8,900	6,963	Two 38-in., one 75-in., and two 100-in.	72	..	..	165	13,000	19.6
Fürst Bismarck	Ditto	1891	503	57 3	38 0	8.777	13.224	22 6	10,200	8,000	Two $43\frac{3}{8}$-in., two 67-in., and two $106\frac{1}{4}$-in.	63	47,000	1450	157	16,412	20.7
Campania ..	Fairfield Co. ..	1893	600	65 0	41 6	9.231	14.457	23 0	18,000	12,500	Four 37-in., two 79-in., and four 98-in.	69	82,000	2630	165	30,000	22.01 ‡
St. Louis	Cramp, Philadelphia	1895	536	63 0	42 0	8.50	12.75	26 0	16,000	11,629	Four 28-in., two 55-in., two 77-in., four 77-in.	60	40,320	1144	200	18,000	21.08 ‡
Kaiser Wilhelm der Grosse	Vulcan Company, Stettin	1897	625	66 0	43 0	9.46	14.27	28 0	20,880	14,349	Two 52-in., two 89-in., and four 96.4-in.	68.8	84,285	2618	178	30,000	22.5 ‡ to 23
Oceanic	Harland and Wolff	1899	685	68 5	49 0	10.01	13.98	32 6	28,500	17,274	Two 47.5-in., two 79-in., four 93-in.	72	74,686	1962	192	27,000	20.72 ‡
Deutschland	Vulcan Company, Stettin	1900	662.9	67 0	44 0	9.89	15.06	29 0	23,620	16,502	Four 36.61-in., two 73.6-in., two 103.9-in., and four 106.3-in.	72.8	85,468	2188	220	36,000	23.25 to 23.5‡
Kronprinz Wilhelm	Ditto	1901	663†	66 0	43 0	..	..	29 0	21,300	15,000	Four 34.2-in., two 68.8-in., two 98.4-in., and four 102.3-in.	70.8	93,685	2702	213	36,000	23.25 to 23.5‡
Kaiser Wilhelm II.	Ditto	1903	678	72 0	52 6	9.41	12.9	29 0	26,000	20,000	Four 37.4-in., four 49.2-in., four 74.8-in., and four 112.2-in.	70.86	107,643	3121	225	38,000	23.5‡
La Provence	St. Nazaire Works	1906	597 ft. $1\frac{1}{2}$ in.	64 $7\frac{1}{2}$	41 8	9.23	14.35	26 9	19,160	13,750	Two 47.2-in., two 76.2-in., four 88.18-in.	66.9	58,342	1571	200	30,000	22.05
Lusitania	Clydebank Works	1907	760	88	60 $4\frac{1}{2}$	8.65	12.56	33 6	38,000	32,500	Turbines	..	158,350	4048	195	68,000	25

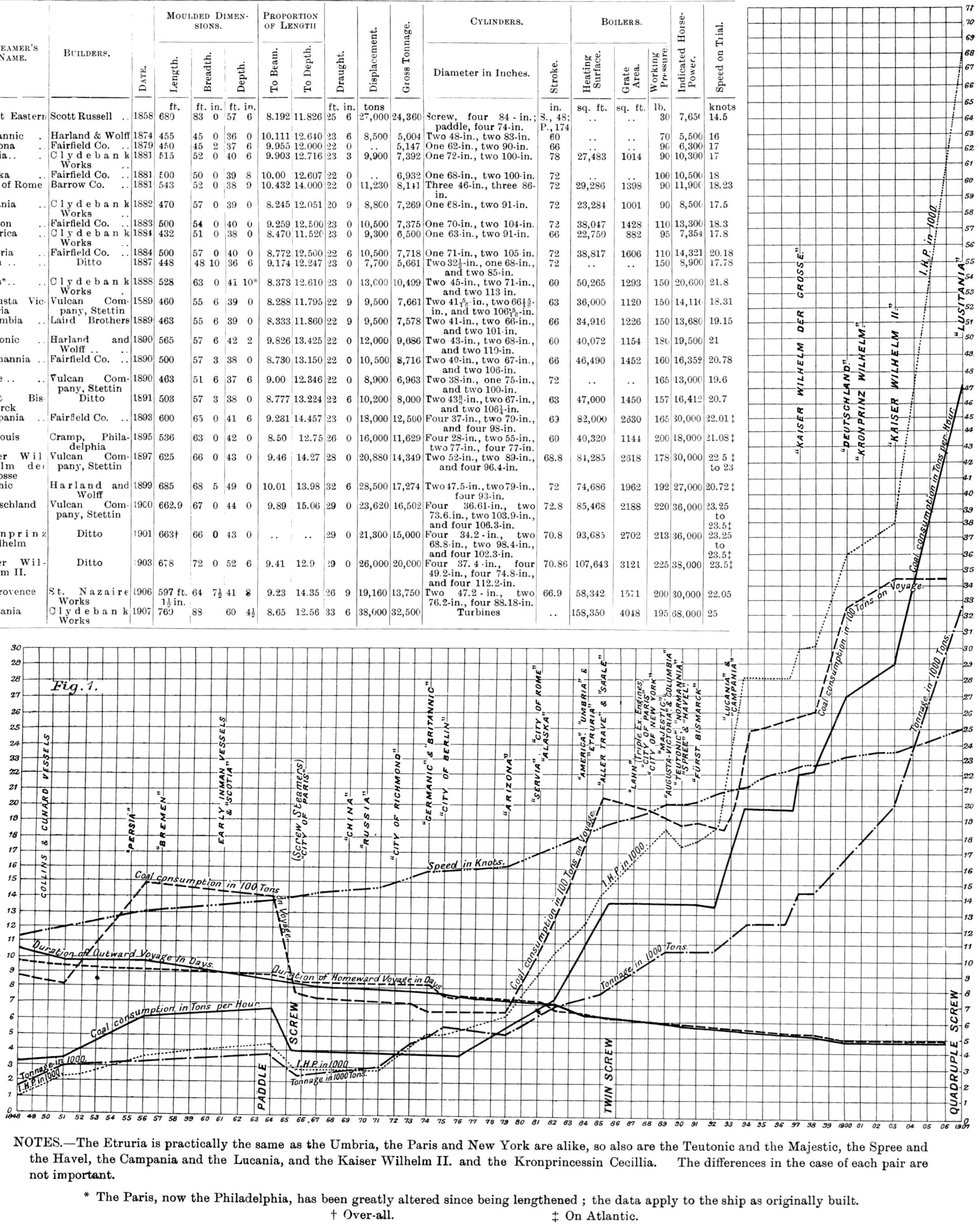

NOTES.—The Etruria is practically the same as the Umbria, the Paris and New York are alike, so also are the Teutonic and the Majestic, the Spree and the Havel, the Campania and the Lucania, and the Kaiser Wilhelm II. and the Kronprincessin Cecillia. The differences in the case of each pair are not important.

* The Paris, now the Philadelphia, has been greatly altered since being lengthened ; the data apply to the ship as originally built.

† Over-all. ‡ On Atlantic.

TABLE II.—*Coal Consumption of Cunard Atlantic Liners.*

—	"Britannia," 1840.	"Persia," 1856.	"Gallia," 1879.	"Umbria," 1884.	"Campania," 1893.	"Lusitania," 1907.
Coal necessary to steam to New York .. tons	570	1400	836	1,900	2,900	5,000*
Cargo carried .. ,,	224	750	1700	1,000	1,620	1,500
Passengers .. ,,	115	250	320	1,225	1,700	2,198
Indicated horse-power..	710	3600	5000	14,500	30,000	68,000
Steam pressure .. lb	9	33	75	110	165	200
Coal per indicated horse-power per hour lb	5.1	3.8	1.9	1.9	1.6	1.45 *
Speed .. .. knots	8.5	13.1	15½	19	22	25

* Estimated.

formance which the Cunard Company determined to excel in their Campania and Lucania, of which

DEVELOPMENT OF INTERNATIONAL COMPETITION.

So far, with but few interruptions, the competition had been between one British line and another, and one British firm of constructors and another, but the German steamship companies had been steadily drawing into line. The North German Lloyd, which had originally entered the lists in 1857, and had shown great enterprise, being the first among the mail lines to adopt triple-expansion engines on the Atlantic, had had their boats built mostly on the Clyde. The advent of the Kaiser Wilhelm der Grosse in 1897 gave the competition an international character. From this time forward, indeed, the German lines and German builders have had undisputed possession of the credit of record speeds on the Atlantic. From

tive may here terminate with Table III., page 12, showing the record passages made by notable ships in successive periods. These may not be the best performances of each ship, as it sometimes happens, as in the case of the Umbria and Etruria, and also of the Campania and Lucania, that, after many years, even when they have been excelled by competing ships, they have done better steaming than when newer. Indeed, it is at once a high tribute to the builders, and to the care with which the ships are worked at sea and tended in harbour, that the Cunarders we have named occupy to-day a high place in the estimation of the public, and, further, contribute to the unique circumstance that on the Atlantic, under the same flag, there is now, or will soon be, a single-screw, a twin-screw, a triple-screw—the Carmania—and a quadruple-screw steamship.

The progress marked since the advent of the

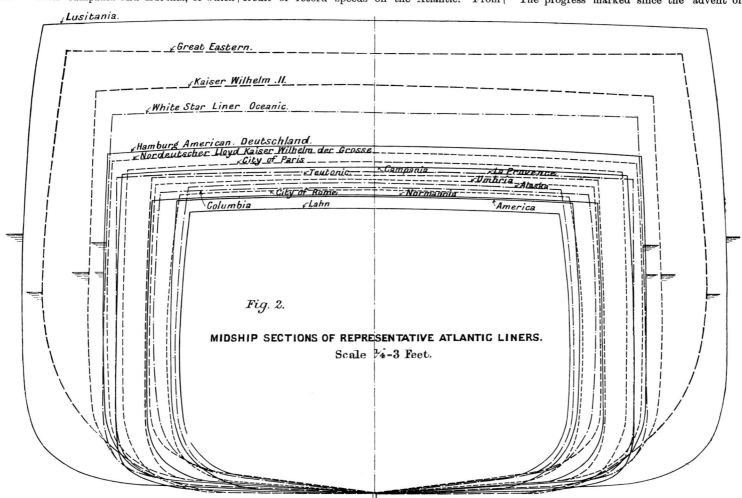

Fig. 2.

MIDSHIP SECTIONS OF REPRESENTATIVE ATLANTIC LINERS.

Scale ¼-3 Feet.

FIG. 2. COMPARATIVE CROSS-SECTIONS OF ATLANTIC LINERS.

we gave a very complete account in our issue of April 21, 1893.* The table on page 10, to which we have already referred, gives the comparative dimensions of these several liners, and it will be seen from the details of the proportions of length to beam and to depth that Clydebank still favoured broad and deep ships, and events have since proved their utility. The broad beam had also the advantage of enabling the ends of the ship to be finer, while minimising the draught for a given displacement ; and here also subsequent progress suggests development of opinion in favour of the beamy ship. The Campania and Lucania were completed for the Cunard Line in 1893, and for several years held the supreme position. They were neither so beamy nor so deep, in proportion to their length, as some of their predecessors, but the length had become 600 ft. between perpendiculars, and the beam 65 ft. The limitations of harbours and docks were beginning to be experienced. The result of the performance on the Atlantic of the Campania and Lucania was to bring down the trans-Atlantic record to just under five days eight hours, the speed developed being, on the outward voyage, 21.82 knots, and on the homeward trip 22.01 knots.

* ENGINEERING, vol. lv., page 463.

the Vulcan Works at Stettin there have come five ships of undoubtedly commendable character. The first we have already named, the second was the Deutschland, of 1898, the third the Kronprinz Wilhelm, of 1901, the fourth the Kaiser Wilhelm II., of 1903, and this year the Kronprincessen Cecillia left on her first voyage on the 9th of August. The dimensions of all these vessels, with the exception of the last, are given in the table on page 10, so that it is not necessary here to refer at length to any of the ships, more particularly as they have been, with the exception of the last, fully illustrated in ENGINEERING.* The last-named is a sister - ship to the Kaiser Wilhelm II., but with slightly greater boiler power, so as to develop 45,000 indicated horse-power, instead of 40,000 indicated horse-power. She will thus probably excel the performance of the Kaiser Wilhelm II., but must fall far short of the results of the new Cunard liners. Our historical narra-

* For Kaiser Wilhelm der Grosse, see ENGINEERING, vol. lxiv., page 415.
For Deutschland, see ENGINEERING, vol. lxx., pages 247, 340, 381, 532, 610, 662, 723, 763, 823.
For Kronprinz Wilhelm, see ENGINEERING, vol. lxxii., page 370.
For Kaiser Wilhelm II., see ENGINEERING, vol. lxxvi., pages 37, 143, 193, 244, 276, 329, 341, 376, 444.

Umbria, 23 years ago, is instructive. The length has been increased fully 50 per cent.; the displacement is more than three times what it was. The power of machinery has been multiplied nearly five-fold, but so great is the difficulty of adding to high speed that the Lusitania, notwithstanding its enormous advance in size and power, will probably add no more than 25 per cent. to the speed.

FAST versus INTERMEDIATE STEAMERS.

Table III., on the next page, indicates the present undoubted supremacy for speed of the German liners on the Atlantic. There are now four ships excelling our fastest steamer in speed, and another is being added. However great the credit to Germany, it may be accepted that there never was, even in German opinion, any doubt as to the ability of the British marine constructor to maintain his position. The opportunity alone has been wanting. In this country there has been a tendency in favour of what is now termed the intermediate ship, and there is much to be said in commendation, from the health-seeking passenger's point of view, of a leisurely voyage, lasting some ten days, instead of the five days from port to port of the high-speed liner. The comfort is the same, and there has consequently been built a greater number of such

TABLE III.—*Some Recent Record Performances.*

Record-Breaking Steamers.		Time.			Speed	Best Day's Run.
		days	hrs.	min.	knots	
In 1840 Britannia's trip—Liverpool to New York		14	0	0	8½	—
In 1862 Scotia's trip—Liverpool to New York		8	22	0	13	—
Servia, 1884	Outwards	7	10	47	—	—
	Homewards	6	23	57	—	—
Oregon, 1884	Outwards	6	10	9	—	—
	Homewards	6	16	59	—	—
America, 1884. Homewards		6	14	18	—	—
Umbria, or Etruria	Outwards	6	1	44	19.3	501
	Homewards	6	3	12	19.1	—
Paris, or New York	Outwards	5	14	24	20.7	530
	Homewards	5	19	57	20.1	—
Campania, or Lucania, 1904	Outwards	5	7	23	21.82	562
	Homewards	5	8	38	22.01	533
Kaiser Wilhelm der Gross, 1902	Cherbourg - Sandy Hook	5	15	20	22.81	580
Kaiser Wilhelm der Grosse, 1901	Sandy Hook-Plymouth	5	10	0	23	553
Deutschland, 1903	Cherbourg-New York	5	11	54	23.15	—
„ 1900	New York-Plymouth	5	7	38	23.51	—
Kronprinz Wilhelm 1902	Cherbourg-Sandy Hook	5	11	57	23.09	581
Kronprinz Wilhelm 1901	Sandy Hook-Plymouth	5	8	18	23.47	561
Kaiser Wilhelm II., 1904	Cherbourg-Sandy Hook	5	12	44	23.12	583
Kaiser Wilhelm II., 1906	Sandy Hook-Plymouth	5	8	16	23.58	564

The Deutschland's westward mean speed of 23.51 knots, made over a long course, and not, therefore, a record in point of time, is equivalent to steaming from Queenstown to Sandy Hook in about 4 days 23 hours ; and the Kaiser Wilhelm II.'s homeward mean speed of 23.58 knots would bring her to Queenstown in a few minutes' less time.

intermediate ships than of high-speed steamers. These intermediate vessels, which date from the advent of the Oceanic in 1899, are of enormous size, some of them approaching even the dimensions of the Lusitania, but they are only of 18 knots speed, and, as a consequence, need not be of the same low coefficient of fineness. They consequently carry a larger cargo. There is an idea that because of their fuller form they are steadier in a seaway. This, however, is not necessarily the case. Steadiness is largely a question, in high-speed vessels as well as in cargo ships, of a satisfactory disposition of weights, and the conditions applicable to every ship are now so clearly enunciated by builders to the owners that any conditions which may arise, owing to variable quantity and specific gravity of cargo, can be met to ensure the minimum of movement in a normal sea, with a maximum of comfort to the passengers. The real question is one of cost of high speed, and where this is not required the intermediate ship is bound to be favoured by owners. It is suggestive of the popularity of this intermediate type—of its less costly voyage—that there are now in Lloyd's Register 57 vessels of over 10,000 tons gross register owned by Britain, and 31 vessels of the same size owned by Germany. But including the two new Cunarders, we possess eleven vessels able to steam at more than 20 knots, as compared with Germany's seven. In this list are included fast Channel steamers.

With the knowledge that our builders could equal the Germans in marine construction, opinion steadily grew in favour of some definite action being taken. This feeling was intensified when, three or four years ago, an effort was made to bring into one combination, more or less dominated by American management, almost the whole of the prominent Atlantic companies, because, apart altogether from national sentiment, a characteristic to be respected and developed, there was the fear that we might in this way lose vessels which could be of great advantage in time of war. The late Lord Inverclyde, possessing all the hereditary qualities and all the strong national characteristics of his father and grandfather, resolutely opposed any such absorption of the Cunard Line, which, more than any other, had become a national institution. He was, however, handicapped, especially in competition with the German lines, in respect that his company had largely limited themselves to high-speed passenger and mail liners. The German lines, on the other hand, possessed not only the fast boats—which when run in season and out of season can never maintain a high profit—but also ships of the cargo and intermediate type ; indeed, two or three German lines possess, more or less, a monopoly of the export and import trade of the Fatherland. In this way the expensive vessels can be maintained out of the profit of the ordinary

PROFILES OF HISTORICAL ATLANTIC LINERS.

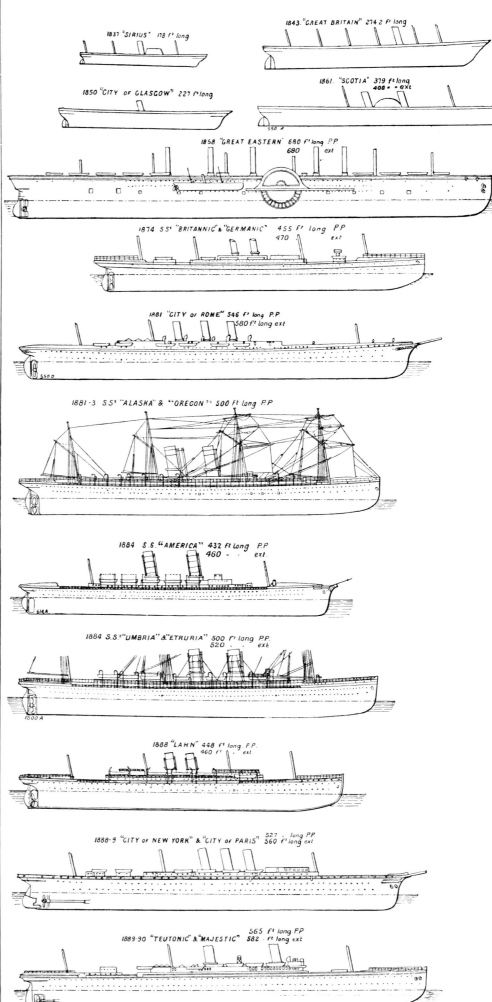

1837 "SIRIUS" 178 ft long

1843. "GREAT BRITAIN" 274 2 ft long

1850 "CITY OF GLASGOW" 227 ft long

1861. "SCOTIA" 379 ft long
400 - ext

1858 "GREAT EASTERN" 680 ft long P.P
680 ext

1874 S.S.' "BRITANNIC" & "GERMANIC" 455 ft long P.P
470 ext

1881 "CITY OF ROME" 546 ft long P.P
580 ft long ext

1881-3 S.S.' "ALASKA" & "OREGON" 500 ft long P.P

1884 S.S. "AMERICA" 432 ft long P.P
460 - ext

1884 S.S.' "UMBRIA" & "ETRURIA" 500 ft long P.P
520 - ext

1888 "LAHN" 448 ft long P.P.
460 ft - ext

1888-9 "CITY OF NEW YORK" & "CITY OF PARIS" 527 - long P.P
560 ft long ext

1889-90 "TEUTONIC" & "MAJESTIC" 565 ft long FP
582 ft long ext

PROFILES OF HISTORICAL ATLANTIC LINERS.

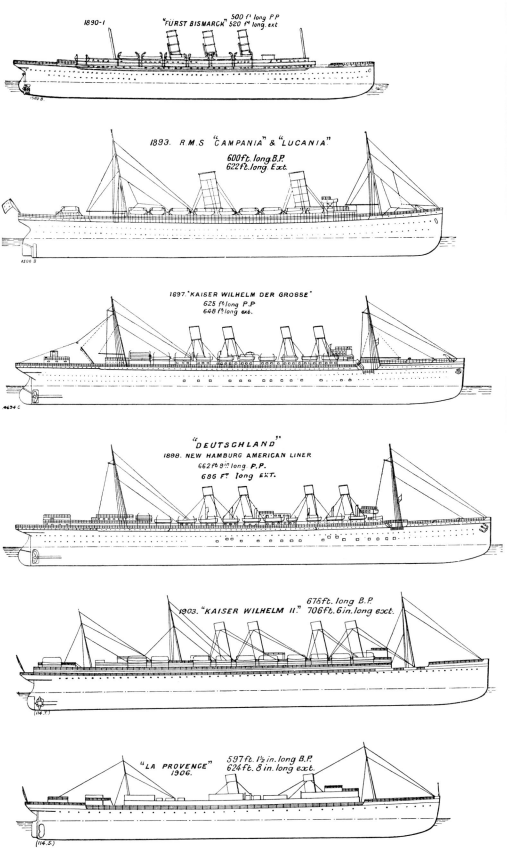

1890-1 "FÜRST BISMARCK" 500 ft. long P.P
520 ft. long. ext

1893. R.M.S "CAMPANIA" & "LUCANIA"
600 ft. long B.P.
622 ft. long Ext.

1897. "KAISER WILHELM DER GROSSE"
625 ft. long P.P.
648 ft. long ext.

"DEUTSCHLAND"
1898. NEW HAMBURG AMERICAN LINER
662 ft. 9 in. long P.P.
686 ft. long EXT.

1903. "KAISER WILHELM II." 676 ft. long B.P.
706 ft. 6 in. long ext.

"LA PROVENCE" 597 ft. 1½ in. long B.P.
1906. 624 ft. 8 in. long ext.

1907. "LUSITANIA" 760 ft. long B.P.
785 ft. long ext.

cargo-carriers. At the same time, the German lines have been assisted in many ways by indirect Government advantages, particularly in recent times, when the maritime spirit has been, and still is, cultivated with so much assiduity by all, from the Kaiser to the peasant. It was therefore matter for keen satisfaction when Mr. Balfour's Government, in 1903, after long consideration and negotiation, entered into an agreement with the Cunard Company in order that the latter should be maintained as a British institution, with fast ships available at all times for war service.

GOVERNMENT AND CUNARD LINE AGREEMENT ; MAIL AND WAR-SERVICE SUBSIDY.

Under this agreement the Government provided a sum sufficient to pay for the new vessels, not exceeding 2,600,000*l*., secured on debentures at 2¾ per cent. interest, while in addition 150,000*l*. was to be paid per annum, on condition that the company would cause to be built, in the United Kingdom, two steamships of large size, capable of maintaining the minimum average ocean speed of 24½ knots in moderate weather. In the event of this speed not being maintained, and if the speed does not fall below 23½ knots, a deduction is to be made from this annual payment by agreement. The clause in which this speed condition is set out is a matter of very considerable interest, and may here be quoted :—

If in the case of either of the two steamships mentioned in Clause 3 hereof, or any vessel substituted therefor, the company shall, before such steamship sails on her first voyage, fail to adduce to the satisfaction of the Admiralty reasonable proof from trials that such vessel will be capable of maintaining a minimum average ocean speed of 24½ knots an hour in moderate weather, but shall prove to the like satisfaction that such vessel will be capable of maintaining an average ocean speed of not less than 23½ knots an hour under such conditions as aforesaid, then such deduction shall be made from the annual payment of 150,000*l*. to be made by His Majesty's Government under the last preceding clause hereof as shall be agreed upon, or, failing such agreement, shall be determined by arbitration, by an arbitrator appointed by the Lord Chief Justice for the time being, and the decision of such arbitrator shall be final.

The minimum speed seems thus to be 23½ knots, although even then the ships may not be rejected ; but the Cunard Company aim at, and will probably get, 25 knots, costly as that may be in respect of first charge, coal consumption, and upkeep. These two ships, in addition to carrying the mails and maintaining the prestige of Britain— which we regard as a very important commercial asset — are to be at the service of the Government in the event of war. To some it may seem remarkable that such an agreement should be necessary to secure the services of such vessels in emergency, and we may even have the naval critic urging that our cruisers ought to be equal in speed for any duty that the proposed Cunarders may fulfil. But many such forget the enormous difference between an Atlantic liner and a cruiser. In the first place such modern liners have a displacement twice that of the greatest cruiser built. In the merchant ship there is no armour to provide for, there are no guns to take, no ammunition nor naval stores, and the consequence is that the architect can allow for machinery something approaching double the weight per unit of full power. It follows that the same reliability in long-distance full-speed steaming cannot be guaranteed in cruisers. In other words, speed and weight of machinery are the main considerations in the merchant ship, whereas in the cruiser they are important, but probably equal only to gun-power and armour protection. The Cunard ships cannot be equal to a cruiser in the latter qualities for warfare ; but they will be superior to similar ships which in time of stress can be withdrawn from the merchant service of other countries, and utilised for naval work.

It may be contended that patriotism alone ought to ensure that ships flying the British flag should ever be at the country's call ; but the old order, which necessitated British ownership before the Union Jack could be flown, passed away in the adoption of the Limited Liability Act. Where the owning company is registered in this country under this Act the fact alone enables their ships to fly the

British flag, even though not a penny is British capital, and not one shareholder—not even a director—is a British subject. This is not the place to enter into the question as to whether such a condition should be permissible. The British flag is certainly a great advantage to any ship in view of the maintenance of our naval power, and it is a question as to whether a change should not be made.

But the Cunard agreement with the Government involves the maintenance of the company as a purely British concern, one of the clauses of the agreement laying it down that the company will be under British control, "that no foreigner shall be qualified to hold office as a director of the company or to be employed as one of the principal officers of the company; and no shares of the company shall be held by, or in trust for, or be in any way under the control of any foreigner or foreign corporation, or any corporation under foreign control." The Cunard Company altered their Articles of Association to meet these conditions. While carrying on business to the best advantage, the company agree not to raise the freights or charges for the carriage of goods in any of their services; while no undue preference against British subjects is to be given. Plans of all ships to be built to steam 17 knots or upwards are to be submitted for approval; facilities are to be given for periodical inspection by the Admiralty, and for storing guns, ammunition, &c., at the ports; no chartering, except to the Indian Government, is to take place without notice being given to the Government, and the option to similarly charter. The Government is always to have the right of hiring the boats, the rates for such being: for vessels over 22 knots, 25s. per gross register ton per month, and 5s. more if the company provide officers and crew; and for 20 to 22 knots, 20s., and 4s. more for staff; and for slower boats at less rates. In addition to holding the ships at the service of the Government, it has been prescribed in the agreement that all the officers, and three-fourths of the crew, shall be British subjects, and that a large proportion shall belong to the Royal Naval Reserve. The ships are thus to be utilised as a great training school for British officers and seamen, and each month a record is to be made of the *personnel* with this point in view.

As to the mail service, the company shall, during the term of this agreement, convey, by means of mail ships from Liverpool (*viâ* Queenstown), or from Queenstown to New York, once in every week, on such day as may be provided, all such mails as shall for the purpose of such conveyance be tendered or delivered at Liverpool and Queenstown respectively, and shall employ as mail ships the fastest of the steamships for the time being belonging to or chartered by the company. For this mail service there shall be payable to the company a yearly sum after the rate of 68,000*l.* per annum; but whenever in any one week more than 100 tons measurement (that is to say, 4000 cubic feet) of parcel mails (exclusive of empty receptacles) in the aggregate are conveyed in either direction (whether by the mail ships or by any other steamships of the company), a further sum of 26s. 3d. is to be paid for every complete ton measurement of parcel mails in excess of 100 tons measurement; but the Postmaster-General may, at his option, pay the rates of freight for the time being charged by the company on similar parcels to other companies or firms whose business it is to carry parcels; but all parcels for which the said rates of freights are paid by the Postmaster-General shall be carried by the company, subject to terms and conditions similar to those upon which the parcels of such other companies or firms are carried, and not under the terms and conditions of the agreement.

The loan of $2\frac{1}{2}$ millions for the building of the two ships is secured by a charge upon the whole of the company's assets, including all vessels built for or acquired by the company, so long as such steamships, or vessels, or any of them, shall remain the property of the company. The loan is to be repaid by the company by annual instalments, each of which shall be equal to one-twentieth of the total amount of the advance, the term of the agreement being for twenty years.

Under the trust deed under which the loan or debentures are to be issued three trustees hold office, the Government and Cunard Company's nominees electing the third. The company are further to issue to two nominees of His Majesty's Government one 20*l.* share of the company, carrying the same voting power and other rights and privileges as an ordinary 20*l.* share of the company; but, for the purpose of demanding a poll in respect of, and voting against, any special resolution involving any alteration of the company's articles of association, so far as respects the provisions referred to in the agreement, also carrying the following additional rights and privileges—namely, the right to demand a poll upon the occasion of any such special resolution, and the right to give against any such special resolution additional votes equal in number to one-fourth of the number of votes possessed by the company's share, stock or debenture holders for the time being.

THE EVOLUTION OF DESIGN.

The agreement having been arrived at and ratified by Parliament, to the great satisfaction of the community, the Cunard Company entered into negotiations for the construction of the ships. These negotiations were necessarily of a protracted nature, as the conditions called for exceptional dimensions, and the designer was trammelled with the same conditions which made Brunel's scientific achievements in the Great Eastern a practical failure. The great speed aimed at required very considerable accommodation for machinery to attain the necessary power in a vessel with sufficient deck area for passenger-rooms to ensure a satisfactory financial result.

As we know, 30 knots is now attained in destroyers—even 36 knots is aimed at—but the credit side of the balance-sheet of an Atlantic liner requires an increase in passenger accommodation proportionate to the advance in the cost of power for the higher speeds. Apart from this, however, length is conducive to speed, but only if it is associated with deep draught. The limit, however, with existing harbours is soon reached, and the ambition of the naval architect is curbed by the lack of progress of dock authorities. This is not the place to discuss whether this hesitancy on the part of these authorities is justified in the interests of finance. We are concerned only with the problem of the marine constructor, but we cannot help offering the suggestion that the harbour which is most progressive in this respect must attain the greatest measure of prosperity, and it is fortunate for this country that we have, in direct competition for the Atlantic service, two ports hitherto so well managed and so progressive in policy as Liverpool and Southampton, because in such competition lies the hope of a definite advance. Even length is prescribed, and in order to minimise the draught to suit existing harbours, the beam has to be increased beyond all former limits, so as to give a low block coefficient of fineness and enable a fine entry and a sweet run to be planned.

SHIP-RESISTANCE AND THE GENESIS OF MODEL EXPERIMENTS.

The form of the new ships was the subject of very careful experiment, and it is to the credit of Messrs. John Brown and Co., Limited, that, in the early negotiations, they proved more progressive than their coadjutors, being most urgent in their advocacy of exhaustive ship-resistance tests with models; and before describing the results it may be interesting to review the genesis of the system, especially as we know of no publication where this has been done.

From the time of Charles I., and the celebrated disputes arising out of the levying of "ship-money," the types of sailing ships used in the Royal Navy, and also in the mercantile marine, assumed what we may call their modern form. The propelling power, being applied at a considerable height, made it necessary to have vessels which were relatively broad, in order that they might be tolerably stiff when under a heavy press of sail. The proportions which this consideration imposed, therefore, made it impracticable to get a really fast vessel (at least measured by present-day standards), although some of the American and China tea clippers attain speeds of 15 and 16 knots.

Another feature which for a very long time exercised also a governing influence on the absolute size of vessels was the fact that they were constructed of wood. The methods of making connection between the component parts of the structure were far from satisfactory, and hence the upper limit of size was a very moderate one. This can at once be appreciated when it is noted that probably the largest vessel ever built of wood did not exceed 300 ft. in length. The advent of iron (and steel) as materials of construction, together with the use of steam, completely altered the fundamentals of the problem. Size was no longer necessarily limited in the way mentioned above, and no consideration of stability was required in relation to the method of application of the propelling power. When these points were thoroughly appreciated, it was not long before the enterprising mind of Brunel showed, by his marvellous production of the Great Eastern, what was the capability of iron as a structural material.

Simultaneously with the increase of size—a point in itself favourable to speed—came great possibilities in the way of increase of the ratio of length to breadth, a ratio which seems to have been about doubled now that the change from wood to steel is completely accomplished.

We have next to note that the never-ceasing advance in the improvement of the marine steam-engine, and the growth in knowledge of the action of the screw-propeller, furnished the naval architect with increased power, and possibilities of applying it to better advantage as time progressed; and as all these causes, operating in the same direction, conduced to the possibility of material increase in speed of steam vessels, it became an absolute necessity that some systematic attempt should be made in the direction of investigating the elements of resistance pertaining to various forms and proportions of ships; and as trials on full-sized vessels are costly, and at times none too satisfactory, the question of the use of models came in the 'sixties to the front once more, as it had done on previous occasions.

This period was a most momentous one as regards our present subject. The transformation in material was rapidly proceeding, as before described, and Brunel's ship was built. He had, in his researches on the problems confronting him, enlisted the services and interest of the late Mr. William Froude, and this gentleman made certain investigations on the probable behaviour of the Great Eastern, and in doing so had formulated his theory of the rolling of ships. This, as is well known, he laid before the newly-founded Institution of Naval Architects, and the results of these researches and the discussions to which they gave rise will be found in the earlier numbers of the Transactions of this Institution. Mr. Froude, in these researches and in others which are to be found in the records of other societies, established his position as a complete master of the theory of naval architecture, worthy to stand on a footing of equality with any of the great men who have ornamented the profession.

Before, however, tracing in some detail the results of Mr. Froude's labours, it may be well to note the best known amongst the previous investigators on the subject of the resistance of ships.

The immortal Newton may be taken first. He came to the conclusion that the resistance to bodies moving in a fluid varied as the square of the velocity. He also enunciated the "principle of similitude," which is the same principle as that now known in this subject as the "law of comparison." Daniel Bernoulli, D'Alembert, and Euler followed along the line of theoretical investigation. Next the Abbé Bossut, in the year 1776, in association with D'Alembert and the Marquis Condorcet, conducted in Paris a series of experiments for the purpose of verifying existing theories, and, if none of them could be verified, "to serve as a basis for a new solution." Although a large number of experiments were made, the results are now practically unknown or forgotten, and therefore exert no influence on present-day practice. With the introduction of experimental research the theoretical investigation of the subject naturally fell into partial abeyance, and so need not be further noted.

In 1791 a society was formed in London for the "Improvement of Naval Architecture," and under its influence a committee was constituted for the purpose of experimental research. The experiments were performed by Colonel Beaufoy in the Greenland Dock, London, and were carried on at intervals from 1793 to 1798. Unfortunately, these experiments, as also those preceding them in point of date, have left no trace of their influence. In the later days of the sailing ship era in the Royal Navy much attention was given to experimental sailing. Large numbers of vessels, built according to the multitudinous ideas prevailing, were sailed in company and in competition, and there is no doubt that much light would have been shed on the matter under investigation had it not been that the introduction of the steam-engine as the motive power entirely changed the current of professional interest into other channels, with more profitable results.

In the year 1868 the subject of experimental investigation was once more urged, and a committee of the British Association formed to consider the matter. This committee consisted of Mr. Bidder, Captain Galton, Mr. Galton, Professor Rankine, Mr. William Froude, and Mr. Merrifield. A majority of the committee recommended that systematic experiments should be made "on full-sized ships" in some suitable spot—say, for example, in the fiords on the Norwegian coast, or on the inland waters of the West Coast of Scotland.

Mr. William Froude had already been engaged in experimenting upon models, and had dissented from the conclusions formed by the committee. He appealed to the Admiralty to lend their assistance, the upshot being that their Lordships "had been pleased to sanction certain experiments upon models, to be conducted by Mr. Froude, and will cause the results of these experiments to be communicated to such professional bodies as my Lords may deem desirable."

The result is well enough known. Mr. Froude, by his rediscovery of the principle of similitude, under the name of the "law of comparison," and by fully recognising at the outset what extreme care, patience, and persistence are required, and what hours may be spent in getting a single good result from a model experiment, has placed the utility of model experiments beyond the slightest doubt; we might almost say, has made them indispensable, for certainly this is true of the more difficult problems confronting the profession. And in view of the considerable number of experimental establishments now in working order, or in process of construction, to labour the point is absolutely vain.

When, therefore, the problem of the design of the fast Cunarders had assumed some measure of definiteness, it was only natural that assistance from model data should be sought by those in positions of responsibility. When Messrs. John Brown and Co. acquired the shipyard at Clydebank, they at once made up their minds to lay down an experimental tank for the purpose of pursuing their own line of investigation. This tank* was approaching completion when the design of the Cunard vessel had to be considered. It was thought to be undesirable to defer consideration of the matter until their own apparatus was in working order, so they threw their influence into the scale, and the Cunard Company succeeded in inducing the Admiralty to assist. Through the kindness of Sir Philip Watts, K.C.B., and Mr. R. E. Froude, and by the labours of the able staff which so efficiently supports them, assistance of inestimable value was given. A large number of models were run at Haslar, which served to show the effect of possible variations in the principal dimensions of the vessel, and the effect of fulness of form. What was of even still greater importance, unique experiments were made on the subject of the most suitable propellers for the ship, and for their location in relation to the hull and to each other.

Simultaneously with the carrying out of these experiments at Haslar, Messrs. John Brown and Co. secured the services and the hearty co-operation of their friends and neighbours, Messrs. William Denny and Brothers, of Dumbarton, who very cordially placed the tank at Dumbarton at the disposal of Messrs. John Brown and Co. for further experiment.

It is hardly too much to say, therefore, that the experiments made in connection with the Lusitania are quite unique in their volume and range, and serve to prove—were such proof necessary—that no single stone has been left unturned in the effort to give most careful and exhaustive investigation to every point.

Although too late to have any influence on the solution of the problem, it is of interest to add that since the experimental tank at Clydebank has been got into full working order, all these experiments have been repeated there, and are used as a standard set for comparison with other work as occasion arises. From these experiments the most suitable directions of rotation of the various propellers were inferred, and it was found that to rotate the outer propellers inwards, and the inner propellers outwards, gave the best promise of efficiency, and this course was in consequence adopted.

* For an illustrated description of this tank, see ENGINEERING, vol. lxxxi., page 541.

Before leaving this portion of the subject it will be well to note, and it is only just to recognise, the great value of the contributions made to our knowledge of the subject of screw-propeller efficiency by the extensive range of experiments made in the United States Government tank at Washington. Certain of the published researches on the subject of resistance and propulsion have been reprinted in ENGINEERING.*

THE CONTRACT; THE DIMENSIONS OF THE "LUSITANIA."

While the order for one of the two ships was placed with Messrs. John Brown and Co., Limited, the other was awarded to Messrs. C. S. Swan, Hunter, and Wigham Richardson, of Wallsend-on-Tyne, the machinery for the latter vessel being ordered from the Wallsend Slipway and Engineering Company, Limited.

Although the dimensions of the Lusitania are incorporated in the table given on page 10, they may be reproduced here with more detail.

Length over all	785 ft.
,, between perpendiculars	760 ,,
Breadth, moulded	88 ,,
Depth ,, ...	60 ft. $4\frac{1}{2}$ in.
Gross tonnage	32,500 tons
Draught	33 ft. 6 in.
Displacement	38,000 tons
Number of passengers—first ...	552
,, ,, second	460
,, ,, third ...	1186
Type of engine	Parsons turbine
Number and type of boilers ...	Twenty-five cylindrical
Number of furnaces	192
Steam pressure	195 lb.
Total heating surface	158 350 sq. ft.
,, grate area	4,048 ,,
Draught	Howden's
Total indicated horse-power (designed)	68,000
Speed (designed)	25 knots

One important feature dealt with in fixing the designs had reference to the use of the ships as cruisers or scouts in time of war, and the plans which we reproduce on Plate XXXVII. show that the machinery—which is almost entirely under the water-line—has been so disposed in separate compartments, and with coal protection along each side, as to counteract, as far as possible, the effect of the enemy's fire at the water-line. For purposes of attack the Lusitania will be provided with an armament as satisfactory as the armoured cruisers of the County class, because on one of the topmost decks there will be carried, within the shelter of the heavy shell-plating, four 6-in. quick-firing guns attaining a muzzle energy of over 5000 foot-tons, while on the promenade-deck on each side there will be four more guns on central pivot mountings, also able to penetrate $4\frac{3}{4}$-in. armour at 5000 yards range, and 6-in. armour at 3000 yards range. With the great speed, which can be maintained for three or four times the period that any modern cruiser can steam even at only 21 knots, and with the careful subdivision for protection and their satisfactory offensive power, the Lusitania and her consort may be regarded as most effective additions to any fighting squadron. Their advent is therefore a great advantage from the point of view of British sea power.

The rudder and steering-gear are all placed well below the water-line. This is a most important point in respect of protection, should these vessels be ever impressed into the national service. The stern has been suitably shaped in the Lusitania to enable this object to be accomplished satisfactorily.

THE ADOPTION OF STEAM-TURBINES.

The second problem in design was the question of the type of propelling machinery to be adopted. The power of the machinery, for the dimensions and form evolved in the Government tank at Haslar, was 68,000 indicated horse-power. Experience has produced an exact rule as to the efficiency of tank boilers as steam-generators, and thus the capacity of the boiler installation was a more or less fixed quantity; but it was important to determine whether the steam efficiency of the steam-turbine or of the reciprocating engine was greater. Even in a ship where speed is the first desideratum it is incumbent upon the designer to aim at economy, alike in first cost, working expenses, and maintenance charges. Three years ago, when the decision had to be arrived at, there were comparatively few data even as to the steam consumption of turbines, and less as to their durability; but the Cunard Company, with that wisdom which has brought them to the front rank, decided to appoint a commission of experts to investigate and report upon the whole question. The company were equally felicitous in their selection of the experts.

* See ENGINEERING, vol. lxxviii., pages 815 and 838.

This Commission included Mr. James Bain, the Marine Superintendent of the Cunard Company, than whom no one knows better the engine duty of Atlantic liners; Engineer-Rear-Admiral H. J. Oram, C.B., Deputy-Engineer-in-Chief to the Navy, who has intimate knowledge both of the scientific and practical sides of the steam-engine and turbine; Mr. J. T. Milton, Chief Engineer-Surveyor of Lloyd's; and the late Mr. H. J. Brock, of the firm of Messrs. Denny, of Dumbarton, who have built many mercantile ships fitted with Parsons turbines; while the three firms concerned in the construction of the two new ships were represented— Messrs. John Brown and Co., Limited, by Mr. T. Bell; Messrs. C. S. Swan and Hunter, Limited, of Newcastle-on-Tyne, by Sir William H. White, K.C.B.; and the Wallsend Engineering Company by Mr. Andrew Laing.

This Commission entered upon their work with great care, conscious of the responsibility resting upon them; on their decision the success of the new ships largely depended. Admiral Oram, who, as Deputy-Engineer-in-Chief of the Navy, has tackled the question of turbine economy, alike from the scientific and practical standpoint, with enormous advantage to the Navy, was able to put before the Commission very important results as to the performance of destroyers. The late Mr. Brock and Mr. Parsons assisted the Committee with the tests of Channel steamers into which their respective firms had fitted turbine-engines. The resultant data, and a careful consideration of the performance of turbines ashore, encouraged the Committee to make the bold step of recommending for these huge liners the new prime mover. Events have since justified this intuition, and the consequence is that the Cunard liners are in the forefront, not only in speed, but in the method of attaining it. The constructors of the machinery, in accepting the contract for turbine machinery, with the heavy guarantees attached, also displayed characteristic enterprise.

The Clydebank firm entered upon their work in a thoroughly practical way, laying down immediately a complete turbine installation, where, by dynamometric means, they were able to test the power, while at the same time measuring the water consumption. Many questions affecting the details of design were similarly experimentally determined, and the result was that they induced the Cunard Company to at once adopt turbine machinery in a large steamer of 20 knots speed, the order for which had just been placed with them. We have already dealt very fully with the machinery in this ship, the Carmania, and, at the same time, have described the experiments undertaken and the modifications made in the turbine,* so that it is not necessary here to say more regarding this phase of the subject. It may, however, be indicated, as suggestive of the completeness of the experimental plant, that it was subsequently fitted to a Clyde steamer direct from the testing-house, and has since given very satisfactory results, corroborative of the high efficiency attained at the works.

THE FORM OF STERN AND NUMBER OF PROPELLERS.

The adoption of turbines was immediately followed by very careful experiments as to the form of stern suitable for four propellers, and as to the proportions of propellers. Four screws were imperative, whether turbine or reciprocating engines had been adopted, because, as indicated on the table of dimensions on page 10, great ingenuity had to be devised in connection with the distribution of power in the cylinders of the piston engines in immediately preceding Atlantic liners. In the Campania and Lucania, where the total power was

* See ENGINEERING, vol. lxxx., page 719.

30,000 indicated horse-power, two sets of engines were found sufficient, each having three cranks with five cylinders, the high and low pressure being arranged tandemwise, with the intermediate cylinder in the centre. In the next large ship, the Kaiser Wilhelm der Grosse, there were two sets of engines of the four-cylinder triple-expansion type, each cylinder working on a separate crank ; although the power was the same, with a slight increase of steam pressure, the low-pressure cylinders were 96.4 in. in diameter. The Vulcan Company, in their succeeding ships, adopted various systems, in the Kaiser Wilhelm II. fitting four sets of engines, two on each shaft. Each set of engines had three cranks, and the tandem system was again adopted for high and first intermediate cylinders, but the diameter of the low-

upon the triple-screw arrangement in former turbine ships, where such complete independence is unattainable. The division of the power into two complete and independent systems follows the course pursued for so many years in the Royal Navy, whose lead is now so generally adopted in this case enabled the engine-rooms to be well subdivided by watertight bulkheads, and the advantages in general secured have been obtained without the sacrifice of a single point of any importance.

The form of stern devised is well shown in some of the illustrations which are given on Plates IV. and V. To improve the manœuvring, the dead wood was cut away, as shown in the profile of the ship on page 13, and on Fig. 30, Plate XXXVII. As in earlier Clydebank ships, the rudder, of the

dimensions of the turbine, and the velocity of steam being constant, the revolutions are of necessity high. The contention has been made—not always with due regard to experience—that the small high-speed propeller involves some loss in efficiency, especially in a seaway, and, further, detracts from the astern speed, and, indeed, from the general manœuvring power of the ship. Be that as it may, it was decided in the Cunard liners, after very careful consideration, to attain the full speed, with the propellers making about 185 revolutions per minute, and the turbines were proportioned to suit this speed. The peripheral speed being practically more or less constant, owing to the velocity of steam, and only affected by the angle or curvature of the blades, it became necessary to adopt turbines of very large diameter. Thus the rotor-drum of the

Photo. by Elliott and Fry.

Photo. by Lafayette.

pressure cylinder was increased to 112.2 in. This latter dimension has been exceeded only in one or two instances, in compound paddle-engines. The six cranks probably improved the uniformity of turning moment. With tandem cylinders the difficulties of balancing the moving parts were necessarily increased, and it is probable that, as a consequence, some portion of unnecessary weight had to be carried. In any case, the transmission of 20,000 indicated horse-power through a single shaft, setting up enormous torque, imposed a very severe condition even upon the best of steel-makers, and those responsible for the design of the machinery in these new liners were, therefore, well advised in aiming at a reduction to about 16,000 or 17,000 horse-power through any one shaft.

The adoption of four units of machinery and four screw-propellers enabled the machinery to be made in two completely separate sets, one to starboard and the other to port, just as in a vessel with twin-screw reciprocating machinery ; a distinct advance

barn-door type, is supported for about two thirds of its depth. Immediately forward of it, on each side, are the two inner propellers, the shafting for these being entirely borne within the ship, the framing of which was bossed out, and strongly supported by heavy webbing, as explained later. The forward propellers are about 70 ft. ahead of the inside screws, and here also the frames are carried by heavy webs. Owing to the great beam of the ship, and the very fine run, the blades of the outside propellers do not project beyond the beam-line, while, at the same time, all the propellers work in free water, and provision has been made for a satisfactory clearance between the propellers and the skin of the ship.

Another question affecting the efficiency of the propelling machinery had reference to the revolutions at which the propellers were to be run at full speed. In Channel-steamer work, and in small craft generally, a high rotating speed has been adopted, largely as a matter of necessity. Where weight is limited, it is important to minimise the

high-pressure turbines is 96 in. in diameter, and that of the low-pressure turbine 140 in., the blades ranging from $2\frac{1}{4}$ in. to 22 in. in length. The result is to permit the use of a propeller of a diameter and pitch which will certainly remove any question as to relative efficiency, under normal conditions, as to manœuvring power and astern speed, and also as to the influence of head seas. From these points of view, the performance of the ship and the machinery will be watched with very careful interest ; although the results already attained with the Carmania prove that the line of reasoning which has actuated the designers of the propelling machinery of the Lusitania is correct, and therefore there is every likelihood of a full practical success.

PERSONALIA.

Before departing from the consideration of those questions which affect the design, our readers will expect us to say something about those who have been responsible for the work. We have already referred to the services rendered in the national interest by Sir Philip Watts, K.C.B., Director of Naval Construction at the Admiralty, Dr. Froude, of the Haslar experimental tank, and Engineer-Rear-Admiral H. J. Oram, C.B., Deputy-Engineer-in-Chief of the Navy.

Mr. J. G. Dunlop, managing director of Messrs. John Brown and Co., Limited, has, as chief at Clydebank, brought to bear upon the many problems to be solved his great practical experience, which is almost unique in its variety and extent. His staff was eminently fitted to carry to a successful issue all the details of construction. Mr. David McGee, the shipyard director, was trained at Clydebank, and has been intimately associated with the building of many of the Atlantic liners and warships which have had their origin in this establishment, so that he was thoroughly conversant with all the details necessary to ensure success. Mr. Thomas Bell, the engineering director of the works, has also been at Clydebank for many years, and carries into his work an enthusiasm and a courage equal to his great theoretical and practical knowledge. He has been responsible for the work of settling the details of the turbines. Mr. W. J. Luke, naval architect and director, who joined the Clydebank yard some ten years ago, is an Admiralty-trained naval constructor.

He was for several years lecturer on the subject at the Greenwich College. He had ever a penchant for experimental work, and, with the addition of a tank for testing models at Clydebank, found abundant scope for his intuitive mind. Here much useful work has been done, especially in connection with the propeller question. One might almost say, however, that everyone at Clydebank has been actuated by the same spirit as Mr. Dunlop in his determination to ensure an absolute success for the ship.

As regards the Cunard Company, their great reputation is abundant evidence of their splendid administration. The choice as chairman, in succession to the late Lord Inverclyde, of Mr. William Watson, was generally acclaimed as a most felicitous one. The position was difficult, owing to the personality of the late Lord Inverclyde, but events have since shown that Mr. Watson's intimate knowledge of all shipping questions, combined with a determination to maintain the prestige of the company, eminently proves his fitness for the post. He has a splendid staff, whether regard be had to the technical or managerial departments. To Mr. James Bain's work we have already made reference, and he is so well known that no further mention need be made of the great tact and experience with which he has

carried out his duty in connection with the Lusitania.

On Mr. George Thompson will devolve the responsibility for the upkeep and repair of this gigantic installation, and we cannot accord him higher praise than to state that he is a worthy successor to Mr. Bain in the post of superintendent engineer of the Cunard Company. Mr. L. Peskett, the naval architect, has also been closely identified with the work, and to the ultimate success of the vessel his wide acquaintance with all the latest developments in the internal economy of high-class vessels of all the principal trans-Atlantic companies has contributed in no small degree.

In the ultimate success of the Lusitania the staff count for much, because, however successful a ship may be from the point of view of construction, her popularity must depend very largely on the comfort ensured on board. Mr. A. Mearns has taken over the general managership in succession to Mr. A. P. Moorhouse, whose lamented death was recorded a few weeks ago. Here, again, the selection has been a happy one, as Mr. Mearns has been trained in the Cunard Company, than which there is no better school, and, having high administrative qualities, he will greatly assist the directorate in maintaining the place which the Cunard Company have always held in the appreciation of the public.

THE CONSTRUCTION OF THE SHIP.

HAVING dealt with those matters concerning the inception of the scheme, and with the problems in design associated with the speed, we may now turn to the no less important questions which had to be settled before constructional work was commenced. These were associated with the strength of the structure, with the scantlings to ensure an absolutely reliable result, and also with the metals to be used. Incidentally, also, much thought had to be devoted to the supporting of the ship during construction and to her launch ; but there have been so many large ships built at the Clydebank works that these latter questions were relatively unimportant. The ship had to be constructed not only to meet the conditions laid down by Lloyd's, but also to comply with the Admiralty requirements as a transport or armed cruiser.

The calculations of stresses were carried out in the usual way, on the assumption that the material of the hull, if built of mild steel, should not be subjected to a stress exceeding 10 tons per square inch, and on the basis that the vessel might experience the hogging and sagging stresses consequent on meeting with waves of her own length, and of a height from the trough to crest of one-twentieth of the length of the wave. The very careful series of calculations entered into showed that the maximum bending moment was slightly over 1,000,000 foot-tons, and that this occurred through hogging, owing to the vessel riding at the centre of her length on the crest of a wave of maximum size with the ends in the troughs. This stress, of course, is greatest at minimum draught ; that is to say, when the vessel is nearing her destination, and when coal in the bunkers has been greatly reduced. With the two ends supported on waves and the centre sagging, the stress was only about 500,000 foot-tons. With a full cargo of coal, when the displacement will probably be 20 per cent. more than in her arrival condition, the hogging and sagging stresses are considerably less. These conditions are about normal, but the aim of the designer was to meet them so that the strain on the structure would be less even than is usually the case with well-built ships.

In the case of the Lusitania it was decided, before construction was far advanced, to enter upon a series of very careful tests in order to determine whether, and to what extent, increased strength could be imparted to the upper structure by the adoption of high-tensile steel. These tests, which were watched with great interest by the officials of Lloyd's, the Board of Trade, and the Admiralty,

and with even greater interest and solicitude by the Clydebank staff and the Cunard officials, were carried out at Messrs. D. Colville and Co.'s Works at Motherwell. The subject of high-tensile steel, however, has lately engaged so much attention, and the papers read at the recent Engineering Conference in London brought out such a full expression of opinion, that it is scarcely necessary for us here to enlarge on the question. But it is important to state that the ordinary tensile and elongation tests carried out in the interests of the builders by Messrs. David Kirkaldy and Son, London, were supplemented by a great variety of experiments, and these showed that the average ultimate tensile strength of the material selected was 36.8 tons per square inch for normal high-tensile steel and 36.6 tons per square inch for annealed high-tensile steel, as compared with 29.6 tons per square inch for ordinary mild steel. The elongation tests were made with pieces which corresponded more to the length of plates on the section of the ship—namely, 100 in.; and it was found that the ratio of elastic to ultimate stress was 47.7 per cent. for the normal high-tensile steel and 53.4 per cent. for the annealed high-tensile steel, as compared with 43.5 per cent. for the mild steel. Thus the high-tensile steel which was used was 24 per cent. better in ultimate tensile strength than the mild steel, which itself was of a very satisfactory quality. The metal was subjected to tup tests as well as to other severe punishments, including the explosion of heavy charges of dynamite against the plates, as described in page 847 of vol. lxxxiii. of ENGINEERING, and in every instance the results were satisfactory. Generally speaking, the conclusion arrived at from these experiments was that the tensile steel was 36 per cent. better than the mild steel. Those responsible for the design of the ship, being specially solicitous to ensure absolute strength, decided, notwithstanding this great superiority, to reduce the scantlings to the extent only of 10 per cent. ; probably the results justified more, and in future large ships a greater reduction may be made, especially as in big Atlantic liners we are far from that thinness of plate which introduces the newer problem of buckling stresses, associated in recent years with the construction of light torpedo craft.

The reduction in scantlings had the very important advantage that it reduced weight where it was most desirable to economise in this respect, and owing to the thinner plates it further ensured better riveting. It was not deemed prudent to adopt the

high-tensile steel for the rivets, a point upon which there seems some difference of opinion.

THE BUILDING OF THE HULL.

The constructional details of the hull will be readily followed by an examination of the sectional drawings given on page 18, Fig. 7, and of the table of scantlings appended to these sections; while on Plates I. to VIII. we reproduce various photographs illustrating the process of building the hull. The keel is formed of three thicknesses of plates, with no outside butt-straps. Experience has shown this plan to be an advantage, because it facilitates operations in the dry-docking of the vessel. This flat keel is shown in the engraving on Plate I. (Fig. 14). Over this, as shown in the details, Figs. 7 and 10, there is the centre-line keelson, which is well shown in the engraving on page 19 (Fig. 12). There are two corresponding longitudinal main girders—the fifth girder marked F and the margin-plate marked L on the section (Fig. 7). The dimensions of those main girders are given separately in the table of scantlings. In addition, however, there are on each side of the centre-line keelson five other longitudinal girders, and the scantlings of these are given on the table.

The general construction of the double bottom is illustrated by Figs. 15 and 16 on Plates I. and II., the longitudinal in the foreground being one of the intermediate members. This view further shows that, contrary to usual practice, the holes in these intermediate longitudinals for lightening the structure are placed with their larger dimension vertically instead of horizontally. This was because of the comparative closeness of the frames, but as a consequence one may walk in greater comfort through the ballast-tanks. There was no attempt to make these intermediate continuous longitudinals water-tight. The water-tight divisions of the ballast-tanks between the double bottom and deep tank are made by the centre keelson and the two main longitudinals F and L. This double-bottom construction extends for practically the whole length of the vessel, and, as is shown by the section, extends for a considerable part of the length of the vessel up to the lower deck. Fig. 16 on Plate II. illustrates the double-bottom structure aft, and affords an excellent idea of the strength of the structure at and abaft the machinery spaces.

As regards the plating, the only departure from recent practice at Clydebank is the connection of

CROSS-SECTIONS SHOWING SCANTLINGS.

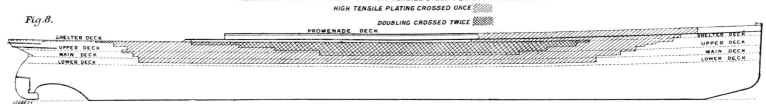

ELEVATION SHOWING EXTENT OF HIGH TENSILE STEEL PLATING ON TOPSIDES.
HIGH TENSILE PLATING CROSSED ONCE
DOUBLING CROSSED TWICE

Fig. 8.

SHELTER DECK
UPPER DECK
MAIN DECK
LOWER DECK
PROMENADE DECK

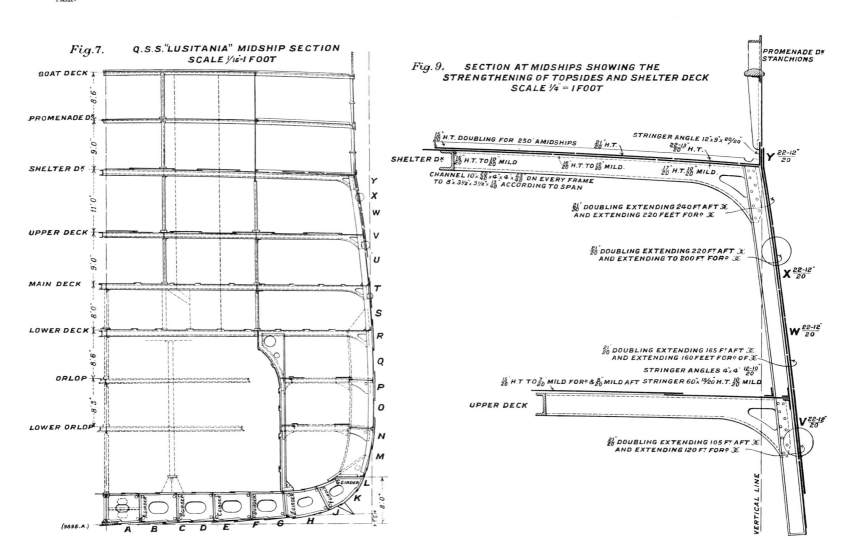

Fig. 7. **Q.S.S. "LUSITANIA" MIDSHIP SECTION**
SCALE 1/16 = 1 FOOT

Fig. 9. **SECTION AT MIDSHIPS SHOWING THE STRENGTHENING OF TOPSIDES AND SHELTER DECK**
SCALE 1/4 = 1 FOOT

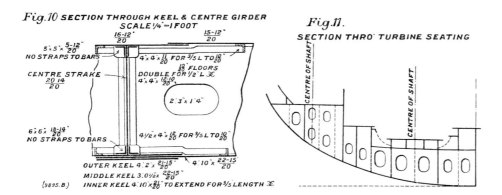

Fig. 10 **SECTION THROUGH KEEL & CENTRE GIRDER**
SCALE 1/4 = 1 FOOT

Fig. 11. **SECTION THRO' TURBINE SEATING**

TABLE OF SCANTLINGS.

Frames.—Inside double bottom, $4\frac{1}{2}$ in. by 4 in. by $\frac{18}{20}$ in. for $\frac{3}{5}$ L amidships to $\frac{13}{20}$ in. joggled ; and reverse frames, 4 in. by 4 in. by $\frac{11}{20}$ in. for $\frac{3}{5}$ L amidships to $\frac{10}{20}$ in. joggled. Outside double-bottom channel, 10 in. by $\frac{19}{20}$ in. by 4 in. by $\frac{19}{20}$ in. for $\frac{3}{5}$ L amidships to shelter-deck, with reverse bar 4 in. by 4 in. by $\frac{12}{20}$ in. angle to lower orlop-deck, to 9 in. by $\frac{19}{20}$ in. by 4 in. by 4 in. by $\frac{12}{20}$ in. for $\frac{3}{5}$ L amidships to shelter-deck, with reverse bar 4 in. by 4 in. by $\frac{12}{20}$ in. angle to lower orlop-deck.

Spacing.—Frames spaced 32 in. for $\frac{3}{5}$ L amidships to 25 in. aft and 26 in. forward.

Floors.—$\frac{15}{20}$ in. under boiler-bearers and where necessary ; elsewhere, $\frac{13}{20}$ in.

Girders.—Centre, 60 in. by $\frac{20-14}{20}$ in. ; G., $\frac{16-12}{20}$ in. ; remainder, $\frac{12-10}{20}$ in. Centre girder angles : top, 5 in. by 5 in. by $\frac{15-12}{20}$ in. ; bottom, 6 in. by 6 in. by $\frac{18-14}{20}$ in. ; other girder angles, 4 in. by 4 in. by $\frac{12-10}{20}$ in. ; margin angle, 6 in. by 6 in. by $\frac{16-12}{20}$ in.

Inner Bottom.—Centre strake, $\frac{16-12}{20}$ in. ; remainder, $\frac{15-12}{20}$ in.

Orlop and Lower Orlop.—Stringer, $\frac{13}{20}$ in. ; face-plate, $6\frac{1}{2}$ in. by $4\frac{1}{2}$ in. by $\frac{13}{20}$ in. ; flanged girder, $\frac{9}{20}$ in. to fore and aft bulkhead.

Lower Deck.—Stringer, 72 in. by $\frac{12-10}{20}$ in. ; remainder, $\frac{8-7}{20}$ in. ;

beams, channel, 10 in. by $3\frac{1}{2}$ in. by $3\frac{1}{2}$ in. by $\frac{12}{20}$ in. on every frame, to 8 in. by $3\frac{1}{2}$ in. by $3\frac{1}{2}$ in. by $\frac{10}{20}$ in , according to span.

Main Deck.—Stringer, 54 in. by $\frac{12-10}{20}$ in. ; next strake, $\frac{10-7}{20}$ in. remainder, $\frac{8-7}{20}$ in.; beams, channel, 10 in. by $\frac{12}{20}$ in. by 4in. by 4 in. by $\frac{12}{20}$ in. on every frame, to 8 in. by $3\frac{1}{2}$ in. by $3\frac{1}{2}$ in. by $\frac{10}{20}$ in., according to span.

Upper Deck.—Stringer, 60 in. by $\frac{15}{20}$ in. high-tensile steel to $\frac{12}{20}$ in. mild ; second strake, $\frac{15}{20}$ in. high tensile to $\frac{9}{20}$ in. mild forward, and $\frac{8}{20}$ in. mild aft ; third stake, $\frac{12}{20}$ in. high tensile to $\frac{9}{20}$ in. mild forward, and $\frac{8}{20}$ in. mild aft ; remainder, $\frac{10}{20}$ in. Beams, channel, 10 in. by $\frac{12}{20}$ in. by 4 in. by 4 in. by $\frac{12}{20}$ in. every frame, to 8 in. by $3\frac{1}{2}$ in. by $3\frac{1}{2}$ in. by $\frac{10}{20}$ in., according to span.

Shelter Deck.—Stringer, $\frac{15}{20}$ in. high tensile to $\frac{12}{20}$ in. mild, doubling $\frac{22-13}{20}$ in. high tensile ; second strake, $\frac{12}{20}$ in. mild, doubling $\frac{21}{20}$ in. high tensile ; third strake, $\frac{12}{20}$ in. mild, doubling $\frac{18}{20}$ in. high tensile ; remainder, $\frac{10-8}{20}$ in. mild. Beams, channel, 10 in. by $\frac{12}{20}$ in. by 4 in. by 4 in. by $\frac{12}{20}$ in. on every frame, to 8 in. by $3\frac{1}{2}$ in. by $3\frac{1}{2}$ in. by $\frac{12}{20}$ in., according to span. Stringer angle, 12 in. by 9 in. by $\frac{20}{20}$ in.

Shell.—Outer keel, 50 in. by $\frac{21-15}{20}$ in. ; middle keel, $36\frac{1}{2}$ in. by $\frac{22-15}{20}$ in. ; inner keel, 58 in. by $\frac{24}{20}$ in. for $\frac{3}{5}$ L amidships. A strake $\frac{22-15}{20}$ in. ; B, C, D, E, F, G, H, J, K, L, M, N, $\frac{21-12}{20}$ in. ; O, P, Q, R, S, T, U, $\frac{20-12}{20}$ in. ; V, W, X, Y, $\frac{22-12}{20}$ in. ; doubling to V $\frac{24}{20}$ in., extends 105 ft. aft of amidships to 120 ft. forward of amidships ; doubling to W $\frac{22}{20}$ in. extends 165 ft. aft of amidships to 160 ft. forward of amidships ; doubling to X and Y $\frac{21}{20}$ in. for 240 ft. aft of amidships to 220 ft. forward of amidships.

Forward, where the vessel is closed in, the plating is $\frac{12}{20}$ in.

F. and A. Continuous Bulkhead.—$\frac{9}{20}$ in. where curved ; remainder, $\frac{10}{20}$ in. ; base angle continuous, 5 in. by 5 in. by $\frac{18}{20}$ in.

Angles.—Under decks in ways of pillars 6 in. by 5 in. by $\frac{18}{20}$ in.

the plates of the garboard strake to the flat keel-plates, which is shown on the detail Fig. 10, and in the view on this page (Fig. 12). Mention may also be made of the longitudinal connecting angles having no butt-straps. The frames and reverse bars up to the margin plate are joggled, to avoid the necessity for slip iron. Practically all the holes in the keel-plates were drilled in place, the plates being subsequently separated so as to remove the burrs from the surfaces; the edges of the holes were slightly reamed, and the whole re-assembled for riveting. The double-bottom plates, as well as most of those used in the main struc-ture of the ship, are at least 32 ft. in length. The connecting - bars of the centre - line girder were riveted first, as it was found by experience necessary to get the garboards in place before any other riveting on the flat keel was proceeded with, owing to the great closing power of the hydraulic riveters used. Fig. 13, below, illustrates the process of riveting by hydraulic power so clearly that no description is called for. The riveters were supplied by Sir William Arrol and Co., Limited, Glasgow.

The floor-plates in the double bottom are placed at 32-in. centres over about 300 ft. in the central part of the ship. At the ends the spacing is 26 in. forward and 25 in. aft, the reduction in spacing being gradual. These floor-plates are 60 in. deep

line) is shown in Fig. 11, while the engraving, Fig. 27 on Plate VII., clearly illustrates the great strength of the structure.

As to the vertical framing from the margin-plate to the shelter deck, it is continuous, as shown in the engraving on Plate VII., Fig. 26. These frames are formed of channels 10 in. by $\frac{2}{4}\frac{0}{0}$ in. by 4 in. by 4 in. by $\frac{2}{4}\frac{3}{0}$ in. for $\frac{3}{5}$ L amidships to 9 in. by $\frac{2}{4}\frac{0}{0}$ in. by 4 in. by 4 in. by $\frac{2}{4}\frac{3}{0}$ in., secured by heavy brackets to the margin-plate, and fortified by web-frames at an average of four frame-spaces apart. The shell-plating covering these vertical frames is arranged for the turn of the bilge in strakes parallel with the sheer line, worked with lapped edges and with lapped butts where they are in one thickness. The plates are generally about 33 ft. long—that is, twelve frame-spaces, plus the lap of the butt; the edges are treble-riveted and the butts quadruple-riveted.

High-tensile steel was used for a considerable number of the upper as well as the sheer-strakes for a great length of the hull amidship. The extent of their use is illustrated by the diagram, Fig. 8. The lightly hatched parts are of one thickness only, and of the same scantling as would have been adopted for mild steel; the more heavily hatched portions are in two thicknesses and of reduced scantling, in consideration of the strength of the material. Throughout the region of doubled

the engine-room, and by the partial bulkheads in the coal-bunkers. The extent of this sub-division will be at once appreciated by reference to the deck plans published on the two-page Plate XXXVII. To the system adopted for automatically closing the doors in these bulkheads we shall refer later.

The midship section, Fig. 7, shows how the longitudinal bulkheads are stiffened and braced to the side. These engine-room bulkheads, being connected to the longitudinal bunker bulkheads, and of strong construction, form valuable girders, contributing to the strength of the ship; and, as they are well stiffened and braced, they are kept up to their work. The main transverse bulkheads have vertical channel stiffeners on one side, 12 in. by $3\frac{1}{2}$ in. by $3\frac{1}{2}$ in. by $\frac{1}{2}\frac{1}{0}$ in. to the lower deck, and flanged stiffeners above, and on the same side hori-zontal girders 32 in. broad, with a face channel 9 in. by $\frac{1}{2}\frac{0}{0}$ in. by 4 in. by 4 in. by $\frac{2}{4}\frac{3}{0}$ in.

The engravings on Plates I. to VIII., illus-trating the construction of the ship, have been grouped generally to show the work, firstly, at the bow, secondly, at the stern, and, thirdly, amidships. Little remains to be written further in elucidation of these views, and of the sections given on page 18, excepting to refer to the stem and stern framings. The stem is of cast steel, and was constructed with rabbets to receive the shell-plating. The weight was 8.3 tons.

FIG. 12. KEEL AND CENTRE-LINE GIRDER.

FIG. 13. HYDRAULIC RIVETING.

amidships, and have a maximum width, at the margin-plate marked L, of 48 in. The floor-plates, as shown in the midship section, Fig. 7, are in one length from the middle line to the fifth keelson, and from this to the margin they are also in one piece. This obviated inconvenience at the turn of the bilge, and proved convenient in the arrange-ment of the floor-plates below. The plates are generally $\frac{1}{2}\frac{0}{0}$ in. thick, except under the boiler bearers, where they are $\frac{1}{2}\frac{2}{0}$ in. The shell-plates on the outer bottom were worked clinker fashion. Nearly all the rivets up to, and including, the margin-plate were put in by hydraulic power. This necessitated the lapping of the plates, as the frames were too close together to admit of the use of riveters of moderate gap. The result will be seen by reference to Fig. 17 on Plate II., and to Fig. 25 on Plate VI. Each strake could therefore be riveted right up to the edge seam, connecting to the next strake to be brought on. In this lower portion of the bottom the edge seams are double-riveted, and the butts have double straps, the outer being double and the inner treble-riveted, with openly-spaced rivets in the third row. The edges of the outer strap are slightly chamfered. From a little above the turn of the bilge the plate edges are sheared in lines approximating to the sheer of the ship, and the strakes below are worked as stealers into the edge of the lowest of the parallel strakes, thus avoiding an excessive number of narrow strakes at the bow and stern, as shown in the engravings just indicated. The framing under the turbine-seating is considerably deeper than elsewhere, and additional fore and aft girders are introduced. A typical section (in out-

thickness hydraulic riveting was adopted. The edges are treble-riveted, and the butts of the doubled portion are strapped outside and inside at the butts of the outside plates, the outer straps taking three rows of rivets, and the inner straps taking four rows; the thickness of the straps is reduced on account of the doubling. The butts of the inside plates are strapped on the inside and quadruple-riveted.

Similar insurance against hogging stresses was extended to the upper decks, and thus a consider-able portion of the shelter and a fair part of the upper deck (Fig. 9) are of high-tensile steel, and were riveted by hydraulic power. This section shows the details of the sheer-strakes, with the beams carrying the shelter and upper decks—a connection which is of considerable importance to the struc-tural strength. The remaining deck-plating is prin-cipally of such a nature as is necessary to provide suitable floorings, and occupies only a secondary place as regards the structural strength of the vessel.

The large openings in the decks—viz., funnels and ventilators—are arranged, as far as practicable, in the same fore-and-aft lines, as shown in the two illustrations on Plate VIII., so that important strakes of plating are run through for long unin-terrupted lengths, and these openings have heavy doublings and well-rounded corners.

The main bulkheads are formed of high-tensile steel, $\frac{1}{2}$ in. thick in the lower parts, and $\frac{9}{2}\frac{}{0}$ in. thick up to the main deck. Above this they are $\frac{6}{2}\frac{}{0}$ in. thick, also of high-tensile steel. There are eleven main transverse bulkheads, and the sub-division is carried considerably further by the longi-tudinal bunker bulkheads, by the two bulkheads in

Figs. 15 to 23 on Plates I. to V. show the stern. The heavy section of double bottom, and the bossing out of the framing for the pro-pelling shafts, are of great interest. The spectacle eyes—monocles would be a more accurate term —for the outer shafts are of cast steel, and well incorporated with the framework of the hull 90 ft. before the after perpendicular. The spectacles for the two inner shafts, which are at 19-ft. 6-in. centres, are also of cast steel, and are riveted to the stern-post. This latter is a steel casting, of a special form, shown on Fig. 22 on Plate V., to support a balanced rudder and to take the steering-gear in duplicate. For the latter the framing and plat-ing had to be flared out, as shown in Fig. 23 on Plate V. The weight of the stern - post is 59 tons 8 cwt., exclusive of the spectacle frames, which, together, weigh 60 tons 4 cwt.

The rudder, which weighs 56 tons 8 cwt., is composed of three steel castings, and the rudder-head is of forged steel; all the parts are con-nected by horizontal flanges, well rabbeted and heavily bolted. The rudder area is 420 square feet; there is one removable pintle.

Before departing from the description of the construction of the hull, a passing reference may be made to the subject of handling the material, as the appliances proved very efficient, and were of low cost. The maximum weight of any unit was about 4 tons, and for this electric jigger cranes were supplied by Messrs. Sir William Arrol and Co., Limited. These were described in ENGINEER-ING, vol. lxxxi., page 163. These are seen in Fig. 29 on Plate VIII. Ordinary jibs on uprights did splendidly for the lighter loads, which were, where necessary, moved in wagons on a standard-gauge railway laid on the deck-plating. These may seem crude methods at a time when so much is spent by some firms on berth structures ; but comment is unnecessary, in view of the short period occupied in the building of the Lusitania. She was launched, weighing 15,500 tons, fourteen months three weeks from the laying of the keel, notwithstanding eight weeks' delay owing to a strike.

With a view to preventing the deterioration of the structure through corrosion, the whole of the internal surfaces of the bunkers and the floors, intercostals, shell-plating, and seatings under turbines and boilers have been coated by Messrs. Wailes, Dove, and Co., Limited, with their patent "Bitumastic" enamel, and the tank-top in way of boilers and machinery, and the fan-room with this company's patent "Bitumastic" covering.

THE LAUNCH OF THE SHIP.

This brings us to the launch, by no means the least important incident in connection with this ship. A detailed description of the launch is given on page 50, and from this some idea can be formed of the extreme precision with which the whole operation was carried out. The event, indeed, was commonplace so far as incident was concerned, but this result was only secured by careful attention to every detail in the preparation. In a paper read at the spring meeting of the Institution of Naval Archi-tects, by Mr. W. J. Luke,* the details of the launching-gear, and the calculations upon which it was proportioned, were fully set out, and it is not, therefore, necessary to enter here upon a full description. Mr. Luke's paper is well worth study because of the completeness of its detail.

The total time which elapsed from the release of the triggers until the vessel was fully afloat was 86 seconds ; of this period 22 seconds were absorbed in tripping the keel-blocks left under her, and during this operation she only progressed about 1 ft. down the ways. This gives an average speed of 12.2 ft. per second for the remainder of the journey to the water. The velocity was so moderate that the vessel was brought up with her bow about 110 ft. from the shore. The total weight of drags in use was 1000 tons.

PASSENGER ACCOMMODATION OF THE SHIP.

SINCE the date of the launch only a year has been occupied in completing the ship, with her extensive habitable quarters. When one realises that the vessel carries 552 first-class, 460 second-class, and 1186 third-class passengers, in addition to 827 officers and crew, the performance indicates the efficiency of the wood-working department at Clydebank.

Table IV. shows the cabin accommodation for the various classes of passengers.

TABLE IV.—*List of Rooms for Passengers.*

First Class. (552 Passengers.)
36 one-berth rooms.
150 two-berth rooms.
72 three-berth rooms.
Total, 260 rooms.

Second Class. (460 Passengers.)
60 two-berth rooms.
85 four-berth rooms.
Total, 145 rooms.

Third Class. (1186 Passengers.)
40 two-berth rooms.
237 four-berth rooms.
21 six-berth rooms.
4 eight-berth rooms.
Total, 302 rooms.

The arrangement of the cabins is clearly shown on the deck plans published on the two-page Plate XXXVII. All the first and second-class, and many of the third-class, passengers are accommodated above the load water-line, which practically coincides amidships with the lower deck (Fig. 30). The first-class passengers are accommodated in the centre part of the ship—on the boat, promenade, shelter and upper decks—only a few rooms being arranged for this class on the main deck. The second-class quarters are arranged in the after part of the vessel, fully 150 ft. of the length of the ship being given up to them. The third-class passengers have their state-rooms in the forward part of the ship, on the lower and main decks. All the state-rooms, therefore, may be ventilated by natural draught, although, as we shall explain presently, a complete system of artificial draught has been fitted.

All the public rooms, with the single exception of the dining-saloons, are at a higher level than usual. The first-class writing-room and library, lounge, smoking-room, and café are on the boat-deck, and therefore quite 60 ft. above the water-level. A capital idea is afforded of these public rooms and of the immense size of the ship by the two engravings published on Plate IX. These views were taken from the top of the 150-ton hammer-head crane* recently built at the Clydebank Works by Sir William Arrol and Co., Limited. Comparison of the roofs of the lounge and writing-room, seen on Fig. 38, and of the smoking-room, seen on Fig. 39, with the buildings in the works, indicates pretty clearly the great size of the vessel. The reception rooms for the second-class passengers are similarly well placed, the lounge, which is an interesting innovation in this class, is on the boat-deck, while the drawing-room and smoking-room are on the promenade-deck. On the shelter-deck forward there is arranged the smoking-room and ladies' room for the third-class passengers.

The dining-saloons, owing to the great area required, had to be within the moulded dimensions of the ship, so that the width of the room might be the full breadth of the ship. The dining-saloons for the respective classes are therefore on the upper deck. On the shelter-deck there is a second storey to the first-class dining-saloon, surrounding the well, with the great dome above. This magnificent room, with the other saloons in the ship, are fully described on page 51, and illustrated on Plates XXI to XXVIII.

to locate the men as near as possible to their work. The navigating officers have their cabins immediately abaft the bridge, and as there is here a smoke-room, with other conveniences, they are self-contained, and need not from beginning to end of the voyage associate with the passengers. The engineers have exceptionally good quarters in the house on the shelter-deck, surrounding the engine-hatches. Here also there are mess-rooms and other conveniences, the whole accommodation

FIG. 42. ELECTRIC DRIVING-GEAR OF PASSENGER HOIST.

The dining accommodation is as given in Table V.

TABLE V.—*Accommodation of Dining-Saloons.*

				Seats.
First Class.—Upper saloon	...	...	...	150
Lower saloon	...	...	...	350
Children's saloon	...	...	...	40
Total	...	...	...	540
Second Class.—260 seats.				
Third Class.—Main saloon	...	...	...	340
Ladies' room	...	...	...	90
Smoking-room	...	...	...	110
Total	...	...	...	540

In the disposition of the accommodation for the officers and crew, the principle followed has been being in advance of the arrangements made in other large ships. The purser and his staff, and the doctor, have their quarters adjoining the grand entrance on the shelter-deck, so that they are at all time easily accessible. The position of the rooms of the supernumeraries will easily be seen on the deck-plans on Plate XXXVII. Seamen are accommodated forward ; stewards at the extreme after end of the upper, main, and lower decks ; while the firemen, trimmers, &c., have dormitories and extensive bath and lavatory accommodation close by the engine-room hatches. A notable point is that the dormitories are arranged for groups corre-

* See ENGINEERING, vol. lxxxiii., page 433.

* See ENGINEERING, vol. lxxxiii., page 803.

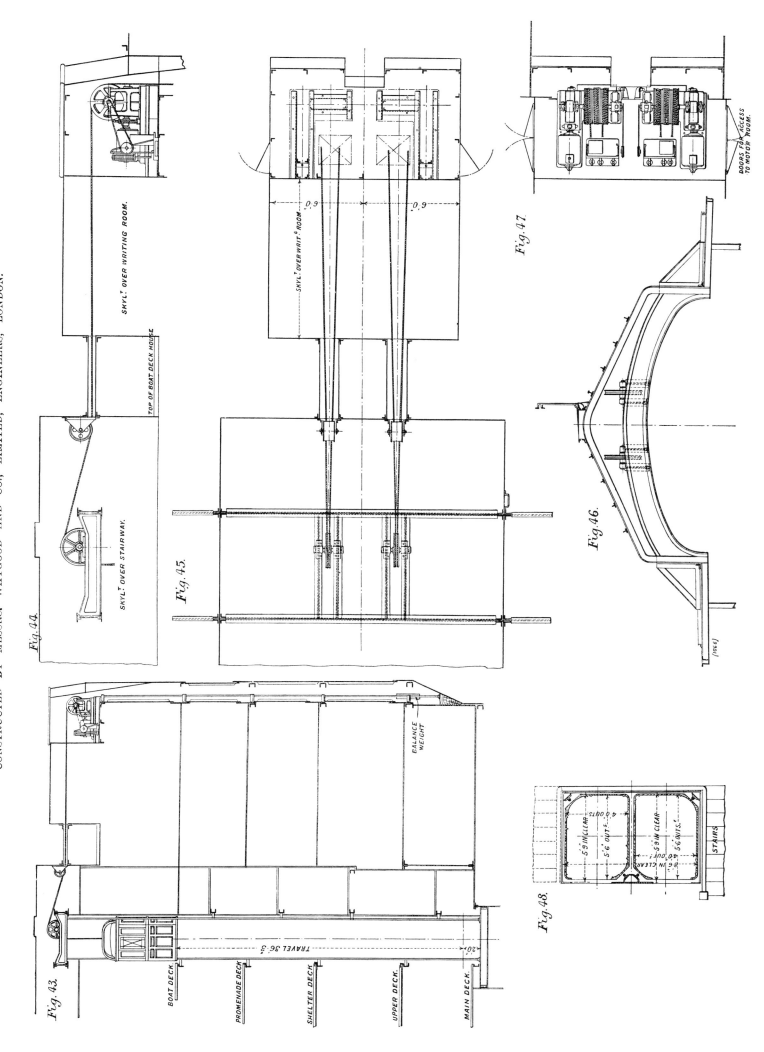

ELECTRIC PASSENGER HOIST.

CONSTRUCTED BY MESSRS. WAYGOOD AND CO., LIMITED, ENGINEERS, LONDON.

Fig. 44.

SKYL.T OVER WRITING ROOM.

TOP OF BOAT DECK HOUSE

SKYL.T OVER STAIRWAY.

Fig. 45.

SKYL.T OVER WRIT.G ROOM.

6.0   6.0

BALANCE WEIGHT

Fig. 43.

TRAVEL 36.3

BOAT DECK.

PROMENADE DECK.

SHELTER DECK.

UPPER DECK.

MAIN DECK.

Fig. 47.

DOORS FOR ACCESS TO MOTOR ROOM.

Fig. 46.

(1066)

Fig. 48.

STAIRS

5.9 IN CLEAR   4.0 OUTS.
5.6 OUT.   5.6 OUTS.
4.0 OUT   5.9 IN CLEAR
8.6 IN CLEAR

BAGGAGE AND SERVICE ELECTRIC HOISTS.

CONSTRUCTED BY MESSRS. WAYGOOD AND CO., LIMITED ENGINEERS, LONDON.

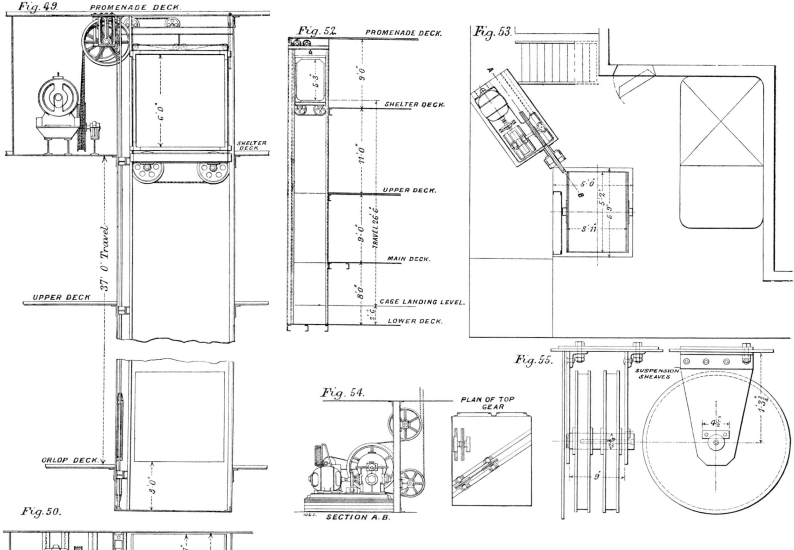

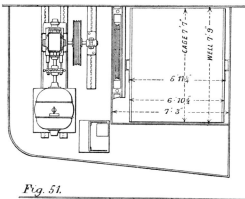

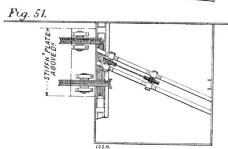

sponding with the number of men in a watch, and thus those going on, or coming off, watch need not disturb the third shift at rest.

The arrangement of the decks conduces to a ready acquaintance of what we may term the topography of the vessel, although the time is probably coming when it may be desirable to name the alleyways like streets, as well as to number the cabins. The arrangement is simplified because the passengers' quarters are above water-level, so that only on the lower and main deck is there need for water-tight bulkheads and doors. The main line of communication for first-class passengers is a broad companionway in the centre of the ship, extending from the main deck up through four levels to the boat-deck. Passengers entering the ship, either from tender, wharf, or landing-stage, will go through doors fitted on the side of the ship at this main-deck level, ascending either by the stairs, or by either of two hoists, to the deck on which their cabin is located. From the entrance-hall or landing on each deck there extend forward and aft main passages, and from these, again, branch alleyways to the cabins. For the second-class passengers there is aft a corresponding companion-way, with large landings or entrance-halls, while forward, again, stairways are provided for the third-class passengers.

It is scarcely necessary to describe at length the arrangement of the several decks, of which plans are given on Plate XXXVII. On the boat-deck (Fig. 31) there are forward cabins of a superior character for sixty-two passengers ; but the principal feature here is the public rooms : the writing-room and library, the lounge and music-room, the smoke-room and the veranda café abaft the engine hatches. Aft there is the second-class lounge and promenade. On this deck there are stowed sixteen boats of the latest design, and the electric lowering gear to be described later is so arranged that the boats can be got to the water in the shortest possible time.

On the promenade-deck there are no public rooms, but here one finds the most interesting rooms, and probably the most successful decorative features in the ship. As shown on the plan (Fig. 32), there are two regal suites of rooms, fully described on page 52, with six *en suite* rooms, and, in addition, large and well-appointed state-rooms for 237 first-class passengers. Aft there are the drawing-room and smoking-room for the second-class passengers.

On the shelter-deck (Fig. 33), which is at the top level of the moulded structure, there are no first-class state-rooms. The forward part is given up to third-class passengers, who have here their smoking and ladies' room, with extensive lavatory accommodation abaft the companion-way. A large part of the promenade space on this deck will also be given up to third-class passengers, and inclement weather will not interfere with open-air recreation, as the forward part is sheltered by a continuation upwards of the skin plating of the ship, as shown in the longitudinal section on Plate XXXVII. Amidships, in the first-class quarters, there is a children's dining-saloon and nursery, with the rooms for officers of the ship : stewards, stewardesses, nurses, pursers, doctors, &c. Here also is located the printing establishment for the publication of the daily bulletin with the ship's news and the Marconigrams from over the seas. The upper floor of the dining-saloon surrounding the well takes up the central part of this deck. Abaft it are the pantries, then the engineers' quarters, and finally 27 rooms for 104 second-class passengers.

Dining-saloons occupy one-third of the length of the upper deck (Fig. 34), while pantries, galleys, bakehouses, and all the other branches of the commissariat department, take up a further large portion. There are, however, over sixty-two rooms, accommodating 147 first-class passengers, and forty-one rooms for 122 second-class passengers on this level.

The immense engine-room staff encroach largely on the main deck (Fig. 35), but there are, nevertheless, at the extreme forward end permanent cabins for 626 third-class passengers ; in the after part 76 cabins for 232 second-class passengers, and in

THERMO-TANK SYSTEM OF VENTILATION.

CONSTRUCTED BY THE THERMO-TANK VENTILATING COMPANY, LIMITED, GLASGOW.

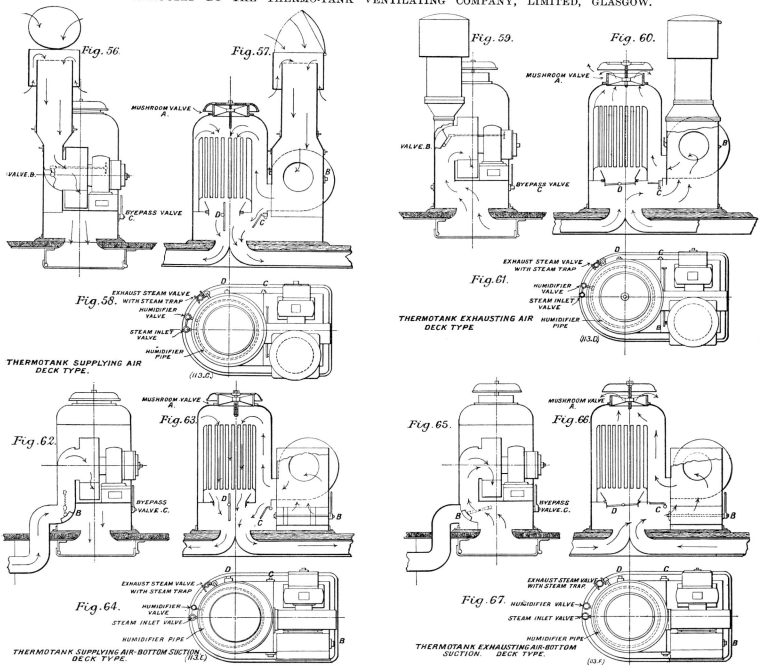

Fig. 56. Fig. 57.

MUSHROOM VALVE A.

VALVE B.

BYEPASS VALVE C.

Fig. 58.
EXHAUST STEAM VALVE WITH STEAM TRAP.
HUMIDIFIER VALVE.
STEAM INLET VALVE.
HUMIDIFIER PIPE.

THERMOTANK SUPPLYING AIR DECK TYPE.
(113.C.)

Fig. 59. Fig. 60.

MUSHROOM VALVE A.

VALVE B.

BYEPASS VALVE C.

Fig. 61.
EXHAUST STEAM VALVE WITH STEAM TRAP.
HUMIDIFIER VALVE.
STEAM INLET VALVE.
HUMIDIFIER PIPE.

THERMOTANK EXHAUSTING AIR DECK TYPE
(113.D.)

Fig. 62. Fig. 63.

MUSHROOM VALVE A.

BYEPASS VALVE C.

Fig. 64.
EXHAUST STEAM VALVE WITH STEAM TRAP.
HUMIDIFIER VALVE.
STEAM INLET VALVE.
HUMIDIFIER PIPE.

THERMOTANK SUPPLYING AIR-BOTTOM SUCTION. DECK TYPE.
(113.E.)

Fig. 65. Fig. 66.

MUSHROOM VALVE A.

BYEPASS VALVE C.

Fig. 67.
EXHAUST STEAM VALVE WITH STEAM TRAP.
HUMIDIFIER VALVE.
STEAM INLET VALVE.
HUMIDIFIER PIPE.

THERMOTANK EXHAUSTING AIR-BOTTOM SUCTION. DECK TYPE.
(113.F.)

the centre of the ship 58 first-class cabins for 111 passengers.

On the lower deck (Fig. 36) there are permanent cabins for 100 third-class passengers, and towards the forward end portable berths are shown for 428 passengers. The space which may thus be occupied can, however, be converted into holds for cargo or stores.

The hold plan (Fig. 37) does not call here for special comment, as it will be dealt with more fully when we come to describe the machinery of the ship.

As to the area of promenading space, a clear idea is obtainable from the engravings on Plates IX. and X. The views on the first of these plates (Figs. 38 and 39), to which we have already referred, show the boat-deck. This is a fine promenade; while on the deck below, 1½ acres in extent, there is again a great walking-track, 3⅓ times round which measure a mile. Fig. 40 on Plate X. shows this promenade-deck, while Fig. 41 on the same plate is suggestive of the great height of the bridge, although the view is only from the forecastle head. This illustration is further suggestive of the great area which these vessels present against wind pressure when steaming at full speed in the teeth of a gale.*

It seems almost superfluous to indicate the many

* See ENGINEERING, vol. lxxv., page 876.

contrivances introduced for the convenience of passengers. There is a well-equipped bureau, where all information can be obtained. Many of the principal cabins are connected with each other and the bureau, &c., by telephones. In a word, from first to last there has been a determination to excel the most admirably equipped hotels on land.

A noteworthy feature in the vessel is the sanitary arrangements, which have been carried out largely by Messrs. Shanks and Co., Limited, Barrhead. The large proportions of bath-rooms and lavatories is specially notable, as well as their convenient distribution. The sanitation throughout is of the most complete kind, the system of flushing, trapping, &c., being far in advance of anything hitherto carried out on a large scale, while the plumbing work is perfect.

Hospitals have been arranged on the shelter-deck amidships, separate hospitals being arranged for infectious diseases for both sexes. These hospitals have been fitted out in the most complete manner, and have dispensary, lavatories, and bath-rooms.

THE PASSENGER HOISTS.

A feature in the arrangements for the comfort of passengers is the complete equipment of lifts for passengers, baggage service, &c., by Messrs. R.

Waygood and Co., Limited, London. In all eleven lifts and hoists have been installed by this firm, all worked by electric current supplied by the ship's generating plant at a pressure of 110 to 120 volts.

Of these hoists, we illustrate on pages 20 and 21 (Figs. 42 to 47) the two passenger lifts running within the stair-well, and probably the most interesting in the ship. These travel through a height of 36 ft. 3 in. between the main and boat-decks, opening on to the splendid vestibules or halls on each deck leading to the various public saloons or to the alleyways through the extensive ranges of cabins. The cars are constructed in polished mahogany, and are each guided by two round steel guides attached to the staircase framing. Special safety apparatus on the cars come into operation on the failure of the lifting-ropes. This apparatus has a positive action, and is not dependent on springs. Each car is raised by steel cables, which pass through the double dome roof of the staircase, over top sheaves, and thence horizontally to the winding-gear, which is fixed at the boat deck-house level (Fig. 43). The counterbalance weights travel in a trunkway, forming a ventilator, the counterweights being guided by round steel guides attached to suitable brackets to the trunkway (Fig. 43).

The lifting-gear is clearly illustrated by Fig. 42. The cables for each lift are two in number, of best crucible-steel wire, attached to the winding-drum. Two independent ropes are also attached to the drum

375-KILOWATT TURBO-GENERATOR.

CONSTRUCTED BY MESSRS. C. A. PARSONS AND CO., LIMITED, ENGINEERS, NEWCASTLE-ON-TYNE.

Fig. 68.

and connected to the counterbalance weights already referred to, to ensure a positive drive. The winding-gear is of the worm-and-wheel type, the worm being of steel, cut from the solid, while the wheel has a centre of cast iron with a phosphor-bronze tooth-ring, into which the teeth are hobbed. The worm and wheel are enclosed in a cast-iron box, forming an oil bath. The worm-shaft is fitted with special adjustable thrust-bearings in order to reduce friction, and the winding-drum is securely keyed to the worm-wheel shaft. This winding-drum is turned and grooved with right and left-hand spiral grooves, in which the lifting-cables coil. The brake-gear is of the electric mechanical type, actuated by a magnet, so arranged that the brake is released when current is switched on, and is applied automatically on the current being cut off by the control.

The magnetically-operated controller is worked from the car by means of a special car-switch having an "up," "down," and "stop" position. The main controller consists of a panel, upon which are mounted an "up" and "down" circuit-breaker, each operated by a magnet and a rheostat actuated by a solenoid, and provided with air retardation. Each of the two circuit-breakers is fitted with a magnetic blow-out, and the contacts, which are of copper, are so arranged that although the current is interrupted at four points, the actual breaking is performed in the field of this blow-out, thus readily disrupting the arc and preventing destructive arcing. The rheostat cuts out the main resistance (which is in series with the armature at starting) in sixteen steps, and is connected to a resistance frame fixed behind the controller panel, and constructed of fireproof materials. The car-switches are of cylindrical type, with a movable self-centering handle, so that in the event of the attendant releasing the handle for any purpose, it at once flies to the "off" position, cutting off the controller and stopping the lift. The controller is also fitted with a special type of automatic cut-off switch, positively driven from the drum-shaft of the machine, and arranged so that, should the attendant omit to switch off the current when approaching the top or bottom levels, the corresponding automatic switch will come into action and will stop the lift before any damage is done.

Each car is fitted with Waygood's patent slack-cable switch. In the event of the car or balance-weight, while descending, meeting with any obstruction to cause the ropes to become slack, this switch is immediately opened and cuts off current from the machine by causing the controller to come to its "off" position, simultaneously applying the brake, and, of course, stopping the lift.

In order to afford security against the lift entrance doors being left open, or inadvertently opened, these are all fitted with automatic locks and electric contacts, arranged so that any door can only be opened when the lift-car is opposite it. Nor can the car be moved away until the doors are closed. An electric bell and indicator is provided in each car, with a push at each deck, to enable the car to be called by passengers.

TABLE VI.—*Capacity of Passenger and Baggage Hoists.*

Load.	Speed. ft. per min.	Travel.	Motors. B.H.P.
Two passenger lifts:—			
10 cwt.	150	From main deck to top deck, 36 ft. 3 in.	8
Two baggage-lifts:—			
40 cwt.	100	From orlop-deck to shelter-deck	15
Two service-lifts:—			
10 cwt.	100	From lower deck to shelter-deck	5
Three food-lifts:—			
2 cwt.	60	10 ft. to 11 ft.	1½
Two ash-hoists:—			
2 cwt.	200	About 60 ft.	3

The two baggage lifts, fitted in a convenient position to the baggage-holds, are each designed to carry a load of 2 tons, and are arranged as shown on page 22 (Figs. 49 to 51). The winding gear is of the worm-

375-KILOWATT TURBO-GENERATOR.

CONSTRUCTED BY MESSRS. C. A. PARSONS AND CO., LIMITED, ENGINEERS, NEWCASTLE-ON-TYNE.

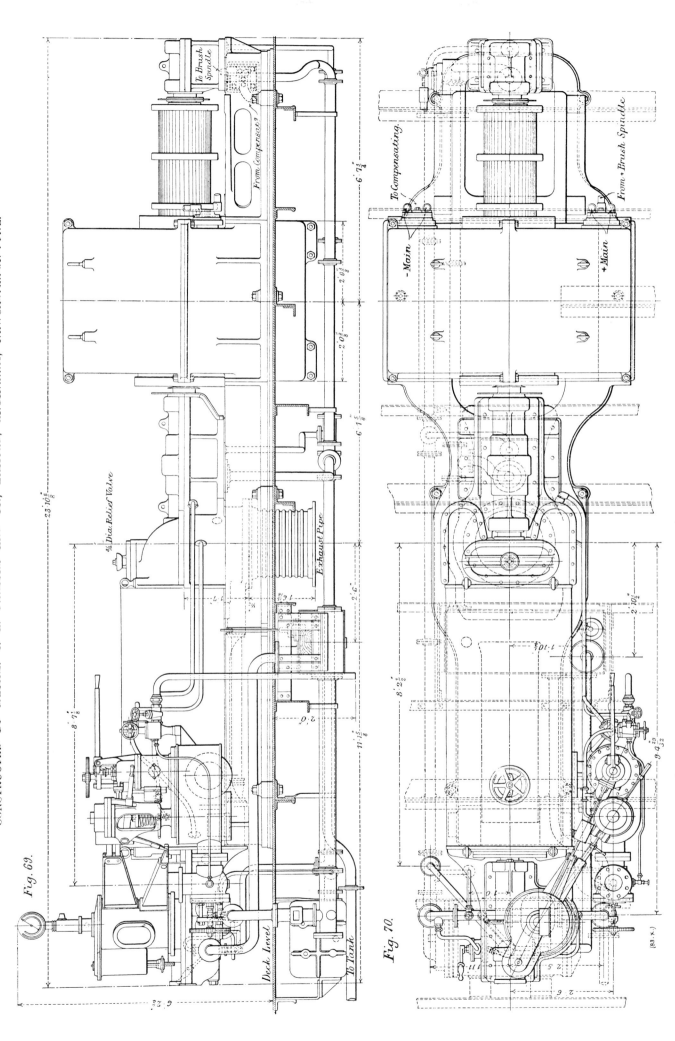

Fig. 69.

Fig. 70.

and-wheel type, somewhat similar to that described for the passenger lifts, but the drive is a friction one. The lifting cables are attached at each end at the top of a trunkway, and they pass around sheaves attached to the cage, and on the balance-weight, being led to the "V" lifting wheel by suitable diverting sheaves, as shown by Figs. 49 to 51. The cars are constructed of steel angle and channel framework, and are guided by steel channels on each side, the counter-balance weights being guided by round steel guides attached to the trunkway. The control of these baggage lifts is very similar to that already described for the passenger lifts, but instead of a car-switch being fitted, sets of "up," "down," and "stop" buttons are fixed in the cars, and also on each deck-level.

There are, further, two 10-cwt. service lifts, illustrated on page 22 (Figs. 52 to 55), the general construction and working being similar to the two baggage lifts. There are also three small service lifts for carrying food, as well as two electric friction hoist-gears for raising ashes from the stokehold. Table VI., above, shows the capacity of these lifts.

THE VENTILATION OF THE SHIP.

The thermo-tank system, as introduced by the Thermo-Tank Ventilating Company, of Glasgow,

D

has been adopted in connection with the ventilation of the ship, and two typical arrangements are illustrated on page 23, by Figs. 56 to 67. This system aims specially at ensuring to all the living quarters of the ship a continuous supply of fresh air, which is not only warmed to the requisite degree, but is also humidified, so that none of the bad effects of over drying can be felt. In cold weather the warmed air is discharged, through a regulated louvre, into each apartment, near the level of the ceiling ; as it cools it gradually sinks to a lower level, carrying with it any carbonic-acid gas to the passage ways, where means are provided for allowing it to pass outside. In warm weather, or when heating is not necessary, the reverse action takes place, as the louvres near the ceiling constitute the exhaust, with the result that the warm impure gases leave the top of the room, and fresh atmospheric air comes in at the floor-level.

The thermo-tank generally consists of an electric motor operating a fan which discharges air to the outside of a tube heater. The air then passes through the tubes, and comes in close contact with the heater surface, flowing thence to the main distributing-trunks. Two valves are used for controlling the passage of air : one for regulating the temperature, while the mushroom valve on the top is provided for the exhaust air. It will be noted that the air passes round the outside of the heater on its way to the tubes, so that the loss from radiation is very small, the outer casing of the thermo-tank being quite cool on all occasions. The heater is warmed by steam from the main boilers, entering at the top, with an exhaust at the bottom. The pressure of steam is reduced to about 30 lb., and a relief-valve is fitted to blow off at from 80 lb. to 100 lb. pressure. The heater and all its connections are tested to the full boiler pressure. The air is humidified by means of a special valve admitting steam in a fine spray, by means of small needle-holes in a copper hoop surrounding the heater. Tests carried out to compare the efficiency of the thermo-tank system with that of the ordinary heaters show that where the steam-heated system took three hours to attain a given temperature, the thermo-tank only required fifteen minutes. The consumption of steam is small, as all the heat is abstracted, only water being drained off to the feed-tank.

The first-class accommodation is connected to twenty-four thermo-tanks, which are arranged principally on the boat-deck houses. These are seen at the base of the funnel in Fig. 38, Plate IX. The second-class accommodation is connected to nine thermo-tanks, the third-class to eleven, and the officers' and crew's accommodation to five, these being arranged mostly on the top of deck-houses, &c. The thermo-tanks in the fore-end of the ship are placed between decks, and obtain their supply of fresh air from the after end of the navigating-bridge, so that in this way a continuous supply of fresh air is ensured in the worst weather, there being no cowl-heads or openings forward of the flying-bridge. Although the thermo tanks are arranged principally on the top of the boat-deck houses, the fresh-air supply is obtained from gratings opening out on the promenade-deck shelter. This has been done so as to avoid the smells from galleys, w.c's, &c., which all exhaust above the boat-deck houses. When the thermo-tanks are exhausting, of course, the cowl-head provided for the purpose can then be used.

The thermo-tanks are capable of changing the air, either by exhaust or supply, in the various compartments to which they are connected at least from six to eight times per hour, and they are also capable of maintaining a temperature of at least 65 deg. Fahr. in the coldest weather. In addition they are interconnected, so that in case of the breakdown of any thermo-tank, a supply can always be obtained from another.

The diagrammatic drawings on page 23 illustrate the working of thermo-tanks as follows :—

Figs. 56 to 58 illustrate the working of deck-type thermo-tanks when supplying fresh, warm, or cold air to the various compartments, and Figs. 59 to 61 show the same when exhausting.

Figs. 62 to 64 show the working of bottom-suction deck-type thermo-tanks when supplying fresh, warm, or cold air to the various compartments, and Figs. 65 to 67 show the same when exhausting.

The work of the thermo-tanks is further augmented by means of twelve powerful exhaust-fans, which are connected by means of trunks respectively to all the galleys and pantries, bath-rooms,

TABLE VII.—SUMMARY OF OFFICIAL TRIALS OF TURBO-GENERATORS.

Number of machine	1034.			1077.		1078.			1079.
Date of test	4/8/06	4/8/06	4/8/06	14/8/06	13/8/06	13/8/06	13/8/06	14/8/06
Load	Full	Three-quarter	Half	Full	Full	Three-quarter	Half	Full
Stop-valve pressure	167	167	173	166	158	161	160	164
Barometer in inches of mercury	29.77	29.77	29.77	29.54	29.4	29.4	29.4	29.54
Back pressure in pounds	5	5	5	4.95	4.86	5	5	5
Speed—revolutions per minute	1200	1200	1200	1200	1200	1200	1200	1200
Voltage	111	111.2	113.6	115.2	107	109.8	112.3	114.5
Average kilowatts	373.27	288.9	188.42	375.38	371.75	285.28	188.3	373.31
Field volts	87.6	88.73	86.06	92.46	87.5	89.6	90.6	92.68
„ amperes..	33.31	31.15	30.9	30.76	30.8	30.8	30.8	31.5
Average quantity of water per hour in pounds	17,831	15,017	11,419	17,301	17,888	15,104	11,649	17,546
Water consumption per kilowatt-hour in pounds	47.76	51.97	60.60	46.08	48.14	52.94	61.86	47

lavatories, and w.c's, these fans being of sufficient capacity to change the air in the above-mentioned compartments at least fifteen times per hour. In addition to the living quarters, the holds and other compartments, forward and aft, are also mechanically ventilated, so that all natural ventilation requiring cowl-heads, or openings through decks, has been dispensed with.

ELECTRIC LIGHTING.

An extensive electric generating station is arranged on a flat deck abaft the engine-room, as shown on the section, Fig. 85, on Plate XXXIX., and details of the applications of electricity are given on page 53. There are four generating sets, each of 375 kilowatts capacity, the voltage being 110 to 120. The prime movers are Parsons turbines, and it is interesting to recall that the Clydebank firm was among the first, if not the first, to fit turbo-

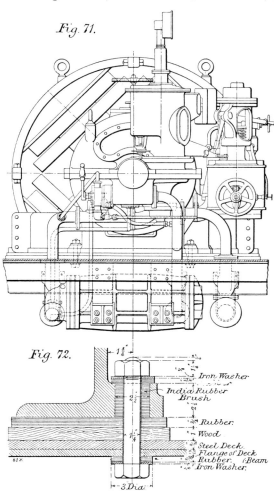

Fig. 71.

Fig. 72.

FIGS. 71 AND 72. DETAILS OF TURBO-GENERATOR.

generators on ships, and on that occasion the vessel also was for the Atlantic trade. Fig. 68 on page 24 is a view of one generating set, with the turbine casing removed, showing the blading in the various expansions, while Figs. 69 and 70 on page 25, and Figs. 71 and 72 on the present page, show the general arrangement of a set, and details of deck-fixing. The turbines were designed to give full load when exhausting into a back pressure of 10 lb. They run the dynamos at 1200 revolutions per minute ; but an overload of 10 per cent. for two hours is pro-

vided for. Each dynamo is shunt wound. The armature is of the surface drum-wound type, with one turn per section. No relative movement between the conductors and commutator bars is possible, but as an additional safeguard, the connections between these are made flexible. Special driving-horns in the ends of the core are provided. The insulation of the whole machine was tested with an alternating pressure of 2000 volts between the conductors and the frame, and the insulation resistance after the above test was to be not less than one-half of a megohm for the whole machine, one megohm for the armature winding, one megohm for the field-winding, and one megohm for each of the brush-holders.

Tests were made of the various turbo-generators at the Heaton-on-Tyne Works of the constructors —Messrs. C. A. Parsons and Co., Limited—and the results for all four engines are given in Table VII. It will be noted that at half load the water consumption was in one case 60.60 lb., and in another 61.86 lb. per kilowatt-hour ; at three-quarter load the consumption was 52 lb. to 53 lb., and at full load from 46 lb. to 48 lb., the back pressure in each case being about 5 lb. The tests were carried out in the presence of representatives of Messrs. John Brown and Co., Limited, and the Cunard Company.

COMMISSARIAT DEPARTMENT.

Certainly not the least interesting part of the vessel is the portion devoted to the kitchens. The Cunard Company has always been famous for its high-class cuisine. It can easily be understood that the kitchens in the Lusitania quite eclipse anything afloat. The saloon kitchen and pantries extend right across the ship, and 126 ft. fore and aft. This department is equipped with every modern device for the preparation of food under the best conditions. The main range, probably the largest in the world, has a hot-plate containing over 250 square feet ; there are no less than a dozen steam-ovens, half-a-dozen steam-stockpots, half a dozen hot-closets, and as many *bains maries*. Electricity has been largely employed, and works the large patent roasters, bread-making, meat slicing, potato-peeling, triturating, cream-freezing, whisking, and other like machines. Owing to the splendid system of ventilation there is a total absence of stuffiness.

There are about twenty pantries and still-rooms, into which several novel features have been introduced. Those for the main saloon are in direct communication with the kitchens, thus ensuring everything being served hot and fresh. Such tiresome work as bread-cutting, sandwich-making, dish-washing, &c., is done by electric machinery. The hot-presses and *bains maries* are really beautiful productions, being finished in black enamel and burnished white metal. Eggs are automatically boiled and timed.

Coffee is made and milk heated under the most cleanly conditions. Each pantry has a scullery in connection, where the dirty crockery is washed in the well-known "Vortex" electrically-driven machines.

The third-class passengers are well provided for, the kitchens being capable of dealing with food for 3000 passengers or troops. All the steam used for cooking purposes is specially evaporated, and is absolutely clean. This is an improvement which will be much appreciated by first-class cooks. The whole of the kitchen, pantry, and bakery plant has been supplied and fitted on board by Messrs Henry Wilson and Co., Limited, Liverpool.

THE REFRIGERATING MACHINERY.

Two complete and independent installations of refrigerating machinery are fitted on board the ship, one for the preservation of the ship's provisions, and the other for the carriage of perishable cargo. Both have been constructed by the Liverpool Refrigeration Company, Limited, and must be described together. The ship's provision-machine is situate near the forward end of the

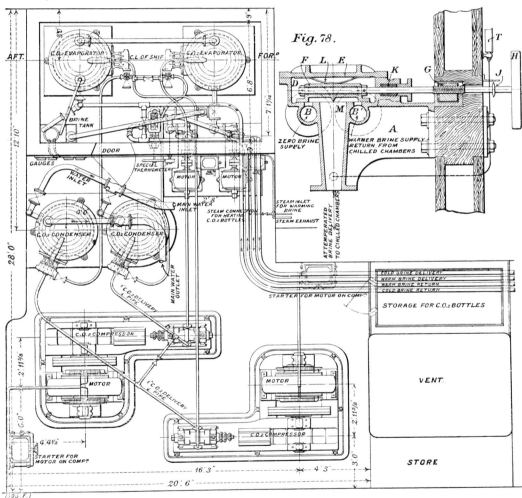

Fig. 75. BULKHEAD REMOVED

Fig. 76. REFRIG. HOUSE

Fig. 77.

Fig. 78.

FIGS. 75 TO 78. DETAILS OF REFRIGERATING PLANT.

turbine engine-room on the main-deck level, and the chambers on the lower deck, port, and starboard sides at some distance forward of the machine. These chambers have been insulated at the Clydebank Works with granulated cork in combination with specially-treated damp and rot-proof paper, with linings of white-pine boards. The chambers are divided into compartments for beef, mutton, poultry and game, bacon, milk, fruits and vegetables, and ice, and the wine and beer and spirit-chambers are also lightly insulated and cooled to a suitable temperature.

The chambers have a total capacity inside insulation of about 13,000 cubic feet, and, in addition, there is a large cold larder on the upper deck, besides cold boxes in the first and second-class bars

and still-room. There is also an installation for the supply of cooled water for drinking and other purposes. In this connection every possible requirement has been thought out and arranged, not only for the preservation of the perishable provisions in bulk, but also for the convenience of the catering and culinary departments generally.

The installation is of the carbonic-anhydride type, illustrated on Plate XI. and on the present page. It consists of a horizontal compound duplex machine, mounted on a cast-iron box-bed, which is divided by a longitudinal bulkhead into two portions, each of which contains an independent set of gas-condenser coils. These coils are of special soft-iron lapwelded tube, galvanised on the outside. The compound steam-cylinders drive from their tail-rods two horizontal double-acting CO_2 compressors. The crank-shaft runs in four bearings, and is in two portions, coupled in the centre and with a distance-plate between the faces of the coupling. A neat arrangement of steam-valves is fitted, so that the engine can work compound or independently as two high-pressure engines. By taking out the coupling-bolts and distance-plate each side of the machine can be run quite independently of the other. Cross-connections are provided, so that either compressor can deliver into either or both gas-condensers, and the machine is the full

equivalent of two independent machines combined on one base.

The evaporator is of the vertical type, the shell enclosing two independent nests of circular coils, one coupled to each compressor, with cross-connections, the same as for the condensers. Two horizontal duplex brass-fitted brine-pumps circulate the brine, and a third, smaller and independent pump is provided for the special duty of pumping the brine supply to the cold larder and refrigerators in the saloon-bars and other places independently of the main pumps. The whole brine distribution forms an entirely closed system. The brine is drawn from the evaporator and delivered into a distributing header, with valves and connections leading to the various pipe sections in the cold rooms. After passing through these the brine returns to a similar collecting-header, and thence back to the evaporator, there being no open brine-tank whatever. All the chambers are cooled with galvanised brine piping, arranged to suit various temperatures required in the several compartments, each of which is regulated independently of any other. The installation is, we believe, the largest and most complete of its kind.

The cargo-refrigeration plant is situate on the shelter-deck, starboard side forward, just abaft the forward funnel hatch. There is an extensive range of cold chambers on the orlop decks forward. These have been insulated at the Clydebank Works with granulated cork in a similar manner to the provision-rooms, already described. There are six chambers in all, the largest ones being divided by longitudinal central bulkheads. They have all been fitted for the carriage of frozen meats and poultry, cheese, bacon, butter, and fruits, and particularly for the carriage of chilled beef. The compartments are quite independent of each other, and can be supplied with brine for cooling at any temperature suitable to the cargo carried. The brine circulates through galvanised wrought-iron piping, and the chambers are fitted with meat-rails and removable hooks for hanging chilled meat, and also removable side tables for the stowage of forequarters. As the machinery is at a considerable distance from the chambers, a brine distribution-house has been fitted on the shelter-deck near to the chambers, from which the regulation and distribution is controlled.

The machinery in this case also is of the carbonic-anhydride type, and special care has been taken to ensure silent running. The plant is in duplicate throughout, and is electrically driven. There are two horizontal gas-compressors, each direct coupled to a powerful electro-motor, shown in Fig. 73, Plate XI. These motors have been specially designed and constructed for the purpose by Messrs. Boothroyd, Hyslop, and Co., of Bootle, and are so arranged, by means of shunt regulation, that they can run at any desired speed from 40 to 110 revolutions per minute. The speed can be regulated with absolute ease by the turning of one hand-wheel only, the motor running at the same speed as the compressor, and no gear-wheels whatever are used. The compressors—Webb and others' patents—embody several new features, which it will be of interest to mention. The outer casing, of soft cast steel, encloses and supports a liner of hard close-grained cast iron, which forms the working bore of the cylinder, but is easily withdrawable from either end of the casing. Two forged-steel headers, carrying the valves, are bolted, one to each end of the casing. The one at the front end is fitted with the stuffing-box and gland, and that at the back end with the plug-cover. The piston is fitted with metallic packing-rings of special metal, very accurately turned and finished, and held in place by a patent split junk-ring head, which, while doing away with all screws, keys, and pins, absolutely secures the rings in place, so that they cannot get adrift as long as the piston is within the cylinder bore. The gland is also fitted with a particular form of metallic packing, and no leather cups are used. The valves and seats are of special hard steel; the valves lift vertically, are of large area, and have no springs whatever. The compressors are constructed so as to be capable of long continuous runs without stop; the absence of leather cups entirely does away with the necessity for frequent renewals of the packing.

The gas-condensers are independent, are of the vertical type, and consist of soft lap-welded coils of wrought iron, galvanised on the outside, and contained in galvanised wrought-steel shells. The evaporators are similarly constructed to the con-

ARRANGEMENT OF BULKHEADS AND WATER-TIGHT DOORS.

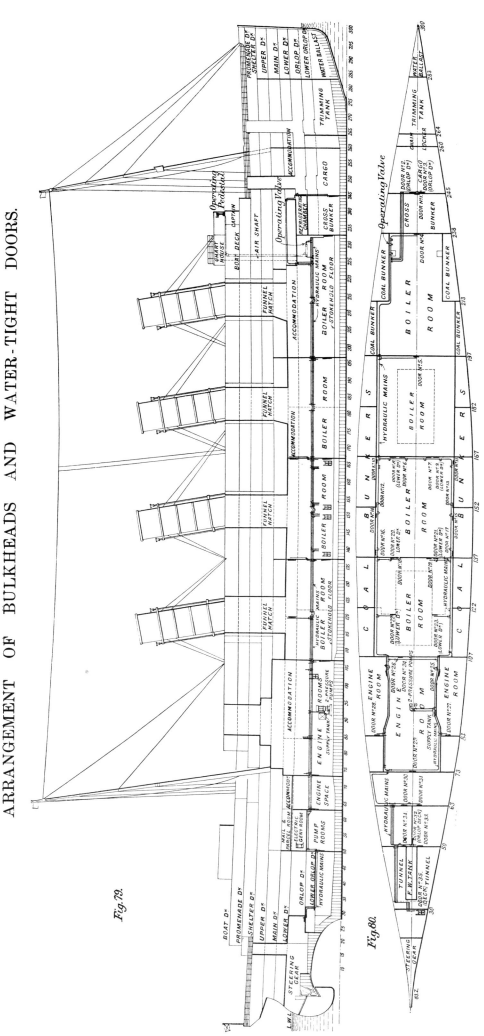

Fig. 79.

Fig. 80.

densers, ample facilities being provided for easy access to the coils for cleaning.

Two high-lift Gwynne centrifugal pumps circulate the brine. These are direct coupled to variable-speed electro-motors by the same makers as the main motors, so arranged that the speed of each pump can be regulated to suit the resistance to be overcome, this resistance varying somewhat, according to the number of chambers in use, and the quantity of brine being circulated. We have already mentioned a large variety of goods that may have to be carried in the chambers, some frozen and others chilled. Frozen goods, of course, require brine at a low temperature for circulation through the cooling-pipes in the chambers, but when carrying chilled beef, for example, brine at a temperature suitable for frozen goods is altogether too cold, and, if circulated, would rapidly freeze the quarters, especially those stowed nearest to the pipes. The temperature must be regulated with great accuracy. The same remark is also applicable to certain fruits and other chilled produce. A brine supply at an accurate and easily regulated temperature is, therefore, of great importance, and in the installation under review special means have been provided so that this can be secured. This warmer brine is circulated by an independent pump, and in the distribution-room mentioned above special duplex headers have been arranged so that either the coldest brine or the warmer brine can be supplied to the cooling-pipes in any one or more chambers, according to the cargo carried, whether chilled or frozen.

Webb and others' patent brine attemperator is illustrated in section in Fig. 78, page 27, and consists of a simple three-ported slide-valve, enclosed in a cast-iron casing, and attached to a screwed spindle with a hand-wheel, so that the movement of the valve over the ports can be accurately regulated as required. The valve is kept up to its face by a suitable coach-spring. A branch from the cold-brine supply main is coupled to one end of the valve-casing, and the return warmer-brine main is coupled to the other end, the mixed or attemperated brine escaping through the central port and pipe, which is connected to the warmer-brine pump. An overflow pipe is connected back to the evaporators.

In working the apparatus, the warmer-brine pump draws from the mixing or attemperating valve-chamber, delivering to the headers already mentioned, thence through the pipes in the chilled chambers back to the attemperator, there to be mixed with any given proportion of the coldest brine necessary to lower its temperature to the required degree. A suitable and specially-constructed pyrometer indicates the temperature, both outside the insulated brine-room. The temperature can be regulated by means of the handle controlling the valve exactly as required, higher or lower to suit, and the control is positive. The brine circulation generally, as in the provision plant, is an entirely closed circuit. There are no brine-tanks, except a small one for mixing brine in the first instance, for charging the machine, or for adding a little from time to time. Any little air or foul gas in the system is automatically disposed of through a small vent pipe carried outside from each evaporator. Though there are a large number of independent circuits, no difficulty whatever is experienced in regulating each exactly as required. With the closed circuit there is no difficulty with air-locks or aeration of the brine, and the system is surprisingly simple, clean, and easy to work.

In both the cargo and provision installations the cold parts of the plants are not individually lagged, but are placed together in a well-insulated chamber or brine-room, where they are always accessible, without the necessity of removing any lagging. The whole of the machinery, piping, and fitting out of both plants has been carried out by the Liverpool Refrigeration Company, Limited, Liverpool, the installation being the latest of a large number of refrigerating plants fitted by this company for the Cunard Line.

THE SAFETY OF THE SHIP.

In describing the construction of the ship, we have referred to the arrangement of bulkheads to ensure the safety of the vessel should any collision or other mishap cause the entry of the seawater. In this respect she will be much safer than almost any other vessel. It will be obvious, however, that if intercommunication is to be maintained freely between the various machinery and other compartments, these bulkheads must be pierced; otherwise serious and innumerable difficulties present themselves. Experience has proved that the absence of such doors is impracticable, and it is necessary to have effective, reliable, and, above all, a quick method of closing the doors. This has been accomplished in the Lusitania by means of the well-known Stone-Lloyd system, constructed by Messrs. J. Stone and Co., Limited, of Deptford. After careful consideration they have preferred hydraulic power for actuating the doors, discarding steam, electricity, and compressed air.

Hydraulic pressure is supplied to each of the doors by a pressure main which runs round the vessel. Pressure is maintained by two steam-driven duplex pumps placed in the engine-room, and continually under steam. A branch from the pressure-main feeds an operating valve, which is placed on the casing of the forward boiler-room, so that the pressure may be led into a small pilot main, called the "closing main," which also runs round the vessel to serve the doors.

The operating valve is connected by telegraph wires and chains to a pedestal on the bridge, so that pressure may be led into the closing main, either from the operating valve itself, or by the pedestal on the bridge. The general arrangement of the system is shown in the section and plan of the Lusitania on page 28 (Figs. 79 and 80), and

sists of a tubular ram, which slides in a casing and is operated externally by a lever. The ram carries at its centre an ordinary slide-valve, which slides over three ports. These ports lead respectively to the opening and closing ends of the cylinder, and to an exhaust main, which runs round the vessel, and delivers into the supply tank. The pressure from the main is constantly behind the slide-valve, so that, according to the position of the latter, the pressure flows either to the closing or to the opening end of the cylinder, the other end meanwhile exhausting. The ram is moved by a controlling handle, which is connected by a rod to the lever, and may be moved from either side of the bulkhead to which it is fitted Thus the door may be opened or closed from either side of the bulkhead. The ram, at its lower end,

which lifts the small mitre-valve off its seat and allows the pressure from the closing main to flow into the tubular ram, past the pilot spindle, which is fluted, and into the exhaust main by suitable ports in the ram and casing. The pressure on its lower end being now relieved, the ram can be operated, as before stated, to open the door. As soon as the handle or lever is released, the pressure in the closing main forces the mitre-valve back on to its seat, and moves the ram back to the "closed" position, and the door is again closed. Thus any man shut in a compartment may escape, and when he is through, the door will immediately close behind him. Warning of the closing of the doors is given by bells at each door ringing continuously as the door is moving.

In conjunction with the pumps and the pressure

FIGS. 81 AND 82. HORIZONTAL AND VERTICAL WATER-TIGHT DOORS (STONE-LLOYD SYSTEM); CONSTRUCTED BY MESSRS. J. STONE AND CO., LIMITED, DEPTFORD.

by the engravings illustrating respectively horizontally and vertically worked doors, with all their mechanism, reproduced on the present page (Figs. 81 and 82).

The doors are of the ordinary wedge type, and are formed of steel plate, suitably stiffened. They are each operated by an hydraulic cylinder, having two pistons connected by a rack, which gears with a pinion carried by a cross-shaft ; the shaft prolonged forms the door-shaft, which, in turn, carries the driving-pinion, gearing with the rack on the door. When space prohibits the fitting of the cylinder in the immediate neighbourhood, intermediate shafting, with bevel wheels, can be arranged, and the cylinder can be placed in any convenient position.

The pistons are of slightly different sizes, so that a larger force is available to open the door, or bring it off its wedges. But the successful working of the system may be said to lie with the controlling valve, which is placed at each door. It con-

runs through a U leather, and the closing main is connected to the space beneath it.

When the officer on the bridge moves over the pedestal handle, and thus opens the operating valve, pressure flows from the pressure main into the closing main, and thence to the under side of the ram, which is consequently forced over. The slide-valve thus uncovers the closing port, and admits pressure to the closing end of the cylinder. To open the door in such a case, it follows that the pressure on the ram must be relieved. This is accomplished in the following way :—Inside the hollow ram is fitted a small mitre-valve, which is held on to its seat by the pressure in the closing main. A pilot spindle runs through the centre of the ram, and terminates at one end against the mitre-valve, and at the other against the lever. Suitable packing against the spindle keeps it pressure-tight. When the lever is moved towards the "open" position, it first depresses this spindle,

main is fitted a governor, on the spindle of which the pressure acts. Any increase over the working pressure of 700 lb. per square inch throttles the steam passing to the pumps. The pressure is thus kept to its normal height, and the pumps are ready at any moment to deliver up to their full capacity.

A circulating-valve is also fitted in the pressure main, and allows a slight flow of water to pass into the exhaust main, and back to the tank. This device keeps the temperature of the water throughout the mains constant, thus preventing injury to the pipes, &c.

As it is desirable that the officer on the bridge should know the position of each door, whether open or closed, an electrical indicator is provided ; this contains a fascia plate, on which a plan of the vessel is engraved. Ruby discs are let into the plate at different points, and are numbered to correspond with the doors they represent, and these are automatically lighted when the door is open.

THE PROPELLING MACHINERY.

As already stated, in view of the immense power requisite to propel the new steamers at the designed speed, the Cunard Company, in September, 1903, called to their aid a committee composed of experienced and eminent engineers, to carefully consider the whole question of machinery design. After several months of deliberation and painstaking investigation, this committee, in March,

1904, finally reported in favour of the adoption of turbine machinery of the Parsons type, and on the two-page Plates XXXVIII. to XLI. we publish detailed drawings of the interesting features of this, the highest power installation ever installed on board a steamship. In these illustrations the general arrangement of the boilers, machinery, and connections is clearly shown.

The steam-producing plant includes twenty-three double-ended and two single-ended boilers, arranged in four compartments, as shown in the section and plan, Figs. 83 and 84 on Plate XXXVIII., and in the cross-sections, Figs. 90 and 91 on Plate XL. The main propelling machinery consists of two high-pressure ahead, two low-pressure ahead, and two astern turbines, as shown in Figs. 85 and 86 on

DOUBLE-ENDED BOILER.

CONSTRUCTED BY MESSRS. JOHN BROWN AND CO., LIMITED, CLYDEBANK.

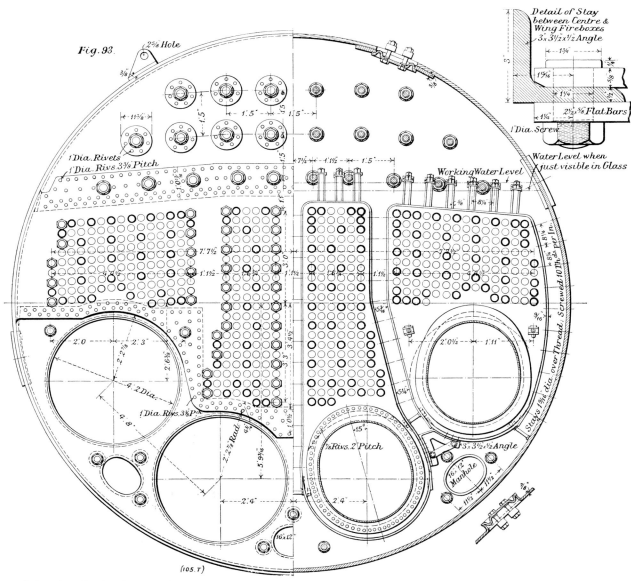

TABLE VIII.—*List of Auxiliary Engines in the Boiler and Machinery Compartments.*

In High and Low-Pressure Engine-Rooms.

Feed-pumps	Six pairs of Weir's	18 in. and 13½ in. by 30 in.
Hotwell pumps ..	Four Weir's	12¼ in. and 14½ in. by 30 in.
Surface-heaters ..	Two Weir's ..	1750 sq. ft. each.
Contact-heaters ..	Ditto	48 in. in dia. casing.
Feed-water filters ..	Two Harris's ..	36 in.
Ditto, auxiliary ..	Ditto ..	20 in.
Auxiliary circulating pumps	Two Allen's, 10 in.	36-in. disc; engine, 7 in. by 6 in.
Auxiliary condensers..	Two Clydebank ..	2000 sq. ft. each.
Bilge-pumps	Four Weir's ..	8 in. and 10 in. by 21 in.
Fresh and condensed water pumps	Two Carruthers'..	Two 6 in., two 6 in. by 6 in.
Water service circulating-pumps	Ditto ..	Two 7½ in., two 10 in. by 12 in.
Sanitary pumps ..	Two Weir's ..	10 in. and 10 in. by 10 in.
Auxiliary air-pumps .	Ditto ..	10 in. and 22 in. by 12 in.
Oil-pumps	Six Weir's.. ..	7 in. and 8½ in. by 15 in.
Gland and jacket drain-tank pump	One Carruthers' duplex	Two 4½ in. and two 5 in. by 5 in.
Sluice-valve engines ..	Two Clydebank ..	Two 6 in. by 6 in.
Reversing engines ..	Four Brown's ..	6 in. by 8 in.

In Pump-Rooms.

Circulating pumps ..	Two sets Allen's ..	Each set with two 18 in. by 10 in. engines and two 32 in. discharges, and two 42-in. discs.
Wet-air pumps ..	Four twin Weir's	14 in. and 40 in. by 24 in.
Dry-air pumps . ..	Ditto	7 in. and 24 in. by 7 in.
Aft water service pump	One Carruthers' duplex	Two 6 in., two 7 in., by 7 in.

Evaporator-Rooms.

Wash deck and fire pumps	One Weir's ..	10 in. and 10 in. by 10 in.
Evaporators	Six Liverpool Engineering Co.'s	
Distillers	Four ditto	

Pumps for evaporators:—Two circulating pumps, two feed-pumps, and two brine-pumps.

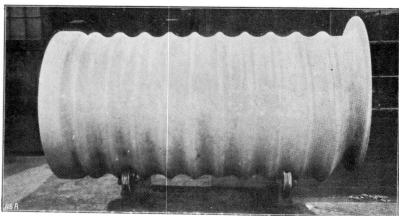

FIG. 96. CAMBERED FURNACE; CONSTRUCTED BY MESSRS. JOHN BROWN AND CO., LTD., SHEFFIELD.

In Boiler-Rooms.

Assistant feed and ash-ejector pumps	Four Weir's ..	14 in. and 10 in. by 14 in.
Ballast-pumps.. ..	Two Carruthers' duplex	Two 8 in., two 10 in. by 10 in.
Ash-ejectors	Eight sets Mechan	
Ash-hoists	Eight sets Crompton	
Forced draught fans and motors :—Eight sets of fans and motors, each set with four fans and two motors ; fans, 66 in. in diameter, Allen's.		
Turbo-dynamo	Four Parsons ..	375 kilowatts

Plate XXXIX. The turbines are of the Parsons type, embodying the latest experience of the Hon. C. A. Parsons and the builders.

Owing to the immense size of these turbines, and in order to comply with the Admiralty's requirements as to subdivision, the main propelling and auxiliary machinery are located in nine different water-tight compartments, as will be seen from Figs. 86 and 87 respectively on Plates XXXIX. and XL. In the largest and most central of these are located the two low-pressure and the two astern turbines, the whole of the feed-pumps, hotwell pumps, oil-pumps, and the pumps for the Stone-Lloyd hydraulic system of closing bulkhead doors. In each of the two wing compartments, separated from this central compartment by longitudinal bulkheads, are placed respec-

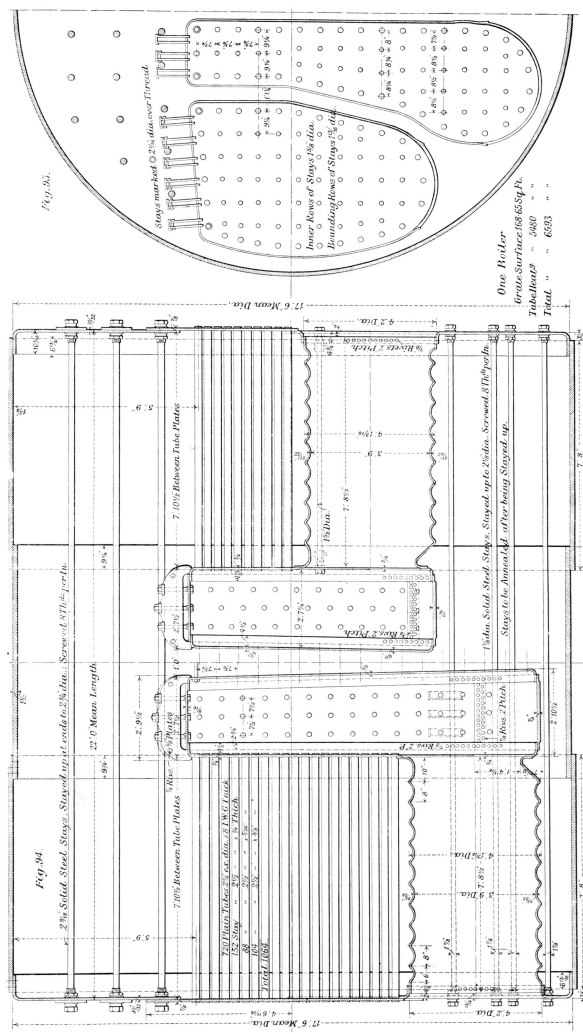

DOUBLE-ENDED BOILER.

CONSTRUCTED BY MESSRS. JOHN BROWN AND CO., LIMITED, CLYDEBANK.

Fig. 95.

Stays marked ○ 2¹¹⁄₁₆ dia. over Thread.

Inner Rows of Stays 1⅞ dia.

Bounding Rows of Stays 1¹⁵⁄₁₆ dia.

One Boiler
Grate Surface 168·65 sq. Ft.
Tube Heat⁹ " 5480 "
Total " 6593 "

Fig. 94.

2¹¹⁄₁₆ Solid Steel Stays. Stayed up at ends to 2⅜ dia.. Screwed 8 Th⁴⁸ per ln.

22′·0″ Mean Length

7·10½″ Between Tube Plates

720 Plain Tubes 2½″ ex. dia. ·8 I.W.G. Thick
152 Stay   " 2½   " × ¾″ Thick
 88   "   " 2½   " × ⁵⁄₁₆   "
104   "   " 2½   " × ⅜″   "
Total 1064

17·6″ Mean Dia.

---

tively the high-pressure turbines, the auxiliary condensers, auxiliary circulating and air-pumps, also the water service, fire and bilge, and fresh-water pumps, as shown on the section, Fig. 87, on the two-page Plate XL. Aft of these, in separate wing compartments, are placed the evaporating and distilling plants, underneath which runs a portion of the high-pressure turbine shafting. In the fifth compartment, extending right across the ship, are placed the four main condensers, and underneath these the feed-tank. Aft of these again are two auxiliary machinery-rooms, each two-storied and each self-contained. In the lower are placed the

main wet-air pumps, dry-air pumps, and main centrifugal circulating pumps; and in each of the upper flats are the electric generating-stations, in which the power is supplied by two Parsons turbo-generators. Abaft these are the shaft tunnels. These are shown in Fig. 87 on Plate XL.

As will be seen from the photograph, Fig. 123 on Plate XIII., but still more clearly from Fig. 121 on the two-page Plate XLI., and Fig. 122 on page 37, the starting-gear is situated on an upper platform at the forward end of the main engine room, and from this position practically everything can be controlled. The main regulating

valves for the high-pressure and the manœuvring turbines are arranged and worked very similarly to those on the Carmania,* the Brown's engines being located on the platform, so that, in the event of any hitch, the valves can be worked at once by hand in place of steam-power.

In Table VIII., on page 30, there is given a list of the auxiliary engines, &c.

STEAM-GENERATING PLANT.

Although the turbines naturally awaken greater

See Engineering, vol. lxxx., page 720.

interest than the steam-generating plant, it will be more consistent with the natural order if, in enter-ing upon a detailed description of the machinery, we deal first with the boilers.

There are, as already stated, twenty-three double-ended and two single-ended boilers in the ship, situated in four separate water-tight compartments, as shown in the longitudinal section and plan on the two-page Plate XXXVIII. Of one of the stokeholds we give a perspective view on page 32 (Fig. 97). The forward boiler-room, designated No. 1, has two single-ended and five double-ended boilers, and in each of Nos. 2, 3, and 4 boiler-rooms

ONE OF THE STOKEHOLDS.

FIG. 97.

there are located six double-ended boilers, in groups of three athwart the ship (Fig. 89 on Plate XL.). In Nos. 2, 3, and 4 boiler-rooms the bunkers are situated on the sides of the boilers and boiler casings ; but in No. 1 boiler-room, on account of the increasing fineness of the ship, recourse had also to be had to a large athwartship bunker, forward of which is a hold available either as a reserve bunker or for general cargo (see Fig. 37 on Plate XXXVII.).

The double-ended boilers, illustrated in detail in Figs. 93 to 95 on pages 30 and 31, are $17\frac{1}{2}$ ft. in diameter by 22 ft. long. In each of these boilers there are 344 stay-tubes and 720 plain tubes, the total being 1064. The total heating surface is 6593 square feet and the grate area 168.65 square feet. As will be seen, there are separate combustion-chambers to each furnace, and the water and steam spaces are exceedingly ample. The single-ended boilers differ from the others only in their length.

The furnaces have a collective grate area of 4048 square feet, while the total heating surface is 158,350 square feet. For each group of boilers there is a separate funnel, all being of the same dimensions, as the heating and grate surfaces of each boiler-room are identical (Figs. 90 and 91 on Plate XL.). These funnels are elliptical in form, the extreme dimensions of the outer funnel being 19 ft. by 26 ft., while the height above the grate-level is 130 ft. We may add that the shells of the boilers are made of high-tensile steel, of a maximum tensile strength of 36 tons to the square inch ; but the fronts and backs, as also all rivets, including those for the shells, are made of ordinary mild steel. The 192 furnaces are of the cambered type, which is a speciality of the Atlas Works, Sheffield, of Messrs. John Brown and Co., Limited. These furnaces, of which one is shown in the photograph reproduced on page 30, Fig. 96, were made to a diameter over ribs of 4 ft. $1\frac{9}{16}$ in., and for a working pressure of 195 lb. per square inch. The front and back ends of these furnaces were finished off in accordance with the latest practice, having their landings turned so as to ensure a perfect fit.

The steam-piping arrangement is shown on the two page Plate XXXVIII. It will be seen that there are four main leads—one from each boiler-room—and that all four are carried right aft to the forward engine-room bulkhead, on the forward side of which a stop-valve is fitted to each of the four lines, which can be worked both from the engine-room and from the boat-deck.

THE FORCED-DRAUGHT FANS.

The forced draught is on the well-known Howden system of heated air and closed ash-pits, the furnace fittings being of James Howden and Co.'s patent built steel type, ensuring the maximum of efficiency and durability with the minimum of weight, the whole installation having been constructed to the designs of James Howden and Co. The forced-draught fans are driven by electric motors. We show in Fig. 89, on Plate XL., the general arrangement of these fans, each of which can be controlled from the engine-room as well as from the fan-rooms.

The fans are well illustrated by the drawings reproduced on page 33 (Figs. 98 to 102). There are thirty-two motor-driven fans, of Messrs. W. H. Allen, Son, and Co.'s manufacture, arranged in pairs, and driven by sixteen electric motors. The fans are throughout of sheet steel, and have impellers of the single-inlet type, 66 in. in diameter, and are capable of producing an air pressure of $3\frac{1}{2}$ in. when running at 450 revolutions per minute. The motors are capable of developing 50 brake horse-power, receiving current at 100 volts, when running at 450 revolutions per minute. These motors, also of Messrs. Allen's manufacture, are completely enclosed, but inspection doors are provided at the commutator end of each motor, which can be readily removed. As the sets have to run in an atmosphere at high temperature, special means have been provided for the ventilation of the motors. As will be seen from the engraving, Fig. 98, the fan next to the commutator end of the motor in each set is provided with a small auxiliary impeller and separate casing, for the sole purpose of supplying air for the ventilation of the motor. This casing is connected so as to deliver the air into the bottom of the commutator casing, the outlet being at the opposite end of the motor-casing. The controllers for these motors are also of Messrs. Allen's manufacture, and are arranged to give a large variation of speed, rising in equal increments from about 185 to 500 revolutions per minute. The construction of these controllers is well shown in the engravings, Figs. 103 and 104 on page 34, the former exhibiting some of the internal parts when removed from the casing. The fans are also provided with water-pressure gauges connected to the fan-casing, and with tachometers.

The twin-screw ship Vera, built at Clydebank in 1897, was the first instance in which steam-driven fans were dispensed with for forced draught in boiler-rooms. The resulting freedom from vibration and noise, and the ready means of regulation from the starting platform, proved so satisfactory that motor-driven fans were subsequently installed, with equally good results, in the sister-ship Alberta, built at Clydebank for the London and South-Western Railway Company, and the s.s. Antrim, built by John Brown and Company in 1905 for the Midland Railway Company. In these ships the controllers were fitted in the engine-rooms, and the fans entirely regulated from that position ; but in the case of the Lusitania the distance from the engine-room to the boiler-rooms is so great that, while it was desired to be able to regulate the fans from the engine-room, it was at the same time also considered advisable to retain the ordinary controllers attached direct to the fans in the boiler-rooms, and this required result has been most satisfactorily attained by the very ingenious apparatus of Messrs. Siemens Brothers, of which we give an illustration on page 34, in Figs. 105 and 106.

When it is desired to alter the position of any one of the fan-controllers, the operator works the switch-handle of the sender to either "fast" or "slow," the handle, when released, being returned to the central position by a spring. This switch causes the motor on the controller to run either forward or backward, and through the gearing to turn the controller barrel either forward or backward. Geared to the controller barrel is the indicator switch, the indicator being situated just

ELECTRICALLY-DRIVEN FANS FOR FORCED DRAUGHT IN BOILERS.

CONSTRUCTED BY MESSRS. W. H. ALLEN, SON, AND CO., LIMITED, ENGINEERS, BEDFORD.

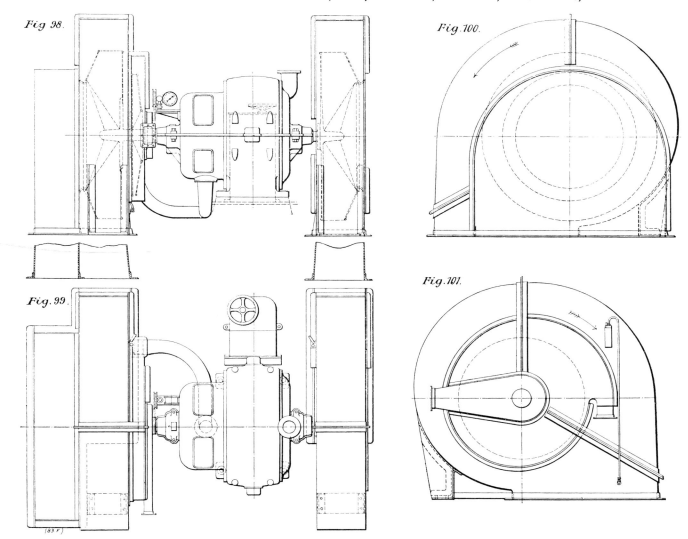

Fig. 98.

Fig. 100.

Fig. 99.

Fig. 101.

FIG. 102.

above the sender switch, and consisting of a revolving drum, on the periphery of which are figures and letters corresponding with those on the top of the controller case; this drum has an electro-magnetic control, worked from the indicator switch geared to the controller barrel, so that the figures or letters on the drum, as seen through the window of the indicator, will correspond with the position of the controller barrel. In order to ensure great accuracy of position of the controller barrel, a bell is placed in the indicator which is connected to a contact-ring in the indicator-switch, having portions of the ring cut away, so that the bell will continue to ring as long as the controller barrel is not in its exact position. It will thus be seen that the operator, when watching the figures on his indicator, can see exactly what is taking place on the controller, the bell telling him whether the controller is in its exact position or not.

The working of the indicator is positive, not step by step, and the instrument is of the same type as is used in the Navy for controlling the firing operations. The motor on the controller is geared to the controller-barrel by means of a slipping-clutch, so that if the operator runs the motor beyond what is necessary to turn the barrel, no harm will be done. The whole apparatus is water-tight. An ammeter is fitted above the indicator to record the amount of current used by the fan.

The air-inlets to the stokeholds have been arranged as trunks extending up to the boat-deck, and, instead of the usual array of cowls, which are always unsightly, especially where, as in this ship, they require to be of great size, they are circular shafts fitted on top with hinged covers. The extent of the opening can be varied, and gear is also arranged so that the cover may be rotated to suit the wind when on the beam. When the vessel is steaming ahead the opening will be, as a rule, towards the bow.

These air-inlet shafts are shown on the boat-deck on both the views reproduced on Plate IX. Fig. 39 also shows the air-inlets for the ventilation of the engine-room, to be described later.

THE DISPOSAL OF ASHES.

One of the difficulties which have to be dealt with in vessels burning such a large amount of coal, as will be the case in this instance, is the disposal of the ashes. As a matter of fact, the expeditious disposal of the ashes has a direct effect on the steaming capabilities of any high-powered vessel, as it is impossible for the firemen to give proper attention to the firing when the stokeholds are

E

CONTROLLING-GEAR FOR ELECTRIC FANS FOR FORCED DRAUGHT.

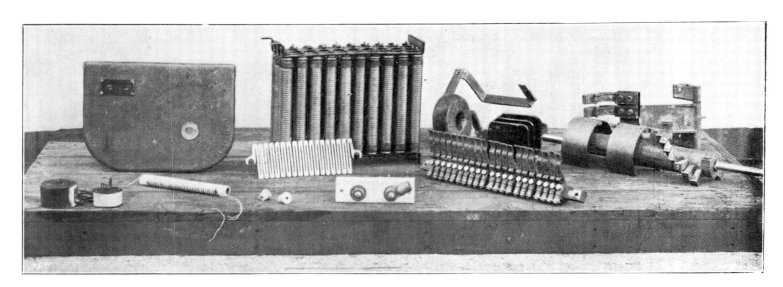

FIG. 103. DETAILS OF ALLEN'S CONTROL-GEAR.

hampered with ashes. Eight See's ash-ejectors are fitted to the Lusitania (and also in the sister vessel), and with this apparatus all that is necessary is for the firemen to shovel the ashes into a hopper in the stokehold, after which they are dealt with by the apparatus without further manual labour on the part of the firemen, and are discharged twenty or more feet clear of the ship's side. As illustrated on Fig. 107 on page 35, the ejector consists of a hopper W, having a hinged watertight cover, secured, when not in use, by butterfly nuts. At the bottom of the hopper a special form of nozzle is fitted, which discharges up the pipe V. This nozzle forms a loose or removable portion of the ejector cock P, and is combined with an escape-valve, which acts as a relief to any shock on the connecting-pipe from the duplex pump due to the sudden closing of the cock. The cock is in communication, by pipe D, with a suitable duplex pump, which draws water from the sea and delivers it under pressure to the ejector-cock.

In order to work the ejector, the discharge-valve Z on the ship's side is first opened, and the duplex pump started, so that sea-water is forced through pipe D. When the water-pressure shown by the pressure-gauge M reaches 200 lb., the ejector cock P is quickly opened, the water from the pump being then discharged through the nozzle up the discharge-pipe V at a pressure of about 150 lb., and the ejector is now working and ready to receive the ashes. The cock can be opened either with the hopper-lid closed or open; but when closed it must be noticed that the air-inlet T is open. The ashes may now be continuously shovelled into the hopper W, the lid of which remains open during the operation and until the whole of the ashes have been removed. When the ashes enter the hopper they are quickly drawn down towards the water-jet by the rush of air, and on reaching the jet are carried up the discharge-pipe, deflected by means of the bend Y shown at the top, and passing through the clack-valve Z, are discharged well clear of the side of the vessel. The valve Z is kept shut when the ejector is not working, and is opened or shut from the stokehold by means of suitable rods or by a patent automatic hydraulic cylinder.

When the whole of the ashes are discharged the ejector-cock P is closed quickly, so that all water that has passed the cock may be discharged overboard, thus leaving the discharge-pipe free of water and ready for further use. The clack-valve Z and the hopper-lid are also now closed until the apparatus is again required. The bend Y is fitted with removable segments X on the top side, which are interchangeable, and easily replaced if worn out by the scour of the ashes. It will be observed that there is no loss of fresh water by the use of this apparatus, and the only steam used is for working the pump, the steam passing back to the condenser in the usual way. Ten to fifteen minutes each watch will suffice to clear each stokehold of ashes.

An alternative system of dealing with the ashes, and for disposing of them when in harbour, has

FIG. 104. ALLEN'S CONTROL-GEAR.

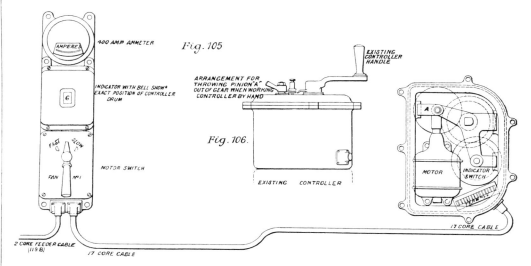

FIGS. 105 AND 106. SIEMENS REGULATOR FOR CONTROL-GEAR.

THE DISPOSAL OF ASHES

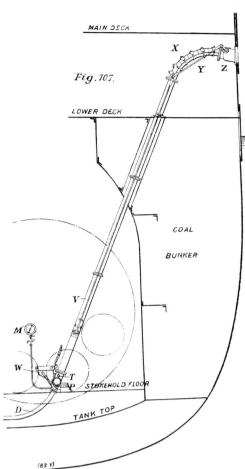

FIG. 107. SEE'S ASH-EJECTOR.

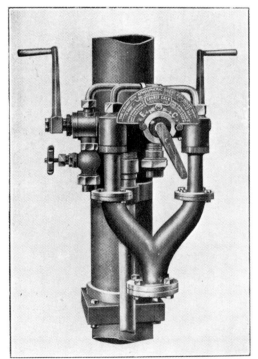

FIG. 111.

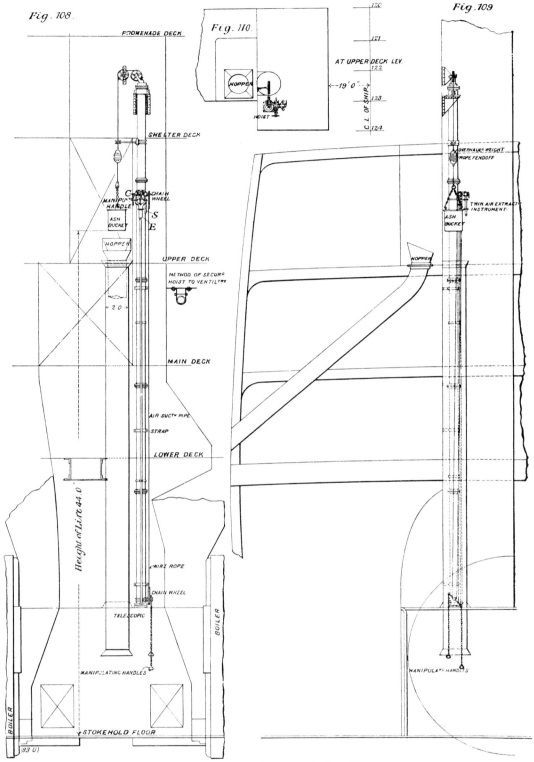

FIGS. 108 TO 111. CROMPTON'S ASH-HOIST.

been fitted by Messrs. T. Albert Crompton and Co., London. This system, known as the Crompton atmospheric silent ash-hoist, is illustrated on this page (Figs. 108 to 111), and the drawings reproduced are largely self-explanatory. In the cylinders or tubes, which are copper-lined throughout, there works a flexible cup piston, to which is attached at one end a steel wire rope, which passes over the swivel-head fixed at the top of the tubes. A pair of clip-hooks is attached to this rope for connecting to the bucket-ropes of each ventilator as may be required to be worked. Inside the ventilators are fixed spindles and patent roller-bearing pulleys for carrying the bucket-ropes down the ventilators, each rope being provided with patent adjustable thimble-eyes for connecting to the ship's bag-hooks or ash-bucket slings in the usual way. At the bottom end of the tubes is a portway chamber, provided with a door for examining or drawing the pistons (shown in Fig. 108), and to this chamber is connected a 1½-in. wrought-iron pipe. At the top end of this pipe is secured the air-evacuator instrument which controls the ash-hoist in all its actions. This evacuator is shown in Figs. 108 and 111. S is a 1-in. steam-pipe from the main and donkey boilers which supplies steam, the velocity of which passing through the evacuator creates the vacuum for working the ash-hoist when the vessel is in port, E being the exhaust-pipe connection to the funnel or to the auxiliary exhaust-tank. C is the vacuum-pipe connection direct to the condenser of the main engines (vacuum side).

This apparatus is worked as follows :—An eighth turn of the operating handle admits steam through the air-evacuator, and at the same time opens up a communication direct to the bottom side of the piston in the tube, thereby creating a vacuum below the piston ; and the atmospheric pressure acting on the top side of the piston forces it down the tube, when the ash-bag or bucket will ascend the ventilator, reaching the door as the piston arrives at the bottom of the tube. A quarter of a turn backwards of the operating handle destroys the vacuum, and the weight of the empty bucket causes the latter to return to the stokehold floor.

When the vessel is at sea the steam is shut off entirely, and the handle of the change-cock (which is shown in Fig. 111) is moved over to C on the name-plate. This change-cock is then in direct communication with the main engine's condenser by the connection marked C in Fig. 111, when the vacuum in the condenser becomes the agent used for working the hoist, the manipulation of the operating handles being exactly the same as before. Whether the hoist is being worked at sea or in port, the operation of moving the change-cock from E to C, or *vice versâ*, is such that it is absolutely impossible for any of the connections to be opened to the atmosphere and the condenser at the same time. Neither is it possible for any steam to pass into the hoist-tubes, irrespective of the position of the operating handles of the air-evacuator—*i.e.*, whether left in after working, or whether any steam passes into the condensers of the main engines when the vessel is in port. The height of lift being a net one, the length of the hoist-tubes is always constructed in proportion thereto, which makes it impossible for any overwinding to occur.

THE TURBINE INSTALLATION.

Having dealt with the boilers and their incidental machinery, we follow the steam to the turbines, which are the most interesting feature in the ship. The turbines are fully illustrated by the drawings reproduced on the two-page Plates XXXIX. to XLI. The high-pressure turbine rotor-drums are 96 in. in diameter, the astern drums 104 in., and the low-pressure drums 140 in.

For such immense turbines it will naturally be inferred that the forgings, &c., required in their construction would also be of very large size. The steel forgings for the turbine-drums, rotor-spindles, and straight shafting were manufactured at Messrs. John Brown and Co.'s Atlas Works, Sheffield. The turbine-drums were all hollow forged, and the low-pressure ahead drums are the largest hollow forgings that have been made up to the present time. The sizes of these drums, as delivered to Clydebank, were as follow:—Outside diameter, 11 ft. 8⅜ in.; inside diameter, 11 ft. 4 in.; length, 8 ft. 2 in.; with metal 3 in. thick. To manufacture these enormous forgings necessitated a good deal of scheming and ingenuity on the part of the staff at the Atlas Works. It may be of interest to give a few data of the forgings for these particular drums. The ingots used were 60 in. in diameter across the flats, and weighed 42 tons each. These were forged down to 54 in. in diameter, and an 18-in. hole trepanned through, making hollow pieces weighing about 27 tons each, which were subsequently expanded into drums 11 ft. 10½ in. outside diameter, as shown in the photograph reproduced on this page (Fig. 112). These forgings were then rough-turned and bored in a lathe that had been specially altered for the purpose. These drums were so large that it was impossible for the railway companies to carry them, and it was necessary to take them by road from Sheffield to Manchester, where they were shipped direct to Glasgow.

The whole of the rotor-spindles and shafting were also manufactured at the Atlas Works, all being, of course, hydraulically forged. The rotor-spindles are extremely large, the majority of them having coupling-flanges 43 in. in diameter, and some being as large as 40 in. in diameter in the body. The intermediate shafting is 20 in. in diameter, and the tail-shafts 22½ in. in diameter by over 30 ft. long. The rotor-spindles, thrust-shafts, and tail-shafts are all made of high-tensile steel.

The throttle-valves, valve-covers, strainers, expansion-joints, &c., are also of very large proportions, and were made as steel castings by the Robert process, which is also one of the specialities of the Atlas Works. The uniformity and superiority of the physical results obtainable by this process are particularly striking, and are attained with less difficulty than by any other method at present in use.

The cast-steel dished wheels on which these drums are shrunk, and a photograph of which we reproduce in Fig. 113 on this page, were supplied by Thomas Firth and Sons, Limited, Sheffield, who have made this particular type of turbine castings a speciality, and have supplied them to practically every firm of turbine-builders in Great Britain. The wheel illustrated was for the low-pressure turbine, and each wheel weighed 11¾ tons. In all, Messrs. Firth supplied about 440 tons of castings. The whole of the castings were subjected to tests and inspection of the Board of Trade and Lloyds. Owing to the great contraction that takes place in steel—double that of cast iron—the greatest possible care has to be exercised in the moulding of such huge wheels to avoid possible failures, and only long foundry experience and skill can overcome the difficulties.

The turbine-blades vary from 2¼ in. to 22 in.

long. In the longer blades the necessary radial and lateral stiffness is obtained by means of three rows of shrouding, in which expansion is allowed for in the same manner as in the Carmania, which was duly illustrated in our issue of December 1,

FIG. 112. FORGING FOR LOW-PRESSURE TURBINE ROTOR; MESSRS. JOHN BROWN AND CO, LIMITED, SHEFFIELD.

FIG. 113. CAST-STEEL DISHED WHEELS FOR LOW-PRESSURE TURBINE ROTOR; MESSRS. THOMAS FIRTH AND SONS, LIMITED, SHEFFIELD.

1905 (see ENGINEERING, vol. lxxx., page 719). It will be remembered that we then explained that the longer blades of the low-pressure turbines were bound together by two circumferential strips laced with copper wire and soldered; and, in order to

prevent distortion, due to the differences of expansion of the drum and the brass strip, very ingenious expansion joints had been devised. The binding strip was divided into short lengths, connected by brass tubes, in which they could slide. In that

article we also described in detail the system followed by the Clydebank firm to ensure absolute balance of all the revolving parts, and this same exhaustive process was again minutely followed by them in the case of the Lusitania. The turbine spindle steam-glands, valves, governors, and system of lubrication, which have answered so admirably in the Carmania, and have been so clearly illustrated by us, are again adopted in the new vessel.

The view published on Plate XII. of the rotor of the high-pressure turbine complete is interesting, as it shows the various stages in the blading for expansion; while the other view on the same page (Fig. 115) is instructive as illustrating the great variety of work undertaken at the Clydebank Works.

The lifting-gear, shown on Figs. 119 and 120 on Plate XLI., is designed on the same lines as that of the Carmania, but is naturally larger and heavier, seeing that the gear for the low-pressure turbine has to be capable of lifting the immense weight of 115 tons; and, as will be judged from the illustrations, the provision of suitable apparatus and means of stowing the immense receiver and exhaust-pipes was one of the many problems which have been so successfully solved by the builders of this vessel.

On page 38 (Figs. 127 to 139) we illustrate the

Lusitania the sequence of steps is practically similar to that in any ordinary installation, there being little scope for novelty in method. The number, size, and arrangement of the auxiliaries form therefore the chief features which call for note.

In Figs. 140 and 141 on page 39 we illustrate the main condensers. These are four in number, arranged in pairs, each unit containing 20,700 square feet of cooling surface, giving an aggregate of 82,800 square feet. A 32-in. bore circulating-water pipe is led to each condenser from the large centrifugal pumps. The two auxiliary condensers, which are situated at the forward end of the high-pressure engine-room, have a collective cooling surface of 4000 square feet, and have separate circulating and air-pumps.

Each of the four main condensers is fitted with the Harris-Anderson patent condenser-tube protector, supplied by the Harris Patent Feed-Water Filter, Limited, for preventing corrosion of the tubes, ferrules, &c. The principle of the system is the introduction into the circulating

ferrule is screwed up, the washer spreads out, thus forming the necessary contact between the tube and tube-plates. Protective metal blocks are secured in the water ends of the condensers, some in direct contact with the tube-plate, and others connected by cables to terminals at the opposite end to the blocks. Any corrosive action likely to attack the tubes is thus transferred to the protector, and pitting of the tubes, ferrules, &c., is avoided.

THE CIRCULATING PUMPS.

The circulating pumps, by Messrs. W. H. Allen, Son, and Co., Limited, Bedford, present some novel features, and of these illustrations are reproduced on Plate XV. and page 39. The main circulating engines consist of eight "Conqueror" type centrifugal pumps, having suction and discharge branches 22 in. in diameter, and arranged in four pairs, the discharge branches from each pair uniting into one common discharge of 32-in. diameter. Each pair of pumps is driven by a single-cylinder high-speed forced-lubrication engine of Messrs. Allen's well-known standard type, the engines again being arranged in pairs. Thus the main pumping machinery is grouped into two sets, the arrangement of one set being well shown in the photograph reproduced on Plate XV. (Fig. 142). The engine shafts can be coupled together in pairs, the engines running as two pairs of two-cylinder high-pressure engines, an arrangement of weights having been provided whereby the balance is exceedingly good under these conditions. The steam distribution, as shown in the cross-section, Fig. 143 on Plate XV., is effected by means of piston-valves, the valve-chest being cast in each case in one piece with the cylinder, the whole being of exceedingly close-grained and tough metal. The cylinders have a diameter of 18 in., with a stroke of 10 in., and together are capable of developing 350 brake horse-power at a speed of 300 revolutions per minute, receiving steam at 160 lb. per square inch, and working against a back pressure of 10 lb. per square inch. The cylinder bodies and covers are well lagged with silicate cotton, and neatly covered with burnished sheet brass, and fitted with the usual drain-cocks and relief-valves, presenting a very smart appearance. Cast in one with each cylinder is a substantial cast-iron distance-piece, which is faced square with the bore of the cylinder for bolting to the top of the engine trunk. This distance-piece is provided with openings, through which access can be obtained to the stuffing-boxes, which are all packed with United States metallic packing.

As stated above, the cylinders are arranged in pairs, each pair standing upon a cast-iron trunk of very rigid design, which carries the slide-faces for the cross-heads; these faces are accurately scraped up and finished square with the top and bottom faces of the trunk. In front are three doors which can be readily removed for inspection and adjustment of the working parts. Special oil and water glands are fitted to the top of the trunk where the piston and valve-rods pass through it. This effectually prevents the oil from working up to the cylinders from the crank-chamber, and precludes water from the cylinders entering the crank-chamber. The whole of the trunks and cylinders complete stand upon a rigid box-section bed-plate, in which is arranged the oil-reservoirs, filters, and oil-pumps, each of these latter fittings being arranged in duplicate, so that the engines may be disconnected from each other and run separately. The oil-pump is of the valveless oscillating type, and is driven from the engine eccentric, and delivers oil under pressure to all the working parts. Each pump is also provided with an oil-pressure regulator, whereby the pressure can be regulated while running.

On the front of the engine-trunk are arranged the oil and steam pressure gauges, in close proximity to the stop-valves; and neat transmission gear is arranged for operating the drain-cocks of the engine; this is well shown in the engraving, Fig. 142 on Plate XV.

Each end of the bed-plate is provided with an extension for bolting to a similar extension of the gun-metal pump-casing. An outer bearing is also provided between the fly-wheel of the engine and the pump. All the main bearings of the engine and pumps are of cast steel, lined with white metal, with the exception of the crosshead bearings, which are of gun-metal. Separate barring gear is also provided for each fly-wheel. Owing to the engines being of the totally-enclosed type, tachometers are

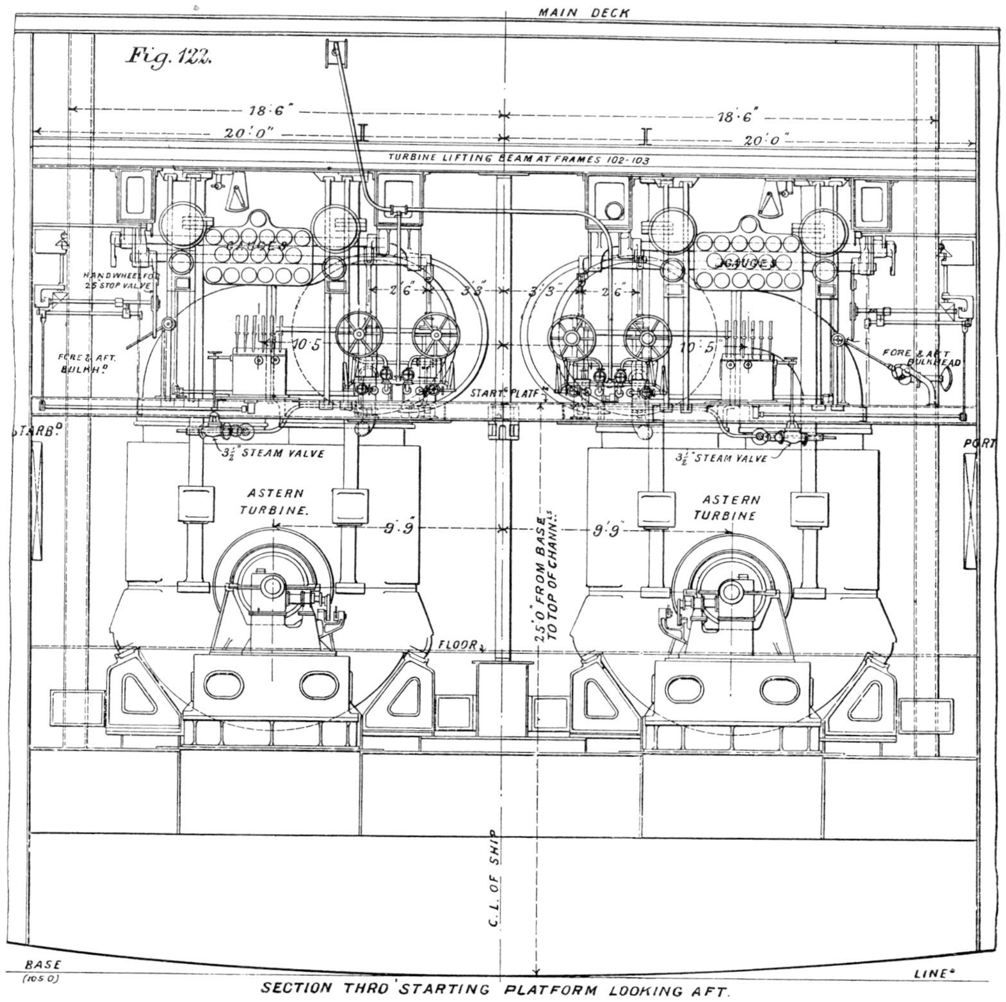

FIG. 122. SECTION THROUGH STARTING PLATFORM.

propeller shafting and stern-tube. Sections are given of the wing-tubes, in which case the shaft is worked by the high-pressure turbines, as well as of the inner tubes, for the shaft worked by the low-pressure turbines; and the drawings are so complete that little need be said in addition to the facts given already in connection with the manufacture of the shafting at the Atlas Works of the company.

Four interesting views of the engine-room are given on Plates XIII. and XIV. The photographs from which these engravings were made are by the photographer at the Clydebank Works—Mr. Lindsay—and are exceptionally good in view of the confined space. Fig. 124 on Plate XIII. is a view of the shaft-tunnel; Fig. 125 on Plate XIV. shows part of the lifting-gear, the photograph having been taken above the turbines; and Fig. 126 on the same plate is a view at the end of the low-pressure turbine, and shows the bearing, &c.

THE CONDENSERS.

The steam having performed its work in the turbine, the next step is to return it in the form of feed water to the boilers. In a leviathan such as the

water of a metal which is electro-positive to the metal forming the tubes of the condenser, the tubes and the electro-positive metal being connected together. The tubes are saved at the expense of the metal that is connected to them. The composition of this protective metal may be altered to suit particular cases. The metal usually employed, however, is electro-positive to nearly all the various alloys of copper and zinc, and it, moreover, retains its protective properties till it is entirely dissolved. There is found to be no trouble with insoluble deposits on its surface. Though not always convenient, the apparatus is sometimes fitted inside the end of the condenser. The makers prefer, however, to provide an independent vessel as a container for the protector, which vessel communicates with the water space by two pipes, which can be closed by valves when desired, thus enabling the protector to be inspected or renewed without interfering with the working of the condenser.

Each tube in the condensers of the Lusitania is brought into metallic contact with the tube-plate by means of a soft-metal washer inserted on the top of the packing in the stuffing-box. When the

PROPELLER SHAFTS AND STERN TUBES.

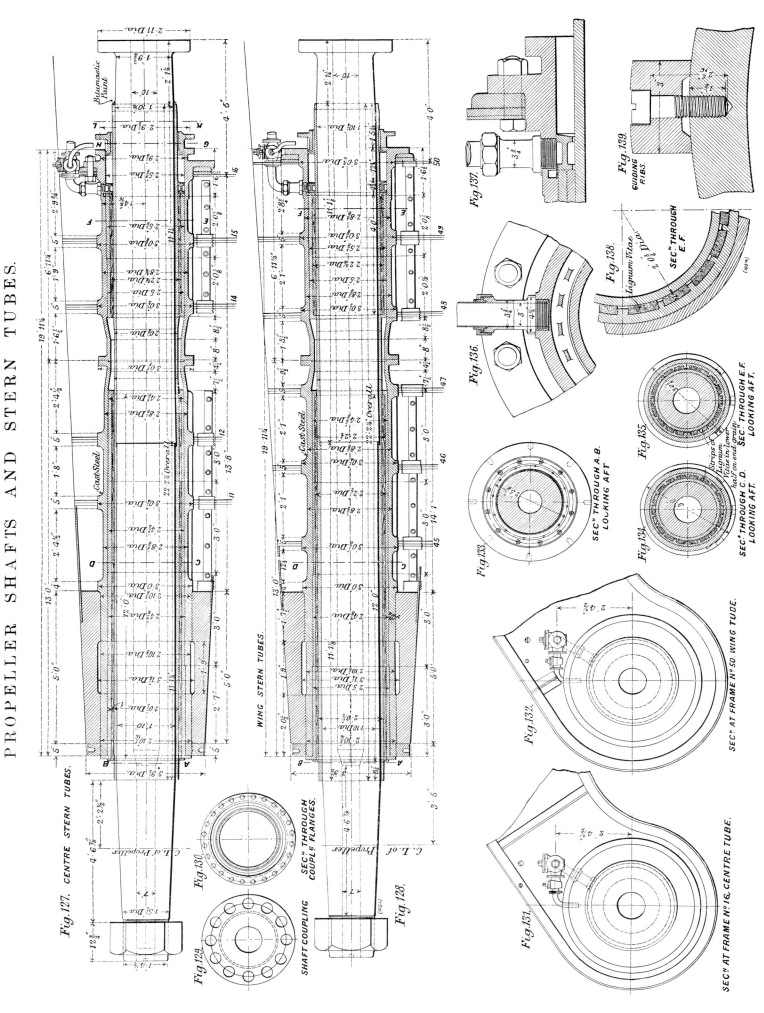

Fig. 127. CENTRE STERN TUBES.

Fig. 128. WING STERN TUBES.

Fig. 129. SHAFT COUPLING.

Fig. 130. SECᴺ THROUGH COUPLᴳ FLANGES.

Fig. 131. SECᴺ AT FRAME Nº 16. CENTRE TUBE.

Fig. 132. SECᴺ AT FRAME Nº 50. WING TUBE.

Fig. 133. SECᴺ THROUGH A. B. LOOKING AFT.

Fig. 134. SECᴺ THROUGH C. D. LOOKING AFT.

Fig. 135. SECᴺ THROUGH E. F. LOOKING AFT.

Fig. 136.

Fig. 137.

Fig. 138. SECᴺ THROUGH E. F.

Fig. 139. GUIDING RIBS.

THE CONDENSERS AND CIRCULATING PUMPS.

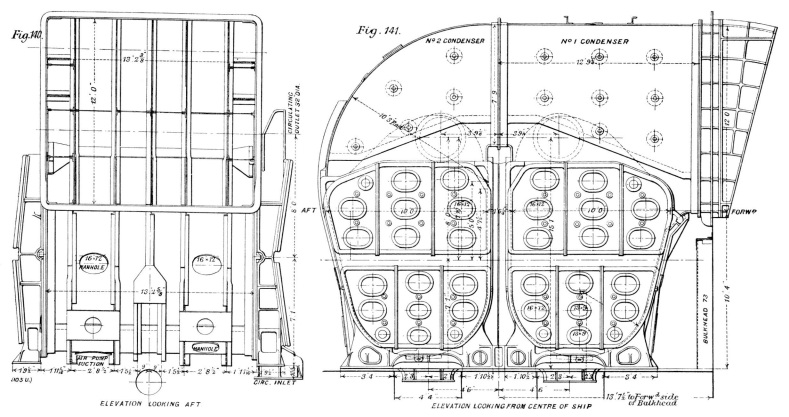

FIGS. 140 AND 141. THE MAIN CONDENSERS.

FIG. 144. ALLEN'S AUXILIARY CIRCULATING PUMP.

also provided for each set to continuously indicate the speed of the machinery.

As stated above, the main pumps are constructed throughout, both casings and impellers, of gun-metal, the casings being $\frac{7}{8}$ in. thick, and the discs having a diameter of 42 in. The pump-shaft is of forged bronze, and carried in bearings external to the pump, the arrangement of which is shown in the drawings and photograph reproduced on Plate XV. The shaft enters the pump-casing at each end through stuffing-boxes having gun-metal glands and special provision for lubrication.

In addition to the above main circulating pumps and engines, two auxiliary circulating pumping-engines have been fitted, each pump being of gun-metal, and having suction and discharge branches 10 in. in diameter, while the diameter of the impeller is 36 in. One of these sets is well shown in the photograph reproduced on this page, the engine being of Messrs. Allen's standard open type, having a single-cylinder 7 in. in diameter, with a stroke of 6 in. The steam distribution is effected by means of a piston valve. The cylinder, valve-chest, and cover are lagged with silicate cotton, and neatly covered with blue sheet steel. The engine bed-plate is rigidly connected to the casing of the pump, and external pump-bearings are provided, being lined with white metal. The piston-rod and valve-rod glands are also fitted with metallic packing of the United States type, and lubrication is provided from a central oil-box, from which oil is carried by pipes to the various bearings. The cylinder is fitted with the usual grease-cup and spring relief valves and drains.

FEED-WATER PUMPS AND HEATERS.

To the condensers, four in number, are connected four Weir wet-air pumps, 40 in. in diameter by 24 in. stroke, illustrated on Plate XVI., by Fig. 145. These are of Messrs. G. and J. Weir's twin type, having two steam cylinders, two pump barrels, with the pump-rods cross-connected by a beam. Steam is admitted to both cylinders by a single valve of the Weir pattern, designed specially for air pump duty, but comprising the usual and distinguishing features of the well-known Weir valve. Gun-metal has been adopted for the pump-barrels, the buckets, foot and head valve-seats, which latter are fitted with Kinghorn valves and gun-metal guards. The cylinders are supported on a cast-iron entablature set on angle wrought-iron columns. The piston-rods are of steel, connected by a cross-head with the pump-rods, which are of manganese-bronze, and work in vertical guides.

In addition to these wet-air pumps, which are capable of maintaining the requisite vacuum when the system is reasonably tight, provision is made

AIR-PUMP, FEED-WATER PUMPS, AND HEATERS.

CONSTRUCTED BY MESSRS. G. AND J. WEIR, LIMITED, ENGINEERS, CATHCART, GLASGOW.

FIG. 147. FEED-PUMP.

FIG. 148. "MONOTYPE" AIR-PUMP.

for unexpected or accidental leakage by fitting four sets of Weir double dry-air pumps, 24 in. in diameter and 7 in. stroke, for dealing with air only. These are illustrated by Fig. 146, also on Plate XVI. In these the air-pump chambers are situated over the steam-cylinders of a double-connected enclosed high-speed engine. These chambers are of gun-metal, and are of the single-acting type. The air passes into the barrel above the buckets through annular openings, and is forced through the head valves on the up-stroke of the pump. The compression of the air results in a certain rise of temperature, which is taken care of by a small supply of circulating water, which passes through the chamber and carries off the heat. Steam is admitted to the engine by a piston-valve controlled by a governor fitted on the shaft in the usual manner.

From the air-pumps the feed water passes to the hotwell, from which it is taken by four Weir hotwell pumps 14½ in. by 30 in., of the firm's light-duty type, fitted with Kinghorn valves, and having gun-metal liners, brackets, and manganese-bronze rods. These pumps are automatically controlled by Weir control-gear fitted in the hotwell, so that the speed of the pumps corresponds to the quantity of water passing into the chamber. The feed water is discharged by these pumps through two Weir surface feed-heaters, where the exhaust steam from all the auxiliaries (with the exception of the turbo generators) is utilised to heat the feed, and as this steam is impregnated with oil, it flows, after condensation, by gravity through an oil-filter into the hotwell tank. In addition to this feed-heater there

FIG. 149. CONTACT FEED-WATER HEATER.

are also fitted two Weir direct-contact heaters (Fig. 149 on this page), into which the exhaust steam from the turbo-generators is led. There is here also control-gear for regulating the speed of the main feed-pumps. These consist of three pairs of Weir standard feed-pumps, 13½ in. in diameter, with a 30 in. stroke, which are supplemented by a duplicate installation of auxiliary feed pumps of the same size and number. These pumps, illustrated by Fig. 147, above, have all gun-metal barrels, with manganese-bronze valves and pump-rods, steel piston-rods, with the requisite suction and discharge stop-valves for drawing from the feed-heaters and discharging to the boilers.

In addition to these auxiliaries, Messrs. G. and J. Weir, Limited, have also supplied four duplex pumps of special design for ash-ejector and auxiliary feed duty, 10 in. in diameter, with a 14-in. stroke, and three duplex pumps for sanitary and wash-deck purposes, also four single direct-acting bilge-pumps, 10 in. in diameter, with a 21-in. stroke. For the supply of oil to the turbine bearings, six of their special direct-acting lubricating-pumps are fitted. For dealing with the water and air from the auxiliary condensers, they have furnished two of their latest type of single direct-acting air pumps, known as the "Monotype" pattern, 22 in. in diameter, with a 12-in. stroke. These represent the latest developments in air-pump design, and are illustrated by Fig. 148, above. The installation of Weir auxiliaries, it will be observed, is very complete and representative, and practically handles the feed-water from the time it leaves the condenser until it is returned to the

FEED WATER FILTERS.

CONSTRUCTED BY THE HARRIS PATENT FEED-WATER FILTER, LIMITED, ENGINEERS, LONDON.

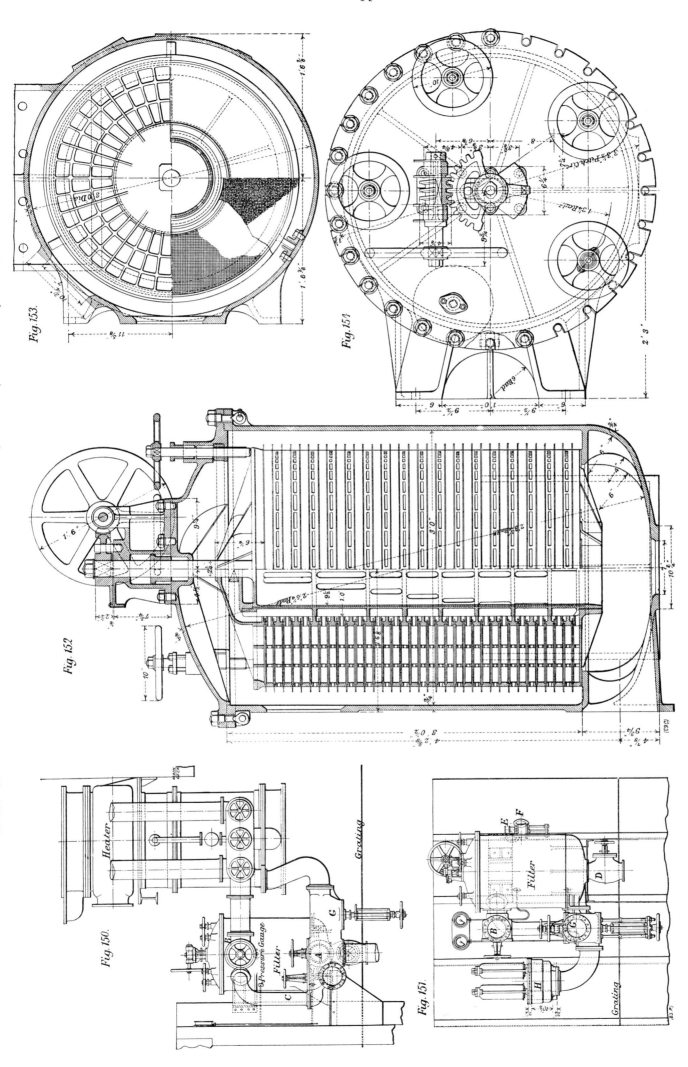

Fig. 153.

Fig. 151.

Fig. 152.

Fig. 150.

Fig. 151.

boilers; a responsible duty which calls for most reliable equipment.

FEED-WATER FILTERS.

Two feed-water filters of the well-known Harris type, supplied by the Harris Patent Feed-Water Filter, Limited, London, are fitted in connection with the hot-well pumps, and filter the water on its passage to the feed-heaters. The filters, which are clearly illustrated on this and the next pages, are each 36 in. in diameter, and of gun-metal throughout, the principal feature in their internal construction being the central sludge outlet—an ingenious arrangement, by which the filtering area is divided into eight separate sections, each of which can be sludged out independently of the others, the whole force of the reversed current of the water, when cleaning, being concentrated on only one-eighth of the surface, so that the cleaning is most efficient, and can be effected in a few minutes without the necessity of opening up. The filters present a most compact appearance, and everything is well arranged to facilitate their ready manipulation.

F

DETAILS OF THE HARRIS FEED-WATER FILTERS.

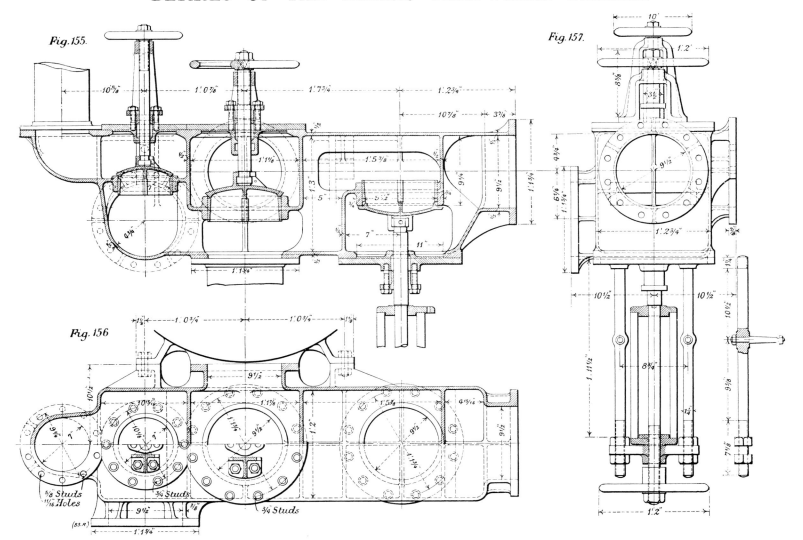

Fig. 155.

Fig. 156

Fig. 157.

Two smaller filters, 20-in. in internal diameter, also in gun-metal, are fitted in connection with the auxiliary machinery. These filters are of the same type as the larger ones, but with all valves self-contained.

DISTILLERS AND EVAPORATORS FOR MAKING-UP THE FEED WATER.

The distilling machinery is of Quiggin's well-known type, and was manufactured by the Liverpool Engineering and Condenser Company, Limited, Brunswick Dock, Liverpool. The complete set is illustrated in Figs. 159 to 162 on the opposite page.

There are two complete sets of plant in the Lusitania, and these supply the whole of the distilled water required for all purposes, the total capacities of each plant being, for cooking and drinking purposes, 18,000 gallons per 24 hours ; for baths and washing, 15,000 gallons per 24 hours ; while the evaporators for feed-make-up purposes for the boilers, when working compound-effect, supply 240 tons per 24 hours, and, when working single high-pressure effect, 350 tons per 24 hours.

Each plant consists of one evaporator for the production of distilled water, and two for feed-make-up purposes, the two latter being arranged to work in series—compound, or separately—single effect. The evaporator is shown in section in Fig. 162, page 43, and the condenser in section in Fig. 160. All the evaporator shells are made of rolled naval brass, double-riveted. This is for the purpose of reducing the weight as far as possible. The ends of the evaporators, all the mountings, as well as the frame and doors, are constructed of gun-metal. The coils are made so that they can be withdrawn bodily, and are all interchangeable, and the coils can be taken out separately for the purpose of cleaning and for inspection ; while in order to facilitate this operation a complete spare heating surface is provided for each size of evaporator, in order that the coils may be replaced by a clean set, when required, in a few minutes. An automatic feed-water

FIG. 158.

regulator, shown in Fig. 161, is provided for each evaporator, and this maintains the water-level in the evaporator at a constant height. It acts in the following manner :—The rise and fall of the water acts on the corrugated float F, the motion of which shuts or opens the pilot-valve P, which in turn governs the control-valve C, by allowing the pressure to increase or decrease in the chamber D on the top of the valve C. The pump is always in communication with the chamber D, the valve C fitting loosely in its casing, and allowing a constant leakage past it for this purpose. The water to the condenser passes through the opening E. Should the valve C wear too slack, the leakage past it to the chamber D may be more than the pilot-valve P can pass, in which case the valve C will not open enough, and the water in the evaporator will fall in consequence. When a new valve is fitted, care

EVAPORATORS AND DISTILLERS FOR MAKING UP FEED WATER.

CONSTRUCTED BY THE LIVERPOOL ENGINEERING AND CONDENSER COMPANY, LTD., LIVERPOOL.

FIG. 159.

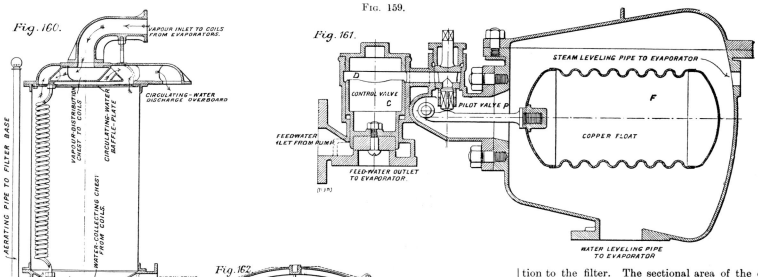

Fig. 160.

VAPOUR INLET TO COILS FROM EVAPORATORS.

CIRCULATING-WATER DISCHARGE OVERBOARD

VAPOUR-DISTRIBUTION CHEST TO COILS

CIRCULATING-WATER BAFFLE-PLATE

WATER-COLLECTING CHEST FROM COILS.

AERATING PIPE TO FILTER BASE

CIRCULATING WATER INLET

FILTER BASE

FILTERING MATERIAL

DISTILLED-WATER OUTLET.

CLEANING-DOOR TO FILTER CASE.

Fig. 161.

CONTROL VALVE C

D

FEEDWATER INLET FROM PUMP.

PILOT VALVE P

FEED-WATER OUTLET TO EVAPORATOR.

STEAM LEVELING PIPE TO EVAPORATOR

F

COPPER FLOAT

WATER LEVELING PIPE TO EVAPORATOR

Fig. 162.

VAPOUR OUTLET

BAFFLE PLATES

GUNMETAL DISTRIBUTION PIPE

WATER LEVEL

BOILER STEAM TO COILS.

DOOR

DIVIDED COLLECTING PIPE FOR CONDENSED STEAM FROM COILS.

RUNNER BAR

must be taken that it does not fit too tight, as the leakage past it would then be insufficient; the control-valve would remain open too long, and the water would then rise in the evaporator. The evaporator shells are lagged with hair-felt, and sheathed with galvanised sheet steel.

The condensers have coils of solid-drawn copper, and are tinned inside and outside; the coils can be withdrawn bodily with the cover by simply unscrewing a nut on the spigot end at the bottom connec-

tion to the filter. The sectional area of the coils diminishes from top to bottom, but each coil has a parallel surface throughout. The inlet for the steam is of full bore where the steam enters, but is gradually reduced in area to a crescent section, until at the outlet end it is only about one-third of the original sectional area. The volume of the steam is reduced as it condenses, and is kept in contact with the condensing surface, owing to the diminishing area of the coil. It is claimed that in this way the surface is rendered much more effective than it would be if the coils were of the same sectional area throughout. The filter, which is charged with animal charcoal and limestone chips, is in the base of the condenser. As a means of aerating the distilled water there is a pipe fitted, which is tapped from an iron-pipe connection, and there is a door for access to the filter. The circulating water enters and flows, as shown. There are two condensers in each set. The shells of the condensers are of galvanised mild steel.

In each set of apparatus there are three pumps—namely, one vertical duplex circulating pump, one vertical duplex evaporator feed-pump, and one vertical single direct-acting type brine-pump for pumping the brine from the low-pressure evaporator (when working compound effect); after the water has been diluted and cooled with sea-water it is pumped overboard. All these pumps are made with solid gun-metal water ends.

PUMPS FOR SUNDRY DUTIES.

In the engine-room there are a great variety of pumps for sundry duties. Many of these have been

GENERAL ARRANGEMENT OF AUXILIARY MACHINERY AND DISCHARGE-PIPES.

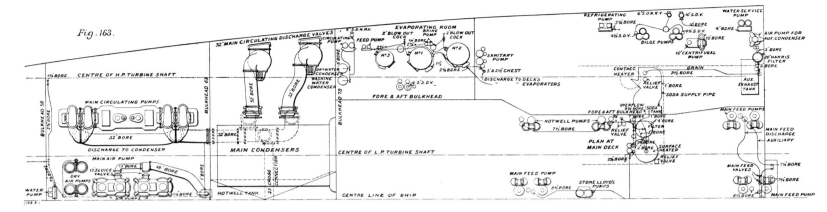

Fig. 163.

supplied by Messrs. J. H. Carruthers and Co., Limited, Polmadie, Glasgow. An illustration of a set of their typical ballast-pumps is given below; the others are of similar design. The arrangement of framing in this type gives very free access to all the moving parts. All the important

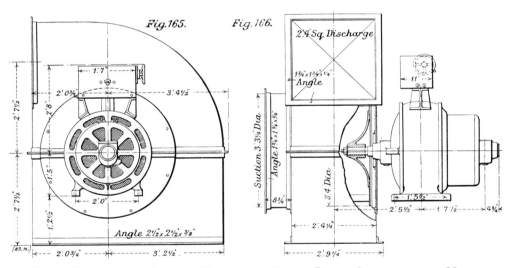

FIGS. 165 AND 166. FANS FOR VENTILATING ENGINE-ROOM; CONSTRUCTED BY MESSRS. LAURENCE, SCOTT, AND CO., LIMITED, NORWICH.

FIG. 164. CARRUTHERS' BALLAST PUMPS.

joints of the valve gear are adjustable. The water valves are easily examined through the front doors of the pump.

Among the pumps supplied are the following :—

Two for ballast service, with
cylinders ... ... 8 in. and 10 in. by 10 in.
Two for water service, with
cylinders ... . 7½ ,, 10 ,, 12 ,,
Two for washing decks ... 6 ,, 6 ,, 6 ,,
One for sanitary service ... 6 ,, 7 ,, 7 ,,

All of the pumps have gun-metal ends.

VENTILATION OF THE ENGINE-ROOM.

Messrs. Laurence, Scott, and Co., Limited, Norwich, supplied twelve fans of 35 in., two of 30 in., and two of 25 in. diameter, all electrically driven and adapted for the ventilation of the engine-room. The outputs specified were respectively 26,000 and 14,000 cubic feet per minute, with free discharge at 315 and 450 revolutions per minute, the fans being direct driven and carried on an extension of the motor spindle. The company's standard type of semi-enclosed motor was adopted, fitted with gauze grids, the magnets being series wound for the reasons given below. In view of the high temperature of the situations in which some of these fans work, the motors were made large, and the temperature rise in a six hours' run was kept

below 50 deg. Fahr. The armature is all built up on a cast-iron quill, and is self-contained and independent of the shaft, on to which it is slipped when completed. Series winding was adopted for the magnets, as this gives better regulation of the load than shunt winding would do. The power required by a centrifugal fan at a constant speed goes up

rapidly as the resistance to its free discharge is removed, reaching a maximum when disconnected altogether from its air-trunks. The variation in speed of a series-wound motor tends to correct the effect of variations in the resistance to discharge of the air, and keeps the load on the motor and the volume of air more nearly constant than would be the case if a shunt motor were used. The series winding also gives a simple method of speed-control without the use of resistances. For slow speed all four field coils are arranged in series with each other and the armature. For full speed the field coils are arranged in two parallel circuits, each of two coils in series, these being still in series with the armature. The motor is then running with a lower resistance in series with the armature and with a weaker field, and therefore at a higher speed. The barrel-controller shown is protected by an overload and no-voltage device. In the event either of an overload or failure of supply, the barrel carrying the contacts flies to the "off" position, even if the operating handle is being held "on." The fans are Messrs. Davidson and Co.'s make, of the well-known Sirocco type, and, like the motors, are amply large for the work.

ARRANGEMENT OF AUXILIARY MACHINERY.

The plan which we publish on this page (Fig. 163) shows the position of the various auxiliary engines which are described and illustrated in the preceding pages. This plan applies to the port side of the ship, but the disposition of the auxiliaries on the starboard side corresponds almost exactly. The plan should be studied in conjunction with the

section and plan of the main propelling machinery on the two-page Plate XXXIX. (Figs. 85 and 86) and the sections, Figs. 87 and 92, on the two-page Plate XL.

The first point of interest is the cross-connection between the port and starboard condensing plant. Either will suffice for the full duty in the event of

one giving out through any cause. The condensers are in a separate compartment abaft the main central engine-room, and over the two shafts driven by the low-pressure turbines, as shown also in Figs. 85 and 86, on Plate XXXIX. The circulating pumps and the air-pumps are in a compartment abaft the condensers. The air-pumps are accommodated between the shafts, and are at a lower level than the circulating pumps.

The evaporator and distilling plant are in a compartment in the wings of the ship, over the outer shafts and abaft the high-pressure turbine. In this way space is admirably economised. It will be understood by those who have studied the preceding figures that the high-pressure turbines in the wing compartments are not in the same athwartship line as the low-pressure turbines, the former being considerably in advance, as shown by the vacant spaces in Fig. 163. This disposition of the turbines has enabled the larger of the auxiliary engines to be grouped in the forward part of the central engine compartment in the vacant space around the astern turbines, which, as shown in the longitudinal section, Fig. 85, Plate XXXIX., are at the forward end of this centre engine compartment. Two main feed-pumps occupy a central position, and the hotwell pumps are in the wing; while to the forward of them, but on a higher level, are the filters and the feed-water heaters. Still further forward, against the main engine-room bulkhead, are two other main feed-pumps. The higher level of the surface heater, and other auxiliaries, is shown on the cross section, Fig. 92, on Plate XL. The arrangement, however, is so clearly shown on this plan of the main discharge-pipes that it is not necessary to write further on the subject.

CARGO AND NAVIGATING APPLIANCES.

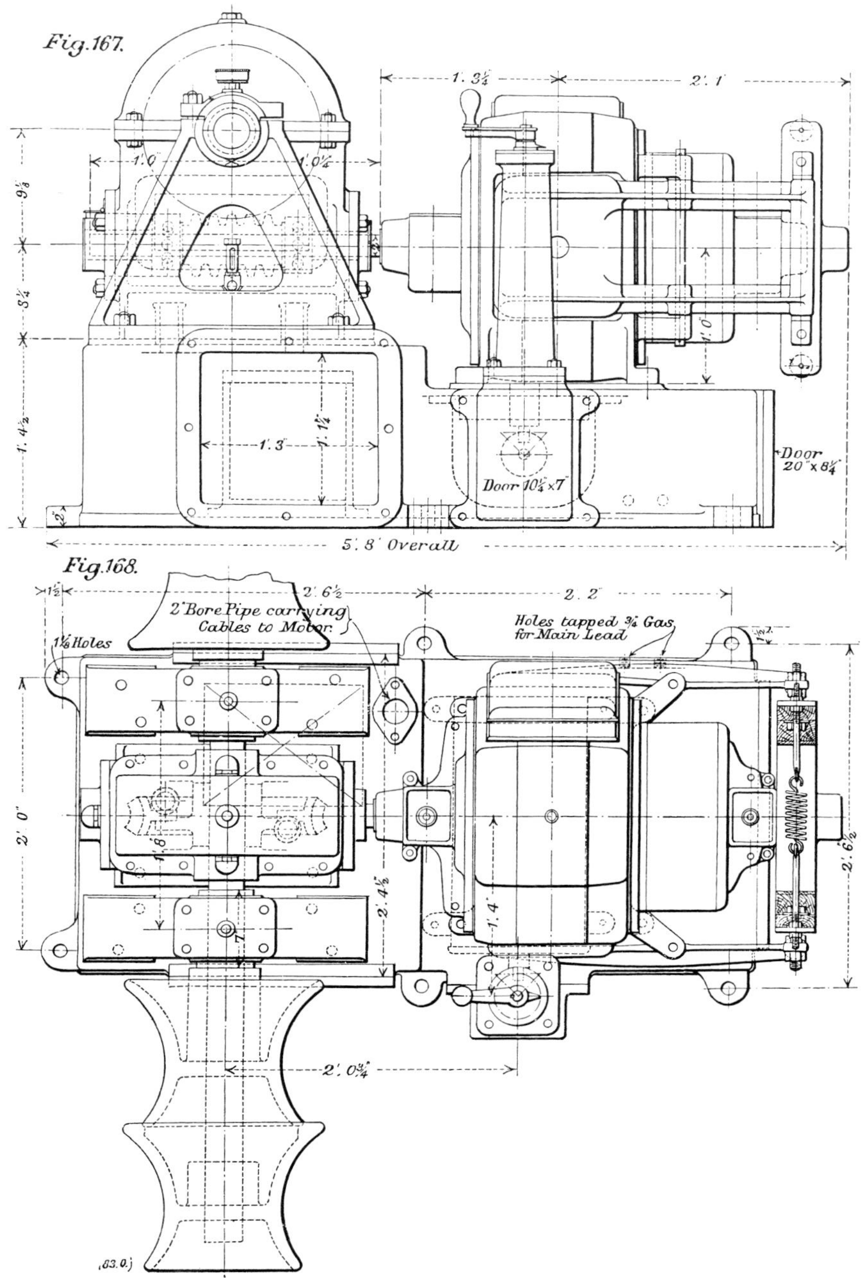

WE come now to the mechanical appliances for the navigation of the ship and for the handling of the little cargo that is carried.

The cargo appliances are not of first-class importance, for the best of all reasons—that the minimum of cargo will be accepted, since it is not profitable to

FIGS. 167 AND 168. ELECTRIC BOAT-HOISTS; CONSTRUCTED BY MESSRS. LAURENCE, SCOTT, AND CO., LIMITED, NORWICH.

add to the load transported at a speed of 25 knots, unless it is at very high freight rates. There are, as shown on the plans on the two-page Plate XXXVII., two holds for cargo, the capacity being 17,500 cubic feet. For coping with this cargo Messrs. John H. Wilson and Co., Limited, Sandhills, Liverpool, have fitted two winches, having two 8-in. cylinders adapted to a stroke of 14-in., which drive single-geared four-drum winches, and a winch with a 12-in. cylinder and a 16-in. stroke, operating a double-purchase warping-winch, with extended barrel-shaft and warping-drums. The arrangement and details of Messrs. Wilson's productions are well known and do not call for special description or illustration. These will be used largely in connection with the handling of cargo taken in the refrigerated holds.

There are also holds for stowage of mails, and a

mail-room for the sorting of letters, &c., before the arrival of the ship in port. This mail-room is aft on the orlop-deck, and the fittings have been carried out under Government supervision. The postal clerks' rooms are overhead, with the sorting-room at hand. There are various appliances for dealing with mails, baggage, &c., and these may now be described before we give details of the machinery in connection with the navigation of the ship.

BOAT-HOISTS.

Four electrically-operated boat-hoisting winches have been fitted. These were manufactured by Messrs. Laurence, Scott, and Co., Limited, Norwich, and are illustrated above (Figs. 167 and 168). The duty specified was to lift a total load of 12 cwt. at a speed of 250 ft. per minute. As two warping-drums are provided on each side, this pull can be distributed over four ropes. As will be seen from the drawings reproduced, the slow-speed shaft, with its four warping-drums, is carried on two substantial pedestal bearings, bolted directly to the box bed-plate on each side of the

separate gear-case. The gear consists of a cast-iron worm-wheel with machine-cut gun-metal rim, mounted on the slow-speed shaft, and engaging with a worm of forged steel carried by an extension of the motor spindle. Ball-thrusts and gun-metal journals are provided in the gear-case, the lower part of which forms an oil-bath for the worm.

The motor, which is of Messrs. Laurence, Scott, and Co.'s "Crane" type, series-wound and water-tight, is rated at 14 brake horse-power when making 600 revolutions and using current of 110 volts pressure. The specification provided that the temperature rise should not exceed 80 deg. Fahr. after one hour's full-load run. The actual temperature rise of the motor used under these conditions was under 60 deg. Fahr., and no difficulty was experienced in dealing with 100 per cent. overload for short periods. Series winding of the magnets was adopted to enable the motor to adapt its speed to various lifts, excessive speed at light loads being prevented by the Scott patent "flapper" brake with which these machines are provided. These brakes depend for their action on the magnetic field of the motor itself, some of the metal round the root of a pole, on either side of the motor, being cut away, so that most of the flux has to pass through steel plates or "flappers" connected to the brake-blocks by pivoted arms. The "flappers" thus experience a pull (tending to close them on to the side of the motor frame) which varies with the strength of the main field, and therefore with the load. The brakes are arranged to come right off with ordinary work, and to come into action gradually as the load is reduced, just enough to prevent the motor attaining an excessive speed when running light. The commutator end-brackets are circular, and are fitted with sheet steel covers pulled down by eccentrics on to a turned surface, with rubber sealing. The covers are slightly flanged, and fit into a turned groove, so that very little moisture can get even as far as the rubber, the arrangement making a satisfactory job, capable of standing anything but actual immersion under pressure. The armature is built up complete on a cast-iron quill independently of the shaft, on which it is secured by a long feather key. The armature can be withdrawn from the worm shaft, if necessary, without disturbing the gear-case, and the omission of an intermediate coupling, possible with this arrangement, makes a compact design.

The controller is of the tramway type, and is placed horizontally inside the deep box-bed under the motor, being operated through bevel-gear by a handle beside the winch. The resistances consist of cast-iron grids, and are also placed in the bed-plate for protection, and are indicated in the illustrations under the gear-box and one pedestal-bearing. The interior of the box-bed is roomy, and is made accessible by several large watertight doors, while ventilation is provided for in a space under the gear-box, where vent-pipes are so arranged as to prevent water getting down to the control-gear.

CRANES AND BAGGAGE-HOISTS.

There are on the vessel four deck-cranes, as well as the same number of baggage and mail-hoists, all constructed by Messrs. Stothert and Pitt, Limited, of Bath. These are illustrated on page 46 (Figs. 169 to 171). The deck-cranes are electrically driven, and are capable of handling loads up to 30 cwt., two at 18-ft. radius and the other two at 26-ft. radius. The superstructure consists of a vertical main frame of plates and angles carrying the lifting and slewing gear, while the jib is formed of a pair of rolled sections braced together. Tie-rods of wire rope are used to enable the jibs to be lowered conveniently. Separate totally-enclosed series-wound motors, working at 110 volts, are provided for lifting and slewing. The lifting motor is rated at 15 brake horse-power at 500 revolutions, and raises the full load at a speed of 100 ft. per minute. The motor drives through worm reduction gear, working in an oil-bath, the worm being of forged steel, and the wheel provided

ELECTRIC CRANES AND BAGGAGE HOISTS.

CONSTRUCTED BY MESSRS. STOTHERT AND PITT, LIMITED, ENGINEERS, BATH.

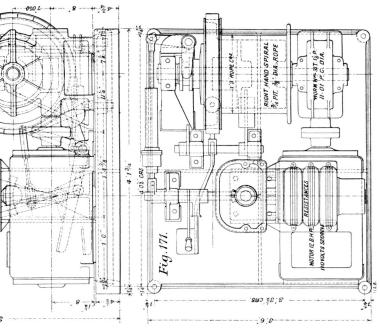

Fig. 170.

Fig. 171.

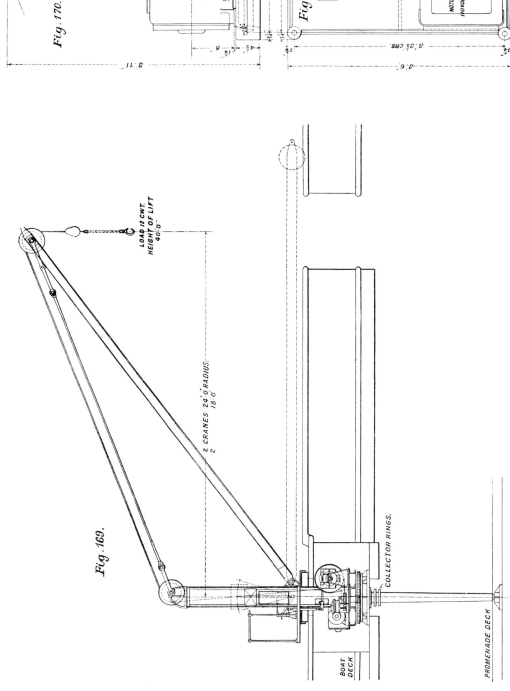

Fig. 169.

with phosphor-bronze teeth. Messrs. Stothert and Pitt's "free-barrel" system is employed for lifting and lowering. In this the barrel runs loose on the shaft, to which it can be connected by means of a coil-clutch. The lever for operating the coil-clutch is connected with the controller-handle in such a way that the same motion which gives current to the motor causes the engagement of the clutch. A powerful foot-brake is also provided, which is also interlocked with the controller-handle, so that it is impossible to work one against the other.

The advantage of the free-barrel system is that the load, after having been lifted to any desired height, may be released immediately and lowered under the control of the foot-brake. Thus no time is lost in bringing the armature and gearing to rest before lowering commences, and the motor has only to run in one direction.

Slewing is performed at the rate of 400 ft. per minute by means of a 2½-brake-horse-power motor running at 750 revolutions. The speed reduction is effected by means of worm and spur-gearing, driving a pinion engaging with the externally-toothed fixed slewing-ring. The weight of the revolving structure is carried on spherical-faced friction-pads in the foot-step, and the horizontal load taken, by rollers bearing in a path turned in the foundation-casting in the boat-deck.

The baggage and mail-hoists have lifting gear of the same type as that of the cranes, many of the parts being interchangeable.

STEAM STEERING-GEAR.

The steering-gear has been supplied by Messrs. Brown Brothers and Co., Limited, Edinburgh, and,

in addition to the gear, there is fitted reserve gear, as illustrated on pages 47 and 48, Figs. 172 to 176. On the rudder-post is a Siemens-Martin cast-steel cross-head, with long press-forged steel connecting-rods in two lengths, with guide-blocks connecting it to the cross-head end of a Siemens-Martin cast-steel tiller. This tiller is supported at its after end by a forged-steel dummy-post fitted into a large cast-iron bracket, which is bolted to the deck. The engines are mounted on the forward end of the tiller, and have cylinders 14 in. in diameter, with a stroke of 14 in. By means of worm-gear, friction-clutch, and spur-gear the engines drive a cast-steel rack, which is made in three pieces, so that when the teeth of the centre part become worn, this part can be replaced independently.

The whole of the moving parts are contained in the engine bed-plate, which has sides cast on it so

as to form an oil-tank, in a pocket in the bottom of which a pair of valveless oil-pumps are placed, driven by the eccentric-rods. These throw the oil into a small tank placed above the working parts, from which it is syphoned by pipes to all the engine bearings. A coil of copper pipe is fitted in the oil-tank for cooling water.

The engine for the reserve Rapson slide-gear is placed forward of the main gear-rack on the lower orlop-deck. It has cylinders 14 in. in diameter, with a 14-in. stroke, and is a duplicate in every way of the engine on the tiller, so far as its working parts are concerned. It is placed so that the crank-shaft lies fore and aft, and the after end of the shaft is prolonged outside the pan, and carries one of a pair of cast steel mitre-wheels. By means of gearing a sprocket-chain is finally driven.

This chain passes to port and starboard, and is

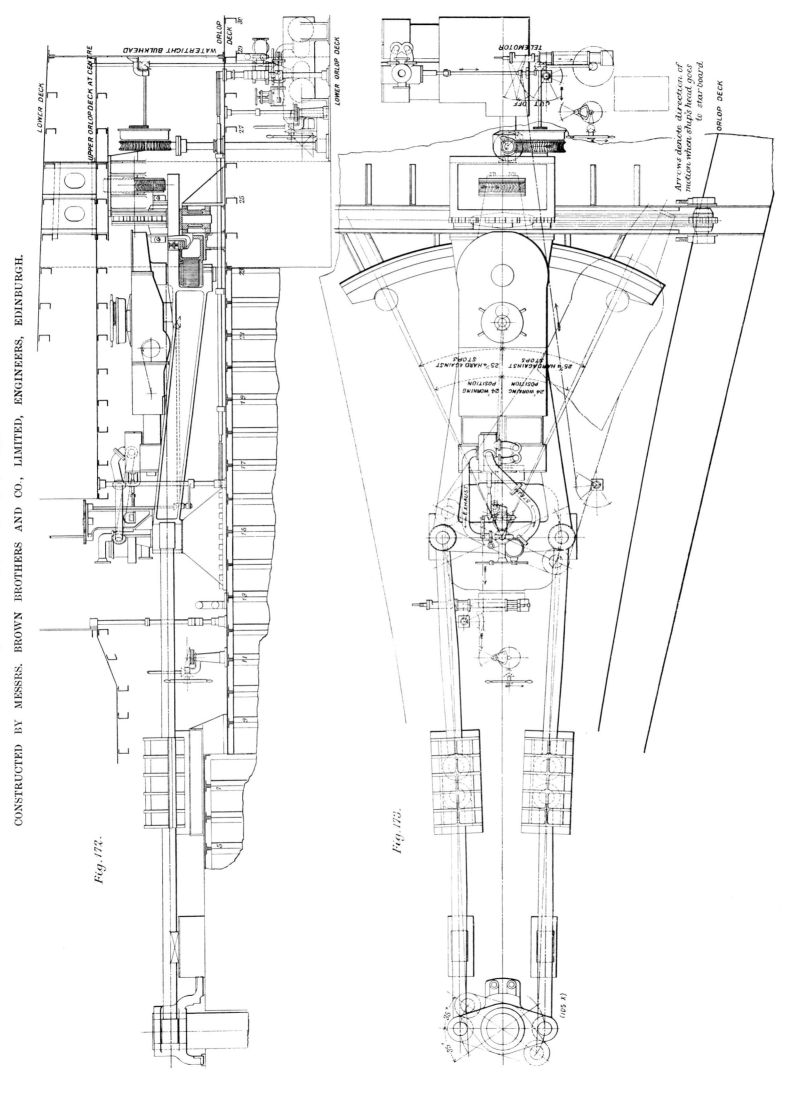

STEAM STEERING-GEAR.

CONSTRUCTED BY MESSRS. BROWN BROTHERS AND CO., LIMITED, ENGINEERS, EDINBURGH.

Fig. 172.

Fig. 173.

STEAM STEERING-GEAR AND ANCHOR-GEAR.

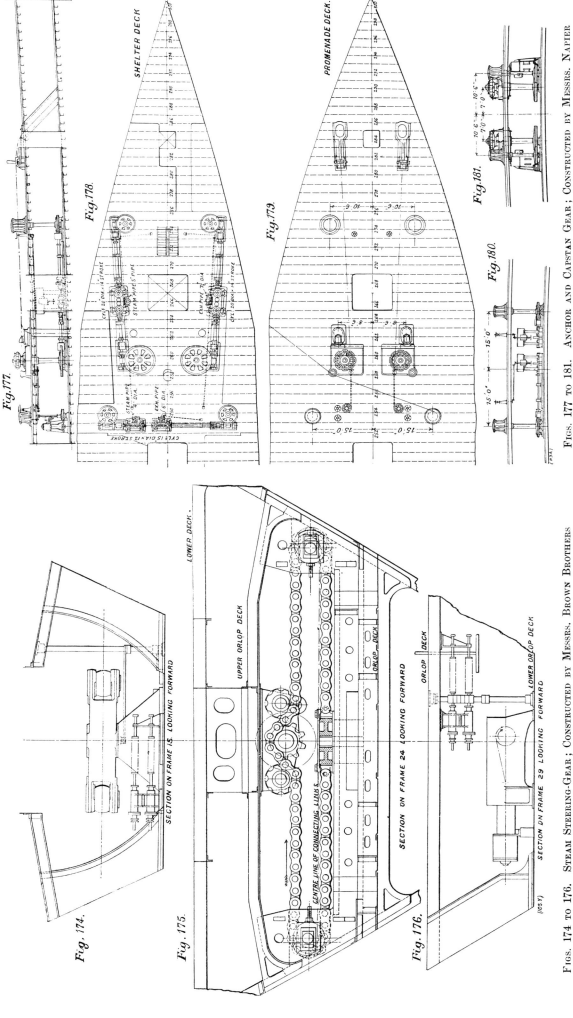

Fig. 174.

Fig. 175.

Fig. 176.

FIGS. 174 TO 176. STEAM STEERING-GEAR; CONSTRUCTED BY MESSRS. BROWN BROTHERS AND CO., LIMITED, EDINBURGH.

Fig. 177.

Fig. 178.

Fig. 179.

Fig. 180.

Fig. 181.

FIGS. 177 TO 181. ANCHOR AND CAPSTAN GEAR; CONSTRUCTED BY MESSRS. NAPIER BROTHERS, LIMITED, GLASGOW.

laid round a cast-iron pulley at each side of the ship. The ends are returned where they lay hold of a bridle which slides in a slot on a prolongation on the top jaw of the forward end of the main tiller. The guide-pulleys, round which the chain is laid, are held in place by means of cast-steel brackets, which can, by means of large screws, be made to take up any slack in the chain.

The rudder moves through an angle of 35 deg. on each side of the centre when the stops of the tele-motor are adjusted ; but the whole gear is arranged so that an angle of 37 deg. is obtained before coming on the rubber-stops. Each set of engines is capable of exerting a torsional strain of 1240 foot-tons on the rudder-stock, the steam pressure in the cylinders being 150 lb., and the back pressure 20 lb.

Two complete telemotors are fitted in the wheel-house on the navigating-bridge, and are worked from a central wheel through a horizontal shaft pro-vided with a clutch, so that each telemotor can be used separately. A complete telemotor is also fitted in the steering-station on the boat-deck aft, under the docking-bridge. Each telemotor has its own independent lead of copper pipes to a set of change-cocks on the athwart bulkhead at the end of the tiller-room, and can be operated from each side of the bulkhead.

Three motor cylinders are provided in each

steering compartment, and each pair has a separate pair of copper pipes led to the change-cocks. The motor cylinders are so arranged that they can be put in or out of gear from either side of the bulk-head. A charging-pump and tank are supplied for each compartment, and the motor cylinders are arranged so that those not in use can be charged by themselves.

ANCHOR, CABLE, WINDLASS, AND CAPSTAN-GEAR.

As will readily be understood, a vessel of such great weight, and presenting such a large area to wind pressure, requires not only strong, but reliable ground tackle, and this was supplied by Messrs. N. Hingley and Sons, Limited, Nether-ton Iron Works, Dudley. The cables, which are illustrated on page 50 (Fig. 187), have a dia-meter of 3¾ in., and are 330 fathoms in length; including shackles the weight is about 125 tons. The vessel carries two swivel pieces for mooring purposes, and they weigh 32 cwt. each. The bower anchors are Hall's improved patent, and weigh 10¼ tons each. Some idea of their proportions will be formed from the engraving on page 50. The cables were made of the highest quality of Netherton iron, which is so well known for this

ANCHOR AND CAPSTAN GEAR.

CONSTRUCTED BY MESSRS. NAPIER BROTHERS, LIMITED, ENGINEERS, GLASGOW.

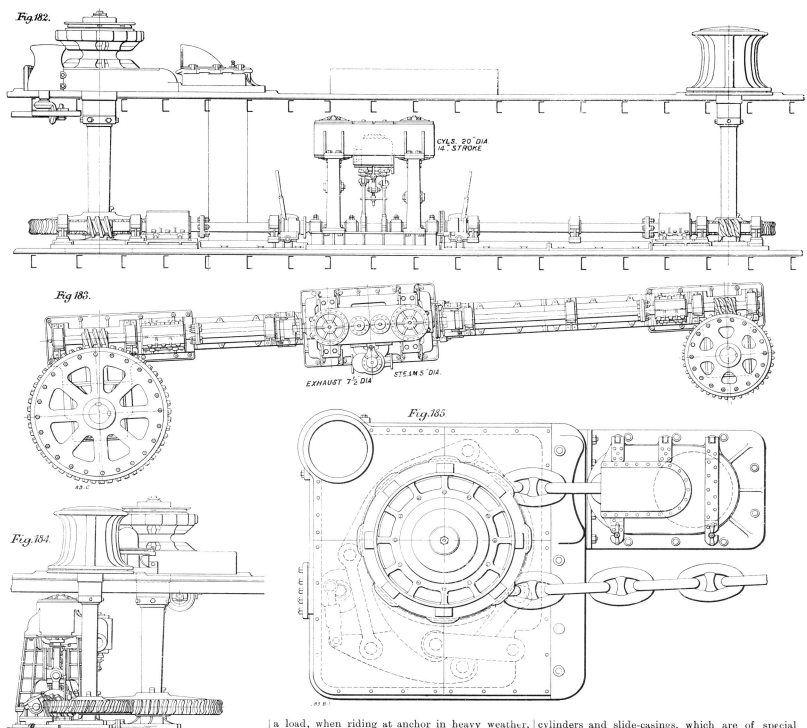

Fig. 182.

Fig. 183.

EXHAUST 7½ DIA.   STEAM 5 DIA.

CYLS. 20" DIA 14" STROKE

Fig. 184.

Fig. 185

purpose, and is made by Messrs. Hingley expressly for this quality of chain. The manufacture of these taxed even the resources of the Netherton Works, although they are considerably ahead of others in the country ; but all went through satisfactorily, and there is no doubt that the outfit of cables and anchors constituted a magnificent piece of work and worthy of the great ship they are for, and the reputation of the firm who made them.

The windlasses for working the 3¾-in. stud link-chain cables are placed on the promenade-deck, and are of the well-known Napier type, manufactured by Messrs. Napier Brothers, Limited, of Glasgow. The drawings of the gear are reproduced on pages 48 and 49 (Figs. 177 to 185). There are two cable-holders mounted on vertical spindles, 16 in. in diameter, in the deck bearings, and fitted at their lower parts with powerful Napier patent differential brakes. These are unequalled for their holding power where heavy loads have to be dealt with in a limited space ; they will hold

a load, when riding at anchor in heavy weather, of about 250 tons, notwithstanding that the brake is not more than 5 ft. in diameter. All parts of these windlasses are made of cast steel, of massive proportions, with gun-metal liners and bearings. The vertical spindles are carried to the shelter-deck, right below the promenade-deck, as shown in Fig. 182, and are connected direct to the engines by a single worm and worm-wheel gear. There is one engine for each windlass (Fig. 182), of ample proportions, and capable of indicating up to a large horse-power with the full boiler pressure. For warping the ship in harbour there are four vertical capstans. The two capstans forward of the windlasses are each driven from one of the windlass engines, and the two immediately aft of the windlasses are each driven by a separate engine of slightly smaller dimensions. This arrangement enables all four capstans to be used simultaneously, the actual hauling power amounting to over 1000 horses. A similar set of four capstans, exactly the same, are fitted at the after part of the vessel. It may be added that nearly every part of the gear, with framing and base-plates, is made of steel, cast or forged, with the exception of the

cylinders and slide-casings, which are of special close-grained cast iron. The object of using steel so exclusively was to provide a maximum of strength with a minimum of weight. Handling-wheels for controlling the different engines, as well as the windlass brakes, are fitted in convenient positions on the promenade-deck.

THE OFFICERS AND CREW.

Finally, there are the captain, engineers, and crew, on whom rests the responsibility for the efficient working of this microcosm, with its most modern of mechanical appliances. From the bridge the captain can control all the gear essential for navigation. The telegraph and telephone communicate with the engine-room, steering engine-room, and the anchor gear and warping capstan stations forward and aft ; while the telemotor itself controls the steering-engine. As already described, the captain can also open or close the bulkhead doors at will. The wireless telegraph apparatus, on the Marconi system, places him in communication with adjacent ships and with the shore during the whole of the Atlantic voyage, so that from first to last the

G

ANCHORS AND CABLES.

CONSTRUCTED BY MESSRS. HINGLEY AND SONS, LIMITED, NETHERTON IRON WORKS, DUDLEY.

FIG. 186.

FIG. 187.

successful navigation of the ship is ensured so far as mechanism can make it, and the Cunard Company have done their best to effect this result from the *personnel* standpoint.

Captain J. B. Watt, who has been appointed to the command of the Lusitania, joined the Cunard Company in 1873, and has passed through every grade of command. Among the vessels of which he has been captain are the Umbria, Etruria, Lucania, Campania, and Carmania. Captain Watt is a native of Montrose and served his early years in the clipper sailing service.

On the starting platform in the engine-room, already described, the chief engineer has within view recorders indicating the working of all the engines essential to the propulsion of the ship, and from this position, too, most of these engines can be controlled, so that, notwithstanding the great area occupied by the boilers and machinery, there is satisfactory supervision. The chief engineer is Mr. Alex. Duncan, who has been transferred from the Campania. The fact of his being selected for this post speaks volumes for his experience and ability. Mr. Duncan is a native of Renfrew.

The full complement of the ship is as follows :—

Navigation :

Captain and officers	..	...	...	9	
Quartermasters	...	...	...	8	
Boatswains...	...	...	...	3	
Carpenters and joiners ...		...	...	3	
Lamp-trimmer and yeoman	...	...	2	
Masters-at-arms	..	...	...	2	
Marconi telegraphists	...	...	2	
Seamen	...	...	...	...	40— 69

Engineering :

Engineer officers ...	...	...	33	
Refrigerating engineers...	...	...	3	
Firemen	...	...	..	...	192
Trimmers	...	...	...	...	120
Greasers	...	...	...	...	21—369

Personal :

Doctor	...	...	...	...	1
Purser	...	...	...	...	1
Assistant pursers...	...	...	...	2
Chief steward	...	...	...	1
Chief steward's assistants	...	...	2

Chef...	...	...	...	...	...	1
Barbers	...	...	...	...	2
Cooks and bakers...	...	...	...	28
Matrons	...	...	...	...	2
Stewardesses	...	...	...	...	10
Mail-sorters	...	...	...	...	7
Typists	...	...	...	...	2
Leading stewards, bar-keepers, &c.	...	50
Stewards	...	...	...	...	280—289

Grand total	..	...	...	827

And now, in conclusion, we wish to express our indebtedness to all the firms who have so readily placed at our disposal drawings, photographs, and particulars to enable us to give such a complete description of this, the most remarkable ship yet built, whether consideration be had to the size, speed, or safety. Nothing seems to have been omitted to make the steamer the most reliable, as well as the most comfortable of vessels, and we sincerely hope that the enterprise of the Cunard Company, and the great skill and experience of Messrs. John Brown and Co., Limited, will be rewarded with the fullest measure of success.

THE LAUNCH OF THE SHIP.

THE Lusitania was launched on June 7, 1906, and photographs of the ship as she stood on the ways ready for launching are reproduced on Plates XVII. to XIX., while others illustrating the progress of the ship down the ways are given on Plate XX. Immediate interest in the launch was associated with the problem, always fascinating to scientists, of the liberation beyond immediate control of a mass of 16,000 tons to be lowered through about 35 ft. during a longitudinal travel of 800 ft. This problem is the more engrossing, owing to the fact that in the great majority of cases the width of waterway into which ships are launched is narrow relative to the length of the vessel. The river opposite Clydebank is only about 610 ft. in width, while the ship has a length over all of 785 ft. ; but the yard there is perhaps more favourably situated than the majority of establishments on the northern river, by reason of the fact that its launching area includes the confluence of the rivers Clyde and Cart ; and in order to further facilitate the success of the operation, the vessel was built at an angle of 40 deg. to the line of the river, the better to take advantage of this increase in waterway. At the same time, the Clyde Trust carried out deepening and widening operations, in pursuance of their policy of meeting all prospective requirements of shipbuilders. One of these changes in the regularisation of the channel included the cutting away of the corners at the junction of the two rivers, so that it was possible to give the Lusitania a run of 1200 ft.

Although a great number of powerful vessels have been constructed at Clydebank, including some of our largest Atlantic liners, battleships, and armoured cruisers, it was deemed prudent to specially prepare a berth for the Lusitania, not so much because of the length or of the mean load per square foot, but because of the concentrated downward pressure at the forward end at the moment when the stern first became water-borne—a condition which occurred in the launch, when the vessel had travelled 560 ft. down the ways. It is difficult to estimate the extent of this downward thrust, but it may be assumed as amounting on an average to about 20 per cent. of the weight of the vessel; and as it is concentrated on a very limited area, the pressure is momentarily very much more severe than the average pressure on the standing ways, which was about 2 tons per square foot. Piles were driven throughout the area subjected to this special pressure, and were bound on top with cross-ties, so as more effectually to distribute the stress. A large part of the berth, of course, did not require any special strengthening; but the great length of the vessel necessitated her being laid down at a greater angle than in the case of preceding ships, and therefore the berth prepared occupied two former slips and the ground between them.

The vessel was built on keel-blocks which had a declivity of $\frac{7}{16}$ in. per foot, and were spaced at 3-ft. centres. The double bottom was, of course, supported as usual on bilge-blocks; and when operations were commenced in connection with the launching, the standing ways were laid between the bilge-blocks and keel-blocks. The ways were on a mean declivity of $\frac{17}{32}$ in. per foot, with a camber of 16 in. in the whole length. The distance apart of the standing ways was 25 ft. This is, perhaps, less than might have been adopted under normal conditions, but the spacing was determined owing to the position of the bossing out of the hull for the two inner shafts, shown in the view of the stern. This bossing out afforded a most convenient method of housing the tops of the aft poppets; the fine run of the ship would have involved elaborate arrangements to secure all these poppets otherwise, and the outer shafts were at too great a distance from the centre line to be utilised for the purpose. It was considered desirable to run a heavy angle-iron along the outside curve of the inner shaft bossing, to further secure the tops of the poppets. This frame may be seen by close examination of the stern view of the ship on Plate XIX.

The standing ways were built up of oak logs 12 in. by 12 in., and were 6 ft. in width. For the immediate preparation of the launch the standing ways were "payed" with Russian tallow and soft soap, the thickness being about $\frac{3}{8}$ in.; and a few days before the launch the sliding-ways were similarly coated and turned in on top. Like the standing ways, they were built of 12-in. by 12-in. oak timbers, bolted together, the lengths in all cases being connected at the butt-joint by heavy steel fish-plates.

On the sliding-ways the cradle was next built up, and the illustration of the bow, on Plate XIX., gives a good idea of the immense proportions, not only of the ship, but of the forward part of this cradle. The support for the top of the fore-poppets is notable for its great strength. There was built on the ship's structure, as shown, a series of ten deep brackets of plates and angles, each riveted to the shell-plates and frames of the hull. These web-brackets were tied on their outer edge by fore and aft plates, with a horizontal plate securely attached at the bottom, formed to receive the heavy timbering of the fore-poppets. Extending over eight frames aft of this, similar but shorter brackets were built to receive the next range of poppets. In the cradle for recent heavy ships in some other works, the bracket has been made in the form of a casting to lie snugly against the shell-plating of the ship, with a flange into which the tops of the poppets were housed, and this casting was made continuous along the top of the poppets. In the case of the Lusitania, however, it was felt that the use of angles and web-plates would give greater strength where it was most required, and would more effectually overcome the downward thrust, to which we have previously referred. The very fine lines of the ship necessitated a greater length of this temporary steel structure than in former ships. From the outside bottom edge of the shelf formed by these web-brackets there extended downwards underneath the keel, and up to the corresponding webs on the other side of the ship, tie-rods of steel, having shoes fitting on to the keel. The function of these tie-rods was to prevent the shelf from buckling, and to assist the brackets to more effectually withstand the thrust transmitted by the poppets when the stern became water-borne. These rods were then in tension, while the poppets continued in compression. The shoes referred to had a timber packing between them and the keel. The rods were released after the ship was afloat by the undoing of their bolts, which were easily accessible, as the bottom of the steel structure in connection with the fore-poppets was well above the launching water-line of the ship. All the fore-poppets were braced in the fore and aft direction by logs firmly bolted to them, and tripping lines were carried from the forecastle to enable the whole of the forward cradle to be pulled clear of the ship after she was water-borne. On the forward end of each standing way there was laid an hydraulic cylinder, the ram of which abutted on the forward end of the sliding-ways, and both cylinders were coupled to the same supply-pipe, the pressure being 1250 lb. per square inch. These hydraulic rams were for use had the vessel not moved on being liberated.

The aft cradle is illustrated in the stern view, on Plate XIX. The top of the poppets were in this case stowed underneath the bossing for the inner shafts, and secured at their outer edges by heavy angle-irons riveted to the shell. Tripping-lines were here also attached to the various lengths of the sliding ways and the aft-poppets, to enable them to be pulled from underneath the ship. It will be seen that quite a considerable length of the ship at the aft end was not supported during the launch, as it was not practicable to build the launching structure further than the point shown in the engraving.

The cradle extends from about 50 ft. from the stem to about 90 ft. from the aft perpendicular. Between the forward and aft poppets the make-up from the top of the sliding-ways to the bottom shell-plating consisted of the usual packing logs, set up by means of hard-wood wedges.

The photograph from which the stern view is made (Plate XVIII.) shows clearly the construction of the stern, and the relative position of the four propellers. It will be seen that the propellers are of unusual form. The immense area of the three blades is particularly noticeable, and indicates that those responsible for the design have given a much higher ratio of blade surface to disc area than is usual in recent practice. This fact, and the light it will throw upon the propeller problem, will add to the great interest of the Atlantic performance of the ship. Another fact is that while the two inside propellers are arranged to turn outwards when going ahead, the two outer propellers will turn inwards. The analyses of the stream-lines and wave-factors revealed by model experiments justified this unusual arrangement. This also is an interesting development, which will be watched with great attention. Another point is that the edges of the blades are exceedingly fine; and in view of this it was considered advisable to carefully bind them with temporary wood casing, to obviate injury during the stripping of the ship for launching, and during the subsequent completion of the vessel when afloat. This accounts for the somewhat unusual appearance of the propellers in the photographs.

To return to the launching arrangements, reference may now be made to the trigger which takes the place of the ordinary dog-shore. This trigger arrangement has been adopted at Clydebank for some time in connection with large vessels. Three separate triggers were placed on each side, located about 180 ft. apart, and were brought into action simultaneously by the electrical gear operating all six. The keel-blocks, bilge-blocks, and shores having been cleared away, a process which occupied several hours, the ship, resting on her cradle, was held by the six special triggers referred to. The action of these may thus be described. The closing of an electric circuit brought into operation an electromagnet at each station, which released a heavily-weighted lever, forming the end of a series of interlocked bell-crank levers, having at its other end a stop projecting up through the standing ways, and abutting against a steel plate let into a cavity on the bottom of the sliding-ways. The falling of all six weighted levers referred to, each actuating its chain of levers, released the ship on the sliding-ways. The lever, when it fell, also closed a separate electric circuit, which actuated an indicator placed at the station where the whole of the mechanism was controlled. By means of the indicator for each of the six dog-shores, the operator was apprised of the successful action of the gear. But had the mechanism described failed to act as arranged, the triggers could have been knocked down by hand, a workman being stationed at each position for this purpose. As soon as the indicators showed that all six dog-shores had fallen, the operator signalled by electric gear to a large disc on the launching platform, which then showed "All clear." The ship, however, at once moved, thus indicating the success of the operation.

From the time of starting until the vessel was clear of the ways, 86 seconds elapsed. Allowing for the 22 seconds occupied in tripping the blocks left under the vessel, when she only moved 1 ft., the mean velocity was of 12.2 ft. per second. The ship was brought to a state of rest with her bow 110 ft. from the end of the ways—a very satisfactory result. The drags, to accomplish this, consisted of six groups of chains on each side of the ground. With all large ships chain-drags are preferred to anchors or plates, because anchors tear up the ground to an unnecessary extent, and plates do not offer the required resistance owing to their smooth surface. The chains, too, are more easily handled.

The drags weighed over 1000 tons. The groups came into action successively in pairs, one on each side, the heaviest group being the last to come into operation. The first pair were effective immediately the vessel had travelled the full length of the ways, which extended about 85 ft. beyond the after perpendicular; the other pairs of drags acted at average intervals of 10 ft. These drags were connected by steel wire ropes to the ship's sides, by means of chain plates bolted through the shell-plating; the eye-bolts and their positions, relative to each other, on the port side of the ship, are clearly shown on the engraving of the bow on Plate XIX.

When the ship was brought to rest, the wire ropes connected to the drags were unshackled from the chain plates by the withdrawal of a pin from the deck, and the ship was taken charge of by six powerful tugs; these, aided by warping lines carried to the shore, succeeded in safely bringing the vessel into the fitting-out basin of the Clydebank Shipyard. It is an indication of the size of this basin to state that, notwithstanding the enormous length of the vessel, the stern does not project beyond the line of the river banks.

THE SALOONS IN THE SHIP.

THE Lusitania is not only a great step forward from the mechanical engineering standpoint, as is proved in the preceding pages, but marks the highest conception of artistic furnishing and internal decoration. Of this fact there is, we think, complete evidence in the engravings which we give on Plates XXI. to XXVIII.

FIRST-CLASS DINING-SALOON.

The dining-saloon with its great dome is illustrated in Plates XXI and XXII. In order to simultaneously seat 500 passengers there is adopted the unusual arrangement of having two saloons, one on the upper deck, and the other on the deck above and around the well and dome, which form the central decorative feature. The lower saloon is 86 ft. long and the full breadth of the ship, so that it is practically square. The upper saloon is 62 ft. long and 65 ft. broad. It is in the Louis XVI. style; the walls being white, with gilded enrichments, in harmony with that period.

At one end of the apartment is a sideboard of veneered mahogany, with panels of fine gilt bronze work. The dome, which has a height of 30 ft., is elliptical on plan, the main feature being four artistically-treated floral panels. All the carving of the walls and pillars is out of the solid wood; the dome is plaster work of a very fine character. The illustrations we publish give a better idea of the whole than could any description. Like all the other public rooms, this saloon is all of Clydebank workmanship; the wood-carving is by Mr. John Crawford, Glasgow, and the gilding by Messrs. Waring and Gillow, Limited, London. Access to the upper dining-saloon is from the entrance-hall on the shelter-deck. It, of course, follows the same design as the lower or main saloon. Attention is arrested and admiration aroused by the *tout ensemble* from this level. The artistic success of the architect is complete, because it is impossible to recognise the usual limitations in scope and execution involved in the case of a floating structure. The absence of vibration finishes the dissemblance.

On the shelter-deck there are a nursery and a dining-saloon for the children. The scheme of embellishment here also is in the Louis XVI. period, but it is advisedly simpler. Both rooms are spacious (the nursery is 20 ft. by 30 ft.), and they are well adapted for their purpose, with stewardesses' rooms and pantry adjacent.

THE FIRST-CLASS SMOKING-ROOM.

At the after end of the ship, on the boat-deck, is the first-class smoking-room, which is 55 ft. by 50 ft. As shown by the two engravings on Plate XXIII., the interior of this room has been completed according to the eighteenth-century period, and has its walls panelled with Italian walnut, the effect of the beautiful grain and figure of the wood being enhanced by the broad simple spacing of the panels. The furniture, consisting of luxurious sofas, settees, easy chairs, and writing-tables, has been designed and manufactured by that old-established firm, Messrs. Marsh, Jones, and Cribb, of Leeds, who have taken the finest models of the Queen Anne period, and treated them in such a way as to combine the comfort so necessary to the ocean traveller with all the dignity and elegance that is inseparable from these fine examples, so well known and highly prized by all lovers of artistic furniture.

The general tone of colour introduced is an old Italian red, which, blending harmoniously with the mellow tones of the walnut, produces an effect on entering the room of quiet repose and richness, in pleasant contrast to the brightness of the white and gold of other public apartments and alleyways. The fireplace, illustrated by Fig. 197 on Plate XXIII., is a striking feature of this room. Fig. 198 on the same Plate shows a portion of the room at the forward end, the ventilators partly isolating it from the main part of the room. (See the plan, Fig. 31 on Plate XXXVII.

THE WRITING-ROOM AND LIBRARY.

From the grand hall on the boat-deck access is obtained at the fore-end to the writing-room and library, which is 44 ft. by 52 ft. This apartment, which is illustrated by Fig. 199 on Plate XXIV., is decorated in the refined style practised by the Brothers Adam in the latter part of the eighteenth century. The walls are spaced out with beautifully-carved pilasters and mouldings, with panels in delicate grey and cream silk brocade. The windows, glazed with specially etched and other glass, have prettily embroidered valances and curtains of Rose du Barri silk tabouret, which is quite unique, being copied from an old document of the period found at Milton Abbey. The carpet has been specially woven for this room in rose colour, to harmonise with the surroundings. The furniture is in inlaid mahogany, the settees, easy chairs, and writing chairs being upholstered with the same materials as the curtains. The writing-tables are particularly handsome, each having in the centre a finely-chased and mercury gilt lamp. The ceiling—leaded glass and electric fittings—completes a scheme which is most pleasing; and the room will undoubtedly be looked upon as one of the finest—if not the finest—on the vessel. The furniture is by Messrs. Trollope.

THE FIRST-CLASS LOUNGE.

Abaft the entrance-hall on the boat-deck is the first-class lounge, which is 68 ft. by 52 ft. This apartment is magnificent as regards its size and the massiveness of the decoration, as suggested by the engraving Fig. 200 on Plate XXIV. It has been decorated in a late Georgian style, the mahogany panelling being veneered and inlaid in specially-selected and finely-figured woods. The furniture, of mahogany and satin-wood, with inlaid tables, has been arranged in groups. Comfort and durability have been aimed at, as is evidenced by the double-stuffed settees and large easy chairs; whilst the introduction of satinwood pieces and the green colour scheme of the carpets, coverings, cushions, and curtains combine to counteract the usually heavy effect associated with this style of decoration. At the forward and after end of this apartment there are arranged massive marble fireplaces. One of these is illustrated by Fig. 201 on Plate XXV. Over the fireplaces are arranged beautiful enamelled panels, by Alex. Fisher, of London. The roof is raised in dome fashion to a height of 20 ft., and is decorated by plaster work of a high, artistic standard. The glass work of the dome is in twelve panes, each representing a month of the year; these have been supplied by Mr. Oscar Paterson, of Glasgow. The furniture is by Messrs. Waring and Gillow, Limited.

SPECIAL SUITES OF ROOMS.

There are eighty-seven special cabins fitted throughout the ship, mostly on the promenade-deck. Of these a typical illustration is given in Fig. 202 on Plate XXV. These suites have been furnished and decorated by various well-known firms—namely, Messrs. Waring and Gillow, of London; George Trollope and Sons, London; and Wylie and Lochhead, Glasgow. The regal suites, of which there are two sets, comprise dining-room, drawing-room, two bedrooms, with pantry and lavatory attached. The other suites are of two rooms. The suites and some special cabins on the starboard side of the vessel are furnished by Messrs. Waring and Gillow, and those on the port side by Messrs. Trollope. All the special rooms are representative of the styles of various well-known periods, notably English and Colonial Adam, Georgian, William and Mary, Sheraton, Louis XV., Louis XVI., and Empire, most of which by their delicacy and refinement of detail are eminently suited for the purpose of ship decoration. These styles afford many opportunities for the application of decorative effect to practical requirements, and of such opportunities the designers have made full use. Upon every part of the work there has been bestowed careful thought, from the modelled ceilings and ornamental lights to the gilt fittings of the doors and furniture. Satin-wood, hard-wood, mahogany, sycamore, and walnut are the woods chiefly used, and they have been selected in all cases for beautiful figuring, and are enriched in many cases with fine inlays. Others of the state-rooms are carried out in white enamelled mahogany.

The starboard regal suite dining-room is in the Louis XVI. style, in panelled mahogany, with mahogany inlaid furniture; and the drawing-room, in the Colonial Adam style, in sycamore, with inlaid satin-wood furniture. These are, indeed, charming examples of the period.

The regal suite on the port side is again in the Louis XVI. style, and is strikingly effective, the details being based upon the beautiful examples at the Petit Trianon, Versailles. This suite is one of the great features of the ship. The dining-room is panelled with fine Italian walnut, enriched with carved ornaments and mouldings of burnished gold. The buffet writing-table, dining-table, and revolving chairs are also in Italian walnut and gold. The chimney-piece in this room is a particularly fine specimen of Fleur-de-Pecher marble, with marble hearth to match, and a quaint log fire, with fire-dogs complete. The panelled ceiling in white and gold, the green silk curtains, *portière* and carpet complete a very artistic portion of the suite. A sliding glass screen connects this room with the drawing-room of the suite, which is panelled in white, with carved gilt mouldings, enriched with beautifully-painted panels of flowers. The ceiling has been specially designed to meet the arrangement of electric lights; the curtains of heliotrope and cream and the green settees and carpet, a handsome mahogany commode, writing-table, &c., finish a setting quite reminiscent of Fontainebleau. The bed-rooms are both designed in a sumptuous manner; one being a scheme of rose-coloured silk panels, with satin-wood furniture inlaid with green; while the other is richly decorated in white and gold, relieved by most charming Wedgwood cameos. The curtains and *portières* of blue silk brocade are embellished with sprays of flowers.

The remainder of the Trollope suites have been carried out in the same sumptuous manner, with every modern comfort which ingenuity can suggest, each room being provided with telephones, electric lights, radiators, &c. The styles adopted are Empire, Georgian, Queen Anne, Sheraton, and Louis XVI., and each has been treated with a purity of style and colour which denotes the true artist.

On this same deck are arranged a large number of special rooms, by Messrs. Wylie and Lochhead, Glasgow. These rooms also present examples of the refined style of certain definite periods. They represent those developments of the later Renaissance which experience and taste have shown to be most congenial to the complex requirements of modern life. The styles selected are the Louis XV. and Louis XVI., the English, Georgian, and the simpler treatments of the later eighteenth century known as Colonial. The determining character of these apartments is a refined simplicity of treatment. Mouldings of delicate contour, restraint in the carved parts, and quiet harmonies in the colour scheme are the points which will attract the attention earliest. The more detailed examination of each scheme will reveal that, while the essential charm of each style has been preserved, none of the requirements so needful to comfort in ship-life have been sacrificed to decorative effect.

THE GRAND STAIRWAY AND CABINS.

The public rooms on the respective decks are entered in most cases from a grand stairway which begins at the main deck first-class entrance, on a low level at the ship's side, convenient for gangways from the wharves, landing-stages, or tenders, and rises successively to the upper, shelter, promenade, and boat-decks: a total height of 44 ft. Of the main entrance-halls views are given on Plate XXVI.

There is at each deck a spacious hall, 24 ft. long, and in most cases the full breadth of the ship. In addition to the broad companion-way, there are two electrically-worked passenger-lifts, situated in the centre of the stairway, and described in detail on page 23. These rise to a height of 44 ft. above the main deck entrance, and convey passengers to the four decks above. These lifts have gates and surrounding frames, which have been treated with admirable taste; and, instead of being excrescences, lend attraction to the decorative scheme of the stairway. The black and gold metal-work contrasts well with the prevailing whiteness of the surroundings.

On the main deck, in the vicinity of the entrance-hall, are a large number of first-class cabins, suited for passengers of moderate means, or rather of a mödest disposition. They are in the best part of the ship for those who desire quietude on the voyage. A feature of the cabins is their spaciousness. On the next level, the upper deck, there are, extending right forward, groups of first-class cabins. These are of unusual arrangement; the lavatory stands in a recess. The furniture, wardrobes, dressing-table, corner-cupboards, settees, &c., are in mahogany, and the walls of enamel white; while the drapery on beds, the rich red curtains on the door and on the entrance to the lavatory recess, are in figured cretonne.

Abaft the hall on the upper and shelter-decks are the dining-saloons, already described. In the promenade-deck entrance-hall is the enquiry bureau, where the traveller may obtain all the necessary information to enable him to enjoy himself on board, and to plan his land journey when he disembarks. The bureau is of mahogany, and the windows are covered with brass fretwork of a chaste design (Fig. 204, on Plate XXVI.). On this promenade-deck entrance is had to the special suites of rooms, which practically occupy the whole available space on this deck.

Coming next to the last stage of the first-class accommodation—namely, the boat-deck—it may be noted, first, that the top flight of the stairway is elegantly decorated, plentifully supplied with lounge-seats and chairs, all in keeping with the surroundings. There is a handsome marble fire-place, and the prevailing tones of white and gold blend well with the marble adopted. The upholstery is a delicate figured rose-shade tapestry. At the after-end of this deck there has been arranged an outside café, 24 ft. by 50 ft. On the boat-deck, also, are the writing-room, the lounge, and the smoking-room, already described.

Several important parts of the decoration have been supplied by the Bromsgrove Guild, Birmingham. These include the metal-work of the staircase and of the sideboard in the saloon, electric fittings in the saloon, at the staircase, and in the smoking-room; the plaster work of the lounge, smoking-room, writing-room, and staircases. All this work is characterised by high artistic ability and finished workmanship.

SECOND-CLASS ACCOMMODATION.

The second-class accommodation includes a dining-room, drawing-room, smoking-room, and lounge, the latter an innovation in this part of the ship. The lounge, 42 ft. by 40 ft., is illustrated by Fig. 205 on Plate XXVII. It is fitted out in mahogany, and arranged with easy chairs and settees, small tables for the service of coffee, &c. The dining-room, 60 ft. long and the full breadth of the ship, is decorated in the Georgian style, with delicately-carved panels and pillars in white; overhead is a circular well surrounded by a handsomely-carved balustrade. At the fore-end of the saloon a beautiful sideboard of mahogany, of very ornate and admirable design, has been placed.

The second-class drawing-room, 28 ft. by 42 ft.,

is in a grey tone, and of the Louis XVI. style. The rose of the carpet and curtains, the satin-wood furniture, and the general grey of the walls, make an admirable contrast. This room, although termed the "drawing-room," has been furnished with writing-tables and bookcases, so that it serves as drawing-room, writing-room, and library. On the other side of the main second-class entrance on this (the promenade) deck there has been arranged the smoking-room, which is 52 ft. long by 33 ft. wide. It is illustrated on Fig. 206 of Plate XXVII. Like the lounge, it is Georgian in design, with mahogany panelling and furniture, a ceiling of white, and a dome of plaster work. At the forward end is a handsome mosaic panel by Messrs. Guthrie and Wells, Glasgow, representing a river scene in Brittany. Throughout the apartment small square tables and comfortably-upholstered chairs have been arranged. The interior, or sliding windows, have a milky bluish hue, which produces an excellent effect in daylight.

The designs for all the public rooms were made, in consultation with Mr. James Millar, R.S.A., F.R.I.B.A., by Messrs. John Brown and Co.'s own architect, Mr. Robert Whyte.

THIRD-CLASS ACCOMMODATION.

The advance in the convenience and comfort of the third-class accommodation is as marked as in

the cases of the first and second-class. The forward end of the vessel, from the lower to the forecastle decks, is given up entirely to the third-class passengers, located in cabins containing two, four, or six berths, and in these 1186 passengers can be accommodated. The appointments of these rooms are far superior to those of but a few years ago. The third-class dining-room, 79 ft. long by 60 ft. wide, is a special feature, situated forward on the upper deck, and in it there can dine at one sitting 350 passengers. It is fitted out, as shown in the view, Fig. 208, on Plate XXVIII., in polished pine, with square windows over the sidelights; circular reversible seats are fitted, and altogether the saloon has a fine appearance. A piano is placed at the fore-end of the saloon. On the shelter-deck two large public rooms are arranged for the third-class—namely, a ladies' room and a smoking-room. These are fitted up in the same style as the dining-saloon.

The forecastle deck side-plating has been carried well aft, and the promenade or shelter-deck thus enclosed has been fitted with side seats. This forms, for a length of at least 150 ft. on each side of the ship, a comfortable lounge for the third-class passengers. It is open, of course, at the aft end, but is still sheltered from the elements if they are boisterous in any way; so that the third-class passengers cannot be considered to be cabined and confined even in bad weather.

THE APPLICATION OF ELECTRICITY IN THE SHIP.

ILLUSTRATIONS and a detailed description of the four 375 kilowatt Parsons turbo-generators, as well as several electric motors, hoists, &c., incidental to the propelling or navigating machinery, are included in the preceding pages: but there are many varied applications of electricity for the convenience of passengers which may be here described.

We may begin with the switchboard, which is of special design, and of the same type as fitted in H.M.S. Dreadnought and other battleships. No slate or marble is used in its construction, the insulation being of micanite used in the form of sheets, ferrules, and washers. Each dynamo has its own panel, consisting of a cast-steel frame, carrying a double pole reverse-current circuit-breaker, fitted with time-element device, a vertical edgewise ammeter, and a voltmeter, the latter being a double one, to assist in ensuring that the adjoining machine shall run in parallel. A bus-bar voltmeter is also provided. The capacity of these circuit-breakers is 4000 amperes at 115 volts. There are 24 feeder panels, each consisting of a double-pole maximum-current circuit-breaker, of similar design to the dynamo-breakers. They are of a normal carrying capacity of 700 amperes, but can be set for any load above that up to 1300 amperes. The bus-bars are at the back of the board, carried on heavy porcelain insulators. All connections are made at the front, and the whole arrangement is such that any panel can be slipped off the frame without in any way disturbing any other panel. The board is in two halves, one half in each dynamo-room; and in order to guard against the possibility of a total breakdown in the event of either room being flooded, a double pole 5000-ampere switch, is fitted on each board to break the connection between the two boards.

The main cables, which are all of 1 square inch section, insulated with vulcanised rubber, and rendered fireproof by a double covering of asbestos and jute braiding. These cables, measuring 2 in. in external diameter, and amounting in all to approximately 4 miles in length, are carried on porcelain insulators, supported on iron racks on each side of the engine-room and stokehold. Each circuit ends in an auxiliary switchboard, consisting of an enamelled slate base, carrying single-pole switches of 150 amperes, and double-pole fuses of the Dixon's patent blotter type. made by Brook, Hirst, and Co., of Chester. From these boards the electric current is distributed in the usual manner to junction, section, and distribution boards, from the last of which current is taken to the various groups of lamps.

There are about 6300 lamps, mostly of 16 candle-power, with a considerable number of 8 candle-power carbon-filament lamps, "Huntalite," lamps for bracket fittings in the public rooms, and 23 candle-power "Tantalum" metallic-filament lamps. These latter are used throughout all the pendant fittings in both first- and second-class public rooms. The first-class cabins are fitted up with every possible electric fitting conducive to the comfort of the passenger, switches and bell-pushes being placed at the side of every berth and sofa. A reading-lamp is also provided, with two or more sockets where it can be attached, so as to suit the occupants of the cabin, whether sitting at the sofa or reading in bed. Electric radiators or connections for the same are provided in every state-room. Those in the specially fitted-up rooms are of original design, electro-gilt and otherwise, and in keeping with the various styles of furnishings. The second-class cabins are supplied with electric fittings, only slightly less numerous than those of the first-class state-rooms.

Apart from the ventilation of the engine-room, which has been described elsewhere, a very complete system of artificial ventilation and heating of all parts of the ship on the thermo-tank principle has been installed, as already described; and, in addition, there are 14 electrically-driven Sirocco fans for exhausting the air from lavatories, &c. Propeller fans of various sizes, from 12 in. to 24 in. diameter, are also in use for exhausting the air from smoke-rooms, galleys and saloons.

Electric-motors and electric heating are very extensively in use in connection with the galleys and pantries, there being 41 different machines or heaters in operation, performing such various duties as dough mixing, dish washing, ice-cream freezing, knife and boot cleaning, potato peeling, beef and bird roasting.

The telephone arrangements are most complete. There are three distinct systems: (1.) Graham's loud-speaking telephones. In connection with these there are two pillar 'phones on the bridge, enabling the officer on watch to speak to the steering-gear compartment. engine-room starting platform, after-bridge, crow's-nest and forecastle. From the engine-room platform communication can be made to the bridge, chief engineer's office, steering gear, pump-rooms and dynamo-rooms. (2.) Inter-communication system of telephones (Parson-Sloper patent single-circuit system, manufactured by Gent and Co., Leicester). There are 23 instruments fitted, enabling inter-communication to be made, without the intervention of an exchange, between

the captain, officers, stewards, Marconi house, bureau, &c. (3.) An exchange line system on the central battery system. The instruments, of which there are in all 89, and the central exchange board, were supplied and erected by the National Telephone Company. These telephones are fitted up in the regal and en suite state rooms, enabling passengers to communicate with each other, and with the bureau, doctor, purser, chief steward; and also by means of a connection, which will be made to the ship when in harbour, with the National Telephone Company's system on shore on this side of the water, and similarly with the American telephone system when the ship is at New York.

The cabin bells are arranged on Gent's second-call system, specially arranged for night work, enabling the watchman stationed at the bureau to tell whether a call has been made on the stewards, and not attended to. The system consists of groups of indicator boards, with drop-shutter indicators of a special pattern arranged so that if a second call is made a circuit is closed, lighting up a lamp on a tell-tale board, and at the same time ringing a buzzer. The night watchman, on hearing this buzzer, can tell at once from the lamp lighted which of the local indicators has had a call; and on proceeding to this indicator, he can locate the particular state room from which the call has been made.

Among the other numerous applications of electricity for the comfort of the passenger and the safety of the ship, mention may be made of a system of fire alarms, both of the automatic and "break the glass and press" type, with indicators on the bridge and engine-room, signal lamp indicators for the mast-head and bow lamps, submarine signalling apparatus, and electrically-operated steam-whistles. There are 49 electric clocks on the Magneta Company's system. They require no batteries to operate them, and no movable contacts in the master-clock or dials; all are controlled from a master-clock in the chart-room. This master-clock has a setting back or forward arrangement, enabling the officer on the bridge to correct the clocks simultaneously from the chart-room. As this has to be done twice a day, there is a great saving of time over clocks of the usual pattern, which require to be set locally.

The whole of the electric installation has been carried out by the electrical department at Clydebank, and some idea of the amount of work involved may be gathered from the fact that over 150 miles of cable have been fitted into the ship.

THE TRIALS OF THE SHIP.

THE Lusitania, in her official speed and manœuvring trials, carried out under the direction of the technical staff of the Cunard Company and of the Admiralty representatives, met the most sanguine anticipations of all concerned. At a draught of 33 ft., she steamed over 26 knots on the measured mile; on a 48 hours' sea run on long measured distances, at a mean draught of 32 ft. 9 in., she maintained a mean speed of 25.4 knots; and on two runs over a 59 mile course, at a mean draught of 31 ft. 7 in., the speed averaged 26.45 knots. The contract anticipated a speed of 24½ knots on the round voyage on the Atlantic, and this will be easily achieved.

Justification for this view is found in the fact that the long-distance trials represented exactly the conditions of the Atlantic voyage. The unprecedented length of the trial precluded "jockeying." The course of about 303 miles was traversed four times in alternate directions, so as to eliminate the influence of tide and weather. And thus any speed maintained on such a trial may be continued indefinitely, so long as coal and other supplies are available. It is unnecessary to say that the machinery worked satisfactorily. The general result stated carries conviction from this point of view. Before entering upon this, the most crucial test, at midnight on Monday July 29, the Lusitania had

speed, it brought consolation in the fact that it prevented fog. The feature of the trial was the uniformity of the speed on both runs south and on the two runs north, the latter being against the wind and tide. The course, as a glance at the chart would show, was divided into three approximately equal parts by the Codling and Tuskar lights. Compass-bearings taken at these intermediate points proved the uniform rate of steaming. The time taken on the runs south, on Tuesday, and on Wednesday, differed by only two minutes; further proof is unnecessary of the great regularity of steam-supply or of turbine efficiency. The speed on four runs was:

South, from Corsewall	...	26.4 knots
North, from Longship	...	24.3 knots
South, from Corsewall	...	26.3 knots
North, from Longship	...	24.6 knots
Mean speed...	... ...	25.4 knots

We omit second placed decimals, but, in any case, the percentage of error in observation is, with such distance, negligible.

This is a great performance: it exceeds by two nautical miles per hour any similarly long run yet made. The truest significance lies in the uninterrupted mechanical precision with which every unit of the machinery worked. The air pressure in the ashpits of the boilers did not

obtained. Several runs were made to determine the speed for given revolutions or power at various draughts; but unless most complete data were published, general results might be misleading. The main point is that the contract speed has been far exceeded, and that when the vessel enters on the Atlantic service on September 7, she is certain to meet every expectation formed by the owners and builders, and, one might also say, by the general public.

The steering qualities of the vessel have also been tested. When steaming at 15 knots the rudder was put from amidships to hard over, both to port and starboard, in 15 seconds, and the full circle was completed in 8 minutes. Immediately before commencing to turn, the engines were running at the rate of revolution which gave 15 knots. A careful record of revolutions was made on a time basis during the evolution, and it was found at the completion of the circle that the rate of revolution was then 70 per cent. of the rate at 15 knots. The final speed was thus assumed as 10.5 knots, the average speed 13 knots; and the diameter of the circle about 1100 yards; this for a ship of this great length is a most satisfactory performance. The ship, at 22 knots, made the complete circle in 7½ minutes, with 15 deg. of helm. In ordinary steering the vessel answered her helm very rapidly, according to

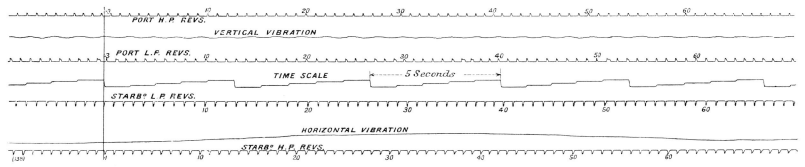

FIG. 209. PALLOGRAM TAKEN ON THE TRIAL AT 22.5 KNOTS, SHOWING VERTICAL AND HORIZONTAL VIBRATIONS.

made several preliminary trials on the Clyde measured mile, not only to tune up the turbine machinery so fully described in the preceding pages, but to standardise the relation between revolutions, power, and speed, so that a series of trials could be made to determine the coal consumption at various speeds. These economy tests began on Saturday, July 27, when, with a large company of guests of the Cunard Company and of Messrs. John Brown and Co., Limited, the owners and builders respectively, the Lusitania left the Clyde for a cruise around Ireland. The vessel was loaded to a draught of 32 ft. 9 in., equal to a displacement of 37,000 tons, and on the cruise the water and coal consumptions were taken while the vessel ran for six hours at speeds of 15, 18, and 21 knots respectively. The results were thoroughly satisfactory, but the data obtained were in connection with service requirements rather than scientific purposes; the results on the Atlantic will be more valuable.

The guests were transferred to the tender at the Mersey Bar on Monday, July 29, and the more exacting tests were entered upon, water and coal consumption data at 23 and 25 knots being taken on the run to the Firth of Clyde, the starting-point of the full sea-speed trials. The course measured out on the chart for the latter was between the Corsewall Light on the Wigtown Coast and the Longship Light at Lands End, and this had to be traversed four times, alternately south and north. The compass bearings gave the distance, which aggregated about 1200 miles. The trial began at midnight on Monday, July 29, and ended about 1 A.M. on Thursday August 1. The weather was favourable, with cloudless days and starlight nights; but on both nights north-west winds freshened to forces of between six and eight, and although this occurred when the vessel was steaming north, and somewhat increased resistance and slightly reduced

at any time reach the maximum of ¾ in. prescribed in the specification by the Cunard Company. The boiler pressure averaged 186 lb. per square inch, while the pressure at the receiver of the high-pressure turbines varied little from 150 lb.; at the low-pressure receiver it was 3½ lb. The mean vacuum was 28.2 in., with an average barometric reading of 29.8 in. The mean revolutions of the four shafts were 188 per minute, and the power, according to the torsionmeter, was 64,600 horse-power. To those not versed in the details of steam-turbine performances, the fact is illuminative that the circumferential or tip velocity of the rotors of the low-pressure turbines was 150 ft. per second, equal to over 9000 ft. per minute. The general procedure in the machinery department accorded with Atlantic practice, and Tuesday's and Wednesday's performance might to all intents and purposes have been two days running, each equal to over 600 miles, on a voyage to New York. This will certainly be the condition a month or six weeks hence.

On returning to the Clyde on Thursday, August 1, the vessel proceeded on two runs between the Corsewall Light and Chicken Rock, the latter the southern extremity of the Isle of Man. The distance is 59 odd miles, and the vessel on the southern run averaged 26.7 knots, and on the northern run 26.2 knots, giving a mean speed of 26.45 knots. This, it must be admitted, is a particularly fine performance, surpassing even the best record made on the measured-mile trials. Following upon this trial further speed tests were made. There were six runs, alternately north and south, between the Holy Isle, on the east coast of Arran, and Ailsa Craig Light; and here again most satisfactory results were achieved. It is not, however, necessary to enter into details regarding these, because they simply bear out the results previously

the testimony of the pilot, and her swing was easily checked.

Although the weather was very fine, alike on the 36 hours' run around Ireland and on the 48 hours' trial on the deep-sea course, there was sufficient swell on the Atlantic in the first-named trip, and between the Tuskar and the Longship Lights on the measured distance runs, to cause pitching and rolling motions to be perceptible, and to afford opportunity for repeated records. In respect to these points a large number of observations gave the period of a single roll from side to side as almost exactly 10 seconds; a single pitch occupied 4 seconds. This latter result calls for no remark, and the slow rolling indicates that, while the vessel has a satisfactory measure of stability, the long period of roll gives assurance that there will be the minimum of discomfort to passengers through this cause.

As to vibration, it has for years been the custom of the Clydebank staff to make observations with Mr. Otto Schlick's pallograph, already described in ENGINEERING (see vol. lv., page 457), and the instrument has been used on every trial of the Lusitania. Mr. Schlick, it will be remembered, enunciated, in a paper read some years ago at the Institution of Naval Architects,[*] a formula for determining approximately for various types of ships the first period of vibration — the slowest period of vibration of which the structure as a whole is capable. The correctness of this formula was borne out by the observations made on the Lusitania. The amplitude of vibration, although very small, was quite dis-

* Mr. Otto Schlick's contributions on the subject of vibrations and the design and application of the Pallograph will be found in ENGINEERING, vol. xxxvii., page 307; vol. lv., pages 375, 457; vol. lvii., pages 401, 406; vol. lix., pages 499, 524.

tinctly marked, and at a draught of 32 ft. 9 in. and a displacement of about 37,000 tons, a first period vibration of a frequency of 62 per minute was clearly recognised on the pallograph records. By referring to the moment of inertia of the transverse section, as given in the paper read at the spring meeting of the Institution of Naval Architects by Mr. W. J. Luke,* and to Mr. Schlick's paper in 1895, and given in ENGINEERING, vol. lix., page 524, it will be seen that this period is thoroughly confirmative of the Schlick formula.

We give on page 54 (Fig. 209) one of many pallograms taken by Schlick's instrument for recording the horizontal and vertical vibrations. This pallogram may be accepted as illustrative of vibrations near the stern in a calm sea, when the turbines were running at about 165 revolutions per minute, which corresponds to a speed of 22.5 knots. The first-period vertical vibration can be quite clearly recognised on the diagram as of a frequency a little faster than 62 per minute. Its amplitude is quite insignificant (as will be seen if the diagram is compared with the similar diagram which we published for the Caronia in our issue of February 10, 1905),† and for the Carmania in our issue of December 1, 1905.‡ In fact, it does no more than serve to identify the *period* of vibration and to confirm Schlick's formula. With a small variation in speed this type of oscillation is quite unobserved; and taken as it was at the after end of the ship, its amplitude is in all probability near to the maximum amplitude for this period of vibration in the vessel. This residual vibration, as it may be called, is due to the action of the propellers; and though it may be possible to modify it in some measure by variation in propeller dimensions and attributes, it seems scarcely possible that it can be entirely eliminated.

It is important to note further from the diagram that there was almost a complete absence of horizontal vibration. The curve indicates the great length of roll of the ship; in the diagram it is seen to be about 18 seconds.

Enough has been written regarding the performance of the ship on trial to show the care and the highly commendable completeness with which the builders and owners have tackled the problems of efficiency, speed, and comfort in trans-Atlantic travel; and all our readers, British and foreign, will associate themselves with our congratulations to the Cunard Company and Messrs. John Brown and Co., Limited, on the splendid success which has rewarded three years of patient and painstaking scientific work.

* See ENGINEERING, vol. lxxxiii., pages 409, 433.

† See ENGINEERING, vol. lxxix., page 189.

‡ See ENGINEERING, vol. lxxx., page 725.

THE BUILDERS OF THE SHIP.

THE story of the evolution of the design and of the construction of the ship and the results of the trials carry conviction as to the experience of Messrs. John Brown and Co., Limited, and their staff, and as to the efficient equipment of their works. Our record of this great achievement in marine construction might, however, be considered incomplete without some review of the works where the Lusitania, with its immense castings, forgings, machinery, and constructional units have been manufactured with so close an approximation to perfection.

Founded between fifty and sixty years ago, John Brown and Co., by enterprising development and judicious combination, have now evolved an organisation so comprehensive that they can produce, complete for service, every type of warship and merchant vessel, with all accessories. The Atlas Steel Works at Sheffield, which date from 1854, produce the iron, steel, armour and the many castings and forgings necessary for all vessels. The Clydebank Shipyard, constructed in 1873, and acquired by the company in 1899, has built a long succession of warships of varied design for many navies, and some of the finest examples of high-speed passenger steamers in successive epochs in the history of naval architecture. The Norfolk Works, at Sheffield, of Messrs. Thomas Firth and Sons, Limited, became practically, although not nominally, allied with John Brown and Co., Limited, in 1903; and as they have made castings for turbine machinery a special study, and have long been noted for their projectile and ordnance forgings, they contribute in an important degree to the general efficiency of the company. Still later the company acquired a large interest in the Coventry Ordnance Works, Limited, in association with Messrs. Cammell, Laird, and Co., Limited, and the Fairfield Shipbuilding and Engineering Company, Limited; and are thus in a position not only to build the hull with its armour, and to construct all the machinery, but to supply the armament and projectiles, of all types of warships. This year the company became allied to Messrs. Harland and Wolff, Limited, of Belfast, by an exchange of shares; and although the two shipbuilding works will continue to be separately managed, the interchange of experience must be a great advantage, and must influence progress in steam construction, apart altogether from financial benefits, with which we are not here concerned.

THE ATLAS WORKS.

In dealing with the establishments of the company and their work, we may take, first, the Atlas Works, Sheffield. The greater part of the 36 acres within the boundaries of these works are covered with buildings. There are in the works forty-three furnaces for producing the iron and other metals used in the various processes of manufacture, which necessitate the use of 400 tons of coal and 100 tons of coke each day of the year. There are ten hydraulic presses, including one of 10,000 tons power, and thirty-three steam-hammers, some of them 80 tons in weight, to work the hot ingots down to the approximate form of the finished product. For manipulating heavy weights there are ninety-four travelling-cranes, two of them having a capacity of 150 tons, one of 100 tons, and most of the others 50 to 60 tons; in addition there are fourteen locomotives in the works, for conveying the products from one shop to another on the many miles of railway running like a network through the establishment. There are 307 machine-tools, many of them of great power, for planing, turning, boring, and otherwise shaping the forgings and castings to finished dimensions. These tools are driven by prime movers developing an aggregate of 12,000 horse-power, which is transmitted to the tools largely through the medium of electricity.

Although the area occupied by the Atlas Works at Sheffield has increased twelvefold since the works were first commenced, the actual turnover of the company has multiplied one-hundredfold—from 30,000*l.* to 3,000,000*l.* sterling per annum. This fact in itself affords a clear evidence of the beneficial influence of modern mechanical methods. The output fifty years ago probably did not exceed 5000 tons per annum, whereas to-day it is close upon 100,000 tons. The 20,000 workers employed in all the works of the company earn in wages about 1,250,000*l.* per annum.

THE MANUFACTURE OF ARMOUR.

Messrs. John Brown and Co., Limited, were among the first firms to manufacture steel; first by puddling, next by the Bessemer process, and finally by the Siemens-Martin furnace. Bessemer found in the firm his first practical collaborators, and this greatly helped to overcome the prejudice then existent against his process. The firm, too, were among the first to manufacture steel for shipbuilding; but a greater step forward, and one of national importance, was the commencement of the manufacture of armour-plates. This was in 1859, when the first armoured ships of the British Navy—the Warrior and Black Prince—were laid down. Instead of adopting the practice of hammering the metal in the plate form, as had been usual for many years for all armour, Messrs. John Brown and Co. put down a mill and rolled the plates, first by the welding of a succession of bars together, and, later, by the use of large ingots. The wrought iron armour was adopted for all ships for several years, the thickness increasing from the 4½-in. plates of the Warrior to the 14-in. plates of the Dreadnought of 1875; although the Inflexible, in 1881, had a double plating, making 24 in. in all.

About the year 1877 guns had so increased in power that it was considered impossible to produce a wrought-iron plate, which, while of reasonable thickness, could withstand the attack from the later 80-ton guns, and the compound plate then came to the front. This was a plate with a steel face and a wrought-iron back (the former representing about one-third of the total thickness), which, under the patent of the late Mr. John Devonshire Ellis, for so long the chairman and managing director of Messrs. John Brown and Co., were united by a process designed to ensure not only a perfect weld, but a comparatively hard face—an important feature entirely lacking in the wrought-iron armour. This face offered so much initial resistance that the projectiles of the time were broken up, or if they struck at an angle, they glanced off. The all-steel plates, introduced about the same time, offered, perhaps, equal resistance to attack, but lacked toughness, which in the case of the compound plate was supplied by the iron back. As the steel plates were thus more liable to break up, compound plates continued in use where thick armour was required.

As far back as 1871, the idea had occurred to the late Mr. J. D. Ellis of applying to iron armour the principle of cementation; and a patent having been applied for, a plate so treated was subjected to firing test. The result, however, was not encouraging, owing to the omission of chilling treatment, which at that time was thought impracticable in the case of such large masses as armour-plates. The patent was, therefore, allowed to lapse, and nothing further was done for the perfection of cemented armour at that time. In 1901, however, Captain Tresidder, a director of Messrs. John Brown and Co., devised a method of chilling armour-plates, for which various British and foreign patents were taken, in the specifications of which mention was made of the suitability of the process for giving dead hardness to the face of any plate where high carbon was present, whether the face was separately made, as by the Ellis compound process, or super-carburised by cementation, as tried by Mr. Ellis on the occasion above referred to.

In connection with this important development in the process of hardening armour, we have further instances of the many cases wherein scientists in different parts of the world work simultaneously, without knowledge of each other's research, towards the same end with similar issue. Harvey, an American engineer, had been experimenting contemporaneously with Captain Tresidder to produce a cemented and chilled plate, and there was one day between the respective applications for patents—the one in America, and the other in England. The Sheffield inventor's date was the earlier; but ultimately, after much negotiation and consulting of lawyers, forces were joined for commercial reasons. This combination of the cementation and chilling processes marked a great advance: a 7-in. plate so treated being a match for a 6-in. shot of 100 lb. striking with a velocity of 1950 foot-seconds; whereas formerly it required a thickness of 10½ in. of all-steel or compound armour to meet this attack.

There was a general feeling, soon after this plate was adopted, that some degree of finality had been reached; but Messrs. Krupp, of Essen, sprang a surprise upon all by perfecting a process whereby an all-steel plate made of excessively high-grade material could, by an elaborate course of treatment, be endowed with not only a face as hard as glass, but also a back as tough as, and much stronger than, wrought iron. The Krupp plate is the plate of to-day; and some idea of its immense resisting power will be formed when it is stated that it is a match for a blow which would conquer a wrought-iron plate of from two and a-half to three times its thickness. As a matter of fact, plates made by the Krupp process for the broadside of ships seldom now exceed 9 in. in. thickness, but for barbettes the usual thickness in first-class ships is 12 in.

The Krupp process was taken up by Messrs. John Brown and Co., and we may indicate briefly its salient features. The material used in the latest plates is a multiple alloy of iron and other metals, and is excessively delicate: so much so, that a large ingot cast from it, if laid down to cool, would almost inevitably fly to pieces. Messrs. John Brown and Co. have their steel furnaces, therefore, close to the hydraulic press. After the steel has been tapped into the ladles, these are

properly conducted, renders it extremely tough. This continuity of treatment and care to avoid cooling is not dictated by economical considerations, but is rendered necessary by the sensitive nature of the material. After the heat treatment, the plate is planed and machined to approximate dimensions, and then is passed to one of the sixteen cementation furnaces in the works, where the face becomes chemically harder by absorption of carbon from charcoal, with which its face is kept in contact during a long exposure to high temperature. The plate is further submitted to several heat processes. It is then set, under a 6000-ton bending press, to the approximate form which it will have when fitted on to the ship. Lastly, it undergoes a final

of the thickness of the wrought iron that would have been perforated by the attack to that of the actual thickness of the plates fired at. Thus the 6-in. Krupp plate would have perforated a wrought-iron plate 17 in. thick, or $2\frac{3}{4}$ times its own thickness. Therefore, its figure of merit is 2.75.

Quality of Plate.	Figure of Merit (being Relative Thickness of Wrought Iron to give Equal Resistance).
Wrought iron	1
Compound of plain steel	1.20 to 1.25
Harvey	1.9 ,, 2.2
Krupp	2.3 ,, 2.8

| 1859-64. Wrought Iron attacked by Round Shot. | 1864-79. Wrought Iron attacked by Pointed Cast-Iron Shot. | 1879-92. Steel attacked by Forged Steel Shot. | 1879-93. Ellis Compound Plate attacked by Forged Steel Shot. | 1890. Nickel Steel attacked by Pointed Cast-Iron Shot. | 1891. Ellis-Tresidder Compound Face-Hardened Plate attacked by Forged Steel Shot |

| 1893-97. Harvey Plate. | 1897. Krupp Plate. | 1897. Krupp 12-in. Plate. | 1897. Krupp 12-in. Plate. |

FIG. 210. ARMOUR PLATES OF SUCCESSIVE EPOCHS ILLUSTRATING INCREASE IN RESISTANCE TO PENETRATION.

hauled along on rails, and raised by an hydraulic lift to higher-level rails, which run over the casting-pit. Here the steel is teemed into a trough, and thence direct into the huge ingot-moulds. As its melting-point is so high, it solidifies upon losing quite a small proportion of its heat, so that it can be taken almost at once to the reheating furnace, preparatory to the treatment under the 10,000-ton press. There it is slabbed down to approximate thickness for rolling in the large mill, special steps being taken to remove a peculiarly adhesive scale that forms upon it. During these several operations the plate frequently requires re-heating, and furnaces for the purpose are provided in convenient positions. The plate is not allowed to cool after being rolled, but is at once passed to the re-heating furnace, and when brought to the required temperature undergoes the first stage of special heat treatment peculiar to the Krupp process, which, if

heat process, followed by chilling, whereby it acquires an intense face hardness. Any alteration or machining subsequent to this last treatment has to be done with powerful electric grinding-machines, as no cutting tools can make any impression upon the face. The holes in the back for the bolts, which attach the plates to the ship, are afterwards bored and tapped, and the plate is then finished and ready for the firing test, or for despatch to the Clydebank or other naval yard.

On the present page there are a series of views showing the progress of armour construction, and on the opposite page a view of a barbette for a British warship. The engravings above show the results of attack on plates of successive periods. The appended Table shows the figures of merit for the various types of armour, as constructed by the company in the successive stages of the evolution of armour. This shows the relation

HEAVY FORGING WORK : SHAFTING.

As typical of forging work, reference may be made to the shafting made at the Atlas Works. Hydraulic presses have for many years been used at the Atlas Works, to the exclusion of hammers, even for light work, as the gradual squeezing action of the hydraulic press is for all purposes more effectual and less severe on the metal than the sudden blows of a hammer. One of the largest shafts made for a land engine was completed by the company in 1901. It was a crankshaft of over 80 tons weight for the engine of an electric-traction station. A general indication is afforded of the size of the shafts completed in this department by the illustrations on Plate XXIX., Figs. 213 and 214. These two views show shafts in the process of being turned by heavy lathes. Both shafts were made for electric machinery—one being an ordinary crankshaft with a straight length for carrying the generator. The diameter in this case is 24 in., and the total weight of the shaft, as shown in the engraving, is 22 tons. In the other illustration the cranks are of the disc type, and the lathe is shown simultaneously boring the holes for the pins of two discs. The total weight of this shaft is 82 tons.

Messrs. John Brown and Co. have several exceptionally powerful presses, ranging from 10,000 tons downwards, and one of these is illustrated on Plate XXIX, with its 100-ton overhead cranes. The press illustrated is very rapid in its work, upwards of 25 strokes per minute being easily attainable. The hydraulic pressure is supplied by a three-cylinder high-pressure pumping-engine in close proximity to the press, and working direct without an accumulator. An air vessel is fitted to maintain a constant pressure and supply of water to the suction valves; and thus there is the minimum of noise and vibration, when the engines are running under full pressure at the high rate of 100 revolu-

by the company with very satisfactory mechanical results.

The machine-shop associated with this forging department consists of three bays, two of them 160 ft. long and 35 ft. and 31 ft. wide respectively, while the third is 194 ft. long and 52 ft. wide; the height of 34 ft. enabling the 70-ton travelling-crane to conveniently manipulate the immense jobs undertaken without interfering with the work done on the floor. One of the bays of this shop is illustrated on Fig. 217, Plate XXXI.; and this view, together with the engravings on Plate XXX., show that the shops are well equipped with the heaviest class of machine-tools, nearly all the well-known makers being represented in the department. There are about 15 lathes, varying from a length of 80 ft. by 48 in. centres to a length of 50 ft. by 66 in. centres, and all are triple- or quadruple-geared.

Amongst the interesting tools in this department is the crank "pinning" machine. When the Admiralty and some foreign Governments com-

BOILER AND FURNACE WORK.

The firm have taken an equally successful part in connection with boiler shells, flues, and tubes. A special press for flanging boiler-ends was laid down in 1879; and as soon as the Siemens open-hearth process for making steel was introduced, furnaces were put down, and, in addition to the rolling of plates, the casting of propellers, propeller-bosses, and the like was undertaken. The triple-compounding of steam-engines encouraged the use of higher boiler pressures, so that a demand sprang up for heavier shell-plates, as well as for a form of furnace that would offer a greater resistance to collapse than the smooth cylindrical type hitherto used. This led to the production at the Atlas Works, in 1885, of the patent ribbed flue, which proved very advantageous to the marine engineer. The latest form of these furnaces was adopted in the Lusitania, as illustrated on page 30. The plant for the manufacture of these flues includes many specially-designed appliances, the whole aim being to

Fig. 211. The Barbette Armour of a Modern Battleship.

tions per minute. The periods during which the maximum power is applied to the press are very frequent, owing to the rapidity of its operation, but they are of very short duration. The load on the engines is thus a severely varying one, alike as to degree and frequency; but the governing arrangements are so effective that the influence on the speed of the pumping-engine is reduced to the minimum.

The press is fitted with special hydraulic pushers for working hollow forgings, such as gun-tubes, cylinder-liners, &c., as with such jobs specially good results are obtained by a rapid stroke. The work of forming such hollow forgings possesses some special features. The ingot-head is cut off in the lathe, and a hole is made through the centre in a horizontal machine by a D-bit. The ingot is then reheated in a furnace at the forge, and afterwards conveyed to the press anvil on the mandril on which it is ultimately to be forged. The forging-press draws the ingot down on the mandril, the job being supported meanwhile from the hydraulic crane. Portions from 5 ft. to 8 ft. in length are thus forged at each heat, and hollow forgings varying in length up to 50 ft. have been produced

menced using double-throw crankshafts in large engines, so as to bring the balancing forces of the reciprocating parts as near to each other as possible, with a view of reducing vibration, it was found impossible, in turning the crank-pins in an ordinary lathe, to overcome a certain amount of spring which made it difficult to maintain true centres. A large crank-pinning machine was therefore erected at the Atlas Works at great expense. In this machine the crank, instead of rotating as in the ordinary lathe, lies in a rigid position while the cutting-tool rotates; and thus the pin can be made absolutely round and perfectly true with the axis of the crank in every direction This splendid tool consists of longitudinal and cross-girders supporting a large frame free to be moved along the girders, and fitted with an internal wheel carrying the tool-boxes. These boxes can be advanced to, or retired from, the crank-pin centre, and at the same time are narrow, so as to be able to work between the crank-webs. The crank rests upon, and is bolted securely to, the girders of the machine; while the wheel revolves and the tools operate on the pin and the ends and sides of the web without necessitating any re-setting of the job.

minimise stress upon the metal and ensure absolute reliability (see Plate XXXI.). The ingots are usually cast in such sizes as to enable two flues to be rolled from each; they are slabbed down in the roughing-mill, and the finishing-rolls form the ribs. Two flue-plates are first placed back to back under a slotting-machine, and shaped at the ends to be flanged; this work is done in pairs, so that the plates will form right and left-handed furnaces respectively.

The plates are then bent in an hydraulic press—one of the special appliances of the firm. This machine consists of a table carrying adjustable ribs, on which the part of the plate to be bent rests, while under it are the three cylinders used in the bending operation. A "fuller," or heavy bar, is rigidly fixed to the framework of the machine, but is removable for the withdrawal of the flue when curved. The flat flue plate is placed between the fuller above and the supporting ribs below, and the latter, rising by the application of the hydraulic power, bend the plate in successive widths to a curve, the radius of which is regulated by the distance apart of the supporting ribs and the duration of the pressing action. As soon as the curvature conforms to the template prepared, the pressure is removed, the plate advanced to bring a new portion under the fuller, and the bending operation completed.

Thus formed to circular shape, the flue is taken to the welding machine. The welding machine is a cleverly designed tool, and is illustrated by one of the engravings (Fig. 220) on Plate XXXI. The anvil is carried on one large bracket, the steam hammer over it on another; and arrangements are provided to enable any length or diameter of flue to be supported immediately on the anvil, the position of which is fixed. Thus, for lateral movement, the platform on which the flue is carried can be traversed by means of gear on the rails placed under the floor level. For vertical movement to suit different diameters of flue, the platform, with rails, &c., can be raised or lowered, and for rotary movement side-bearing wheels are fitted to the movable platform. Both of the arms carry gas furnaces and blowers, coal-gas being preferred because it is considered "easier" on the material. The gas used in this welding-machine is perfectly mixed within the blower, and not at the point of contact as is the usual practice—a difference in method which tends to a more uniform temperature at the point of welding. The hammer is operated by steam, and the work is very quickly and effectually carried out, the flue with its carriage being traversed along immediately under the gas fires and hammer.

The flue is next taken to the rounding-machine, also operated by hydraulic power. This tool has a central column, against which the flue is pressed by suitable shaping blocks conforming to the various flue sections. The outside block is given a reciprocating motion by hydraulic cylinders, and the pressing of the flue in this way against the inner column takes out any of the irregularities due to welding, &c. The heat at which this shaping operation takes place is between 1100 deg and 1200 deg. Fahr. The flanges for securing the flue to the shell-plate and combustion chamber are next formed in hydraulic presses. The flue is then trimmed to the exact dimensions by cold band-saws, with spirally-designed tables which can be moved in any direction, radially, vertically, or horizontally. Slotting machines of special design are used to trim edges which it is not possible to reach with saws. The flue is pickled at a suitable stage in the proceedings, usually before flanging and dressing; and after this operation it is finally annealed in an upright furnace with a movable truck floor. The furnace is air-cooled, so that there is no chance of alteration in form. Thus completed, the flue is passed to the boiler-maker.

ENGINEERING DEPARTMENT.

There are several large machine-shops in the Atlas Works, as a rule, 600 ft. long and 60 ft. wide, with cranes ranging up to 60 tons. Two typical bays are illustrated on Plate XXX., and another by Fig. 217 on Plate XXXI. Electricity is used for driving all the tools, cranes, &c. The planers, mostly of the screw type, are of great size, some taking jobs 15 ft. wide and 10 ft. high. The lathes, all triple or quadruple-geared, vary in length from 80 ft. down to 50 ft., and in the diameter of headstock from 66 in. to 48 in. centres. Some of the tools recently introduced have exceptionally wide pulleys for high belt-speeds, in order to obtain the necessary power for utilising to the utmost the special tool-steel made and used by the company for heavy cutting at high speed. The boring-machines are of massive proportions; a 15-in. hole can be bored out of the solid to form a gun tube at a speed of 1 in. per hour. The boring of shafts with holes of 8 in. to 10 in. in diameter is done at the rate of from 3 in. to 5 in. per hour. The other tools of the department include several large slotting-machines, one of them having a stroke of 8 ft., and the necessary drilling and boring-machines. Special loading arrangements are provided for the despatch of productions.

The productions of the works are varied, as the following list shows :—

Armour-plates by the Krupp, Harvey, and other processes.
Marine and other engine crank-shafts.
Shaftings of all kinds.
Turbine drums of the largest dimensions.
Gun and other forgings.
Patent ribbed boiler flues.
Ellis and Eaves induced-draught apparatus.
Robert patent and crucible steel castings of all descriptions for engineering and colliery purposes.
Siemens crucible and all kinds of tool-steel.
Atlas self-hard steel for high-speed cutting.
Rolled and forged bars, angles, iron and steel T-rings, &c.
Railway tyres, axles, springs, buffers, &c.
Patent wrought-steel wheels.
Foundry and forged pig iron.

There are extensive laboratories, where all material as it arrives in a raw state, or as it leaves in a complete form, is subject to examination, samples being taken at various stages for chemical analysis and mechanical tests. The chemical laboratory, fitted with the usual appliances, has a staff of fourteen chemists, and a great many of the analyses are by combustion. In the case of many of the productions tests are made at frequent stages; in armour manufacture, for instance, there are three or four chemical analyses and five or six mechanical tests. The measure of chemical hardness of armour is determined from drillings taken from the plate, analysed in layers of $\frac{1}{8}$ in. by the combustion method.

The mechanical testing department has a 50-ton horizontal hydraulic testing-machine of the Buckton type, as well as an old-fashioned dead-weight testing apparatus, still useful and accurate, although slow. There are two lathes, four planing-machines, able to deal with pieces 3 ft. square by 3 ft. 6 in. high; a rotary-machine for milling, and other appliances, along with a press of 600-lb. pressure for cold bending. All these machines are practically kept working day and night, the aim being that nothing shall be sent from the works except it be thoroughly reliable. For railway work there is the usual drop-test apparatus.

Finally, it may be stated that the works can produce in a year :—

	Tons.
Armour plate	10,000
Forgings	5,000
Flues	2,000
Castings	2,500
Railway Material	20,000
Pig iron	45,000
All other Manufactures	10,000

PROJECTILES.

The Norfolk Works of Messrs. Thomas Firth and Sons, Limited, which adjoin Messrs. Brown's establishment at Sheffield, have a productive capacity of 40,000 tons of steel per annum. The manufactures are, for the most part, similar to those of the Atlas Works, consisting of forgings for ordnance work, shafting, &c., steel of every kind (including crucible steel of the highest quality for tools, high-speed steel, files, saws, edge-tools, &c.), and railway materials, with the important addition of projectiles. Nickel, chrome, and other alloy steels for motor-car construction are specialties.

The machine-tools in use are able to deal with the largest forgings that the engineer may require; but as the processes of manufacture are, more or less, the same as those carried out at the Atlas Works, and described in the preceding pages, we do not propose to deal completely with the plant at the Norfolk Works. We make an exception, however, of projectiles, as they are not manufactured at the Atlas Works. Indeed, it was partly the desire to be able to produce this important item in the completion of a warship for fighting service that induced Messrs. John Brown and Co., Limited, to become associated with Messrs. Firth, who have for many years been prominently and favourably known for their shot and shell. Messrs. Firth's connection with this department of industry dates from the days of the old round shot, which they produced from crucible steel, with the assistance of dies. They have since taken a leading part in all the succeeding stages, culminating in the modern capped armour-piercing shell, with its great penetrating power.

The manufacturing departments of the Norfolk Works utilised for the production of projectiles include the steel-producing plant, the forge and press departments, and extensive machine-shops. For the melting of steel for projectiles and similar purposes—tool-steel, &c.—there are 148 crucible-holes, each accommodating two crucible-pots; the capacity is over 5000 tons per annum. All projectiles were at one time made from crucible steel; but in the more modern systems of manufacture, especially where special alloys are utilised, it has been as convenient and efficient to utilise the Siemens-Martin open-hearth furnace at the works for this as for other purposes. There are four of these in the Norfolk Works, one of them having a capacity of 45 tons, two of 25 tons, and one of 10 tons. Ingots from the steel-melting department are sent to the forge, where they are worked into bars under hammers ranging from 12 to 30 tons in power (see Fig. 221, on Plate XXXII.).

The process of manufacture differs according to the final form which the projectile is to take. When it is intended to make armour-piercing shot, the blanks—as the embryo projectiles are called—are bored and turned, then hardened and tempered, gas checks or copper bands being subsequently fitted on. Blanks to be manufactured into armour-piercing shell are sent to the punching and drawing-shop, where they are dealt with by a series of hydraulic presses, varying from 500 tons to 100 tons in power. The first process consists in the formation of a cup at the base of the pointed blank, to facilitate the subsequent drawing down into a hollow cylindrical form. The press for the latter purpose, illustrated on Plate XXXII., is of the horizontal double headed type, of 300 tons power, having a cylinder 16 in. in diameter and a stroke of 72 in. The shell cylinder is next machined, hardened, examined and tested. An important part of the work is done in the forge, which is fitted with a modern 12-ton hammer, and many other hammers, as illustrated on Plate XXXII.

For the machining of the projectiles to the correct finished form there are five machine-shops, some of them arranged for doing special work upon all sizes of shot, in order to concentrate as far as possible the experience gained. Two of these shops are illustrated on Plate XXXII. In these several machine-shops there are 146 machine-tools, many of them of special type. The tool for forming the ogival, or pointed nose, is a particular pointing lathe; the cutting-tool accommodating itself to the lessening diameter of the nose by means of a radius bar, secured at one end to a fixture on the frame, and at the other end operating a cross-slide, which again actuates the cutting-tool. One of these machines is shown to the right of the engraving, Fig. 224, on Plate XXXII. The groove for the copper band is cut in an ordinary lathe, with ribs in wavy lines, so as to prevent the band from rotating independently of the projectile in its passage through the rifled bore of the gun. This band is pressed into the groove on the projectile on a special hydraulic press of the horizontal type, with a 15-in. cylinder. For this special duty there is mounted on the cross-head of the ram a die representing half the circumference of the ring, while the head of the press carries a similar die corresponding to the other half; the projectile, with its ring, having been placed in position, the hydraulic pressure exerted through the dies, forces the ring at all points of contact into the groove prepared for it.

The projectile after being hardened is finished to its ultimate true diameter by means of grinding-machines, of which there is a large collection, specially devised for the varied work of the company. These machines are fitted with horizontal spindles for holding the projectile in front of the grinder. The spindle is provided with a hand traversing-slide, so that the machinist has complete control over the operation, and can ensure that the grinding is done to suit the gauge. All so-called solid shot have a small hole bored down the centre, and even shell drawn hollow in the press are sometimes turned internally. This work is done in boring-mills of the horizontal type. The shells are steam heated internally prior to the process of lacquering, and the time and percussion-fuse blocks are screwed at the base in the ordinary way.

Messrs. Firth have also made a speciality of the steel castings for turbine machinery; but as in illustrating the units of the Lusitania machinery on page 36 we have referred to their experience, and the general excellence of the results, we need not here write further on the subject.

THE CLYDEBANK SHIPYARD.

Since it was constructed in 1873, this establishment, situated on the Clyde, near Glasgow, has added to the naval and merchant fleets of several nations a long line of vessels of the highest standard and success. Beginning with the smallest class, the sloop of war, advance has been made step by step to the largest battleships and cruisers in the world; with the result that the managers and staff have accumulated an experience which enables them

SHIP-MODEL EXPERIMENTAL TANK AT THE CLYDEBANK WORKS.

FIG. 225. VIEW OF INTERIOR LOOKING SOUTHWARDS FROM NORTH END, WITH DRY AND WET DOCKS.

to undertake naval work with the assurance of absolute success, and at the same time inspires the naval authorities of Britain and foreign countries with confidence in ordering such vessels. The firm also possess an experimental tank in which to conduct ship-model tests according to the system first introduced by Dr. Froude, by which means it is easy to determine the design that will give the greatest propulsive efficiency, and ensure the highest speed for a given weight and power. By the aid of the special plant in use, the work of ship construction can be effected expeditiously, efficiently, and cheaply.

If further evidence than the success of the Lusitania were required to establish the high place of the works among shipbuilding concerns, there is the fact that the firm are now completing the construction of the 25-knot armoured cruiser Inflexible, than which there is no more powerful cruiser

afloat. They have built or engined warships totalling 180,600 tons displacement and 451,830 horse-power. Their enterprise, too, is reflected in the fact that they have completed, or have in hand, turbine machinery totalling 213,000 horse-power—a greater total than can be credited to any firm in the world. Many of the fast Channel steamers have been built at Clydebank, and the record of Atlantic work is almost unique, as our review of the development of the liner on pages 9 to 12 shows. Mention may be made of the Saxonia, Caronia, and Carmania as well as the Lusitania. The Table on this page gives the names of typical warships built during the past few years. In addition, machinery has been constructed for the battleship Africa, the armoured cruiser Essex, and the fast scout-cruiser Boadicea.

In describing the works, it may be more interesting to review the departments and plant in the

TABLE IX.—SOME TYPICAL WARSHIPS BUILT AT CLYDEBANK WORKS.

	Length.	Displacement.	I.H.P.	Speed.	Guns.
	ft.	tons		knots	
Battleships.					
H.I.J.M.S. Asahi ...	400¾	15,200	15,000	18	Four 12-in., fourteen 6-in., twenty 12-pr., eight 3-pr., four 2½-pr.
H.M.S. Hindustan ...	425	16,350	18,521	19	Four 12-in., four 9.2 in., ten 6-in., twenty-eight smal.
H.M.S. Jupiter ...	390	14,900	12,000	17.5	Four 12-in., twelve 6-in., eighteen 12-pr., twelve 3-pr.
Armoured Cruisers.					
H.M.S. Inflexible ...	530	17,250	—	23.28	Two 9.2-in., sixteen 6-in., fourteen 12-pr., three 3-pr.
H.M.S. Leviathan ...	500	14,110	31,203	23.02	Four 7.5-in., six 6-in., two 12-pr., twenty-two 3-pr.
H.M.S. Antrim ...	450	10,850	21,694	21.77	Two 9.2-in., twelve 6-in., fourteen 12-pr., three 3-pr.
H.M.S. Sutlej ...	440	12,000	21,361	21.61	Two 9.2-in., twelve 6-in., fourteen 12-pr., three 3-pr.
H.M.S. Bacchante ...	440	12,000	21,520	21.75	
Protected Cruisers.					
H.M.S. Terrible ...	500	14,200	25,000	22.4	Two 9.2-in., sixteen 6-in., fourteen 12-pr., eight 3-pr., nine maxims, two 12-pr. (landing).
H.M.S. Ariadne ...	435	11,000	18,000	20.75	Sixteen 6-in., fourteen 12-pr., three 3-pr., two maxims.
H.M.S. Europa ...	435	11,000	16,500	20.5	Sixteen 6-in., fourteen 12-pr., four 3-pr., two maxims.
Torpedo-Boat Destroyer.					
H.M.S. Arab ...	218	470	6,000	31	One 12 pr., five 6-pr.

SHIP-MODEL EXPERIMENTAL TANK AT THE CLYDEBANK WORKS.

FIG. 226. MODEL CUTTING MACHINE.

order of their use and importance in the building of the ship, rather than to adopt an itinerary method ; and it may be said at the outset that the works have a frontage to the River Clyde of 3200 ft., and that the building berths have a length varying from 450 ft. to over 800 ft.

THE EXPERIMENTAL TANK.

The department which first influences the efficiency of the work is the experimental tank. Reference is made on page 14 to the part that research work has played in evolving the design of modern steamers ; and in ENGINEERING, vol. lxxxi., page 541, we described in considerable detail the experimental department at Clydebank ; but our record here might be considered incomplete were no particulars given of the tank and its equipment. The waterway extends for 445 ft., of which 400 ft. is deep, varying from 9 ft. at the north end to 10 ft. at the south end. This fall of 1 ft. is gradual, and is for the purpose of drainage when emptying. The breadth is uniformly 20 ft. At the north end there are wet and dry docks ; of the wet docks, one is for storing models, and the other, placed between the dry docks, is used for loading and trimming purposes. The towing-truck can be run over the central dry dock, and the dynamometer and propeller gears examined from it ; the latter must be raised to clear the dock-sill. Ballast bags and some spare parts are stored in both dry docks. At the south end there is a sloping beach, 25 ft. long, to assist in breaking up the waves formed by the passage of a model through the water. A recess, however, is left up the middle, to prevent screws or models being run aground. The basin, which is

rectangular in cross-section, is formed of concrete, with expanded metal and puddled clay backing.

The building is of brick, and besides the tank proper, provides accommodation for a large drawing-office, a tracer's room, and superintendent's office, with the necessary fireproof record-rooms, &c. Adjoining the tank and in communication with it is a complete new department for model-makers. These assist in the work of the tank by making cores for the casting of paraffin wax models, and in fairing down the latter when they come from the shaping machine.

As it is very necessary to keep the temperature of the tank at or about a uniform degree, winter and summer, a complete system of hot-water piping is installed, and the heat is controlled at the calorifiers, of which there are two at the north end and one at the south end of the building, in rooms for the purpose. The offices and shops are heated on the same system with pipes and radiators.

Light is admitted to the tank by windows on both sides, and from the roof, which is in great part of glass ; while a complete system of electric lighting is installed throughout the buildings.

The models used are generally about 15 ft. long, although exception is made in the case of high-speed torpedo-boat destroyers, when the length is about 11 ft. The model of the Lusitania was made to a scale of $\frac{1}{48}$th, being 15.83 ft. in length ; the speed of this model corresponding to 25 knots was 365 ft. per minute, or about $3\frac{3}{4}$ knots ; but models are always run over a range of speeds lower and higher than that proportionate to the trial speed of the ship ; and they are run at these speeds in three or five conditions of displacement, so that

complete information relating to displacement, speed, and resistance is obtained for each model.

Fig. 225, page 59, shows the north end of the tank. The melting-boxes are supported on the wall. Paraffin wax with a small addition of beeswax is melted in the upper box, and strained into the lower or storage one ; from there it is run off through pipes into a mould in the clay, or casting-box, the mould being carefully prepared to the shape required for the model, with a margin allowed, and having a core of lath and canvas to regulate the thickness.

When the casting has sufficiently set, it is levelled on the top and carried to the cutting or shaping-machine (Fig. 226). As part of the cutting-machine there is a wheeled carriage on planed rails, in which the casting is placed, secured at the middle line, keel upwards, while in front there is a table on which a half-breadth plan of the ship is pinned. Two cutters, which, when at work, rotate at about 2500 revolutions per minute, are adjustable about the centre line of the carriage, and in a vertical direction. For details of this ingenious machine, which cuts the model from half-breadth plans, we must refer the reader to the article in our issue of April 27, 1906, already referred to. This also applies to the dynamometer and screw-trucks, illustrated in Fig. 225, page 59.

This is, as yet, the only electrically-driven tank carriage in this country, motive power in the other cases being supplied by a rope driven from a winding engine. Current is supplied from one of the yard power-stations, but as it would be too irregular if applied direct, it is passed through a motor generator into accumulators, from which it is again discharged through the motor generator at a suitable and regular voltage, and delivered to the

150-TON CRANE AT CLYDEBANK WORKS.

CONSTRUCTED BY SIR WILLIAM ARROL AND CO., LIMITED, GLASGOW.

FIG. 227.

tank. The method of measuring the resistance of a model is that used by the late Dr. Froude, of recording graphically the extension of an accurately-made spiral spring. The extension is magnified twelve times, and each spring is standardised in position before use ; but full details will be found in our article, to which we have already referred.

THE HULL CONSTRUCTIONAL PLANT.

The work of hull construction begins in the case of all ships in the moulding-loft, which is 250 ft. long and 55 ft. wide ; the roof is of light steel principals, with corrugated iron on the purlins, and the sides are entirely of glazing. There are frame-bending shops in the western and eastern yards, each with several angle-iron furnaces, 61 ft. long, and a large floor area of cast-iron blocks for setting the frames, as well as screeve boards for laying them out. There are alongside, also under cover, the usual equipment of punches and shears, with a special hydraulic machine for cutting off the ends of channel bars, and a machine for planing both edges of angles at one operation. A specially noteworthy machine is that for setting the flanges of angle-iron frames to the required bevel. The tools in the platers' shed, as a rule, are designed to work plates up to 35 ft. long and 7 ft. wide. There are about thirty punching and shearing machines. Of special interest are two double punching machines, of the cam and lever pattern, with twin punches at each

side. There are two hydraulic manhole punches, capable of working holes of 36 in. by 22 in., while two other machines of a kindred nature for cutting elliptical and circular manholes are worked with automatic feed. Irregularities in the plates, angles, and channel framing of warships, due to splinter gratings in the air-hatches of protective decks and to other causes, have made necessary the use of band saws for cutting such sections, instead of the ordinary hydraulic shears ; and two powerful saws of this type are in constant use at Clydebank, in addition to the ordinary circular saws, of which there are four. There is an immense hydraulic flanging machine for setting plates for the keel and garboard strakes, as well as for stiffening flanges in bulkheads. It is capable of dealing with plates of any length, being open-ended, but the machine itself is 25 ft. long.

WOOD-WORKING DEPARTMENT.

As can readily be imagined, in an establishment which sends out a large number of high-speed passenger steamers and yachts, the wood-working department is very extensive, occupying about 10 acres of ground, two-thirds of which is covered by drying sheds. The timber for the joiners' shop is accommodated in a building measuring about 360 ft. long by 125 ft. broad, and having 112 portable racks and four patent electrically-driven radial cross-cut and ripping saws, for cutting timber to the

exact size required by the joiners. The store for deck planks is a duplicate of the joiner's shed, the timber being delivered automatically from the planing-machines to any part for stacking. There is ample accommodation, entirely under cover, for storing and seasoning all wood required for the decks of twelve Atlantic liners.

The saw-mill is new, and is situated at the extreme west end of the yard. It is controlled in every part by four overhead travelling cranes, which lift the logs direct from the river, and store them or deliver them to the machines as required. The log department is fitted with machinery of a combined cutting capacity of over 500 logs per week. In the re-conversion and re-sawing of the wood the principal machines used are one large deck planer, one lining and flooring machine, one American planer, one moulding machine, one deal frame, one improved Casson's bench, two small saw benches, two large travelling circular benches, one lightning planer, two pendulum cross-cut saws. In the saw-room there are seven automatic saw-sharpening machines for band-saws, one automatic circular saw-sharpener, one automatic blade-grinder, one punching machine, and two hand-sharpening machines. The wood stove is controlled by a patent thermo tank, by which the temperature can be regulated at will. The entire installation is supplied with steam by two Lancashire boilers, automatically fired by Henderson's patent stoker for sawdust and chips. The buildings, machinery arrangements, &c., were designed by the company's staff.

The joiners, cabinet-makers, and polishers are accommodated in a two-storey brick building, 200 ft. long and 150 ft. broad. The collection of wood-working tools is complete, and is representative of the best British and American practice. It includes sand-papering machines, dove-tailing machines, blind-slotting machines, and special tools for cutting spiral or fluted grooves of balusters, sheer-legs, &c., with the usual planing and moulding machines. The shavings, &c., and sawdust are carried off by a pneumatic conveyor direct into the furnaces of the boilers in an adjacent power station.

THE FITTING-OUT BASIN.

It may not be uninteresting to introduce here a reference to the dock or fitting-out basin. It occupies the central part of the water frontage, and extends for 750 ft. from the river, while the width of the dock is 320 ft. from cope to cope. In addition to the 120-ton sheer-legs, which have done service for so many years, and several 20-ton and 10-ton travelling-cranes, the firm have recently erected two cranes of 150-ton capacity—one on each side of their fitting-out basin—so that they may deal with the heaviest loads for two ships simultaneously without moving the ships to and from the crane berth, as is done in other works, at considerable expense in time and money. One of the new cranes is of the derrick type. The foundations are steel cylinders sunk to a great depth ; and these, together with the structural portion of the crane, were built by, and from designs of, Sir William Arrol and Company, Limited. This crane is placed on the east side of the dock, and has been used in the fitting-out of the Cunard liner Lusitania. The other crane is of the hammer or Titan type, and is placed on the west side of the dock. It consists of a square tower, 125 ft. in height, carrying a horizontal jib of a total length of 240 ft. ; the long arm being 150 ft. in length. The jib is supported upon a ring of live rollers, and is capable of making a complete revolution in either direction, with lifting and racking motions. This is the largest crane of its type yet completed, and a view of it is given on the present page ; but for a description of it we must refer our readers to the full particulars and detailed drawings in ENGINEERING, vol. lxxxiii., page 737.

THE ENGINEERING DEPARTMENT : TURBINE-MAKING MACHINERY.

We now turn to the engineering department of the works, which is compactly arranged near to the head of the fitting-out basin. Some idea of the capacity is provided by the fact that for several years the average output has been over 60,000 indicated horse-power per annum, the number of men engaged in this department alone being from

2700 to 3000 ; while in Plates XXXIII. to XXXV. we give views which suggest the great size of the engineering shops and the magnitude of the work undertaken. Space being limited, we are only able to give one or two facts regarding some of the heavier machine tools.

First mention must be made of the lathe for turning large turbine rotors. This tool, illustrated and described in ENGINEERING, vol. lxxix., page 313, is 82 in. in height of centres, 50 ft. long between centres, and 11 ft. 10 in. wide across the double-slide bed. The width across the base of the loose headstock is 8 ft. 9 in., and across that of the fast headstock 9 ft. 1 in., rendering these parts sufficiently rigid to prevent any irregularity of the rotor before turning affecting the perfect roundness of the finished work. The overall length of the lathe is 72 ft. 6 in., and the gross weight 163 tons. There is also a large and very powerful horizontal boring-mill, illustrated on Plate XXXIV., specially designed for boring turbine casings. This tool was illustrated and described in ENGINEERING, vol. lxxviii., page 659. The overall length is 76 ft., and the total weight 95 tons ; but we must refer the interested reader to our detailed description.

Included amongst other heavier tools are two vertical milling machines, the cutters used varying in diameter up to 18 in. ; the cross-feed is 6 ft., and the transverse-feed is 2 ft. 1 in., the movable tables being 4 ft. in diameter. There is a treble-geared miller, capable of milling a surface 10 ft. by 4 ft. 7 in. by 18 in. deep, the table being fitted with a quick-return power motion. Opposite this latter tool is a triple-geared lathe, 20 ft. between centres, with an independent motion by screw ; the headstock is 33 in., and is provided with rack motion for quick hand traverse ; the saddles are arranged so that they will pass alongside the shifting-head, in order that an extra large job may be faced up. The face-plate is 5 ft. 10 in. in diameter, and can swing 48 in. and 54 in. clear of the back and front saddles respectively. There are two other powerful treble-geared lathes, mounted on one bed, so that a 33-ft. length of shafting can be driven by both heads. Close by is a large radial drill, having a spindle 5 in. in diameter, and fitted with a screw and hand gear ; the jib has a 3-ft. vertical travel, the drilling spindle traverses 8 ft., and the vertical feed is 2 ft. 6 in. There are five slotting machines, the larger having a 20-in. stroke, with compound and rotary table, and another with a 16-in. stroke, with a quick-return motion, admit ting articles up to 5 ft. 4 in. in diameter. Adjoining is a large treble-geared face-place lathe, the plate measuring 11 ft. in diameter. There are together a set of three combined planing and slotting machines, with quick-return motions. One can deal with an area of 21 ft. long by 17½ ft. high, and is arranged to take a cut of cast iron 1 in. deep at a speed of about 15 ft. per minute ; a second can slot and plane over a surface of 20 ft. 6 in. long by 14 ft. high ; the third machine can take a job 15 ft. long by 12 ft. high.

At the north end of the bay there are grouped a set of four horizontal universal, boring, drilling, and tapping machines, and two of these can operate over a continuous vertical surface of about 40 ft. by 10½ ft. These powerful machines have bored cylinders of exceptional diameter, tapping and studding their flanges at a single setting. One of the 5-in. spindles of these machines is fitted with an interchanging wheel arrangement for combing or cutting internal screws of large diameter, by means of a chasing tool held in a small slide on the end of a spindle. Opposite these machines are two powerful treble-geared shafting lathes, whose beds are continuous, and with feeds up to 5 in. per minute. They are 21-in. centres, and each is fitted with two strong duplex sliding saddles, each having front and back duplex rests. The front rests are arranged for tapered work.

It is not possible, however, to give anything like a complete idea of the equipment of the engine works, which also include a well-equipped brass foundry, brass-finishing shop, galvanising shop, sheet-iron department, copper smithy, as well as the boiler works, in all of which electricity is adopted, the modern system of driving the dynamo by producer gas-engines being adopted.

The brass foundry, illustrated on Plate XXXIII., is considered one of the largest and finest in the country, having ample plant and every facility for carrying out all classes of work. The equipment includes air furnaces ranging from 16 tons to 5 tons, drying stoves 20 ft. long by 20 ft. wide, heavy overhead travelling cranes, and hydraulic jib cranes, 2½ cwt. air furnaces and 32 crucible furnaces, hydraulic and hand-moulding machines, besides rumblers, and circular and band-saws. In order to render the foundry self-contained, there is a 3-ton cupola for making the required mouldii g boxes and plates, core bars and core irons, and the other cast-iron necessary for the department. Brass castings up to 25 tons have been dealt with. Adjoining the foundry are the requisite stores for metal, sand, and furnace coal, &c. ; and close by is the hydraulic house, in which is a 60 horse-power and 100 horse-power gas-engine, driving separate three-throw pumps, and supplying two accummulators, 15 in. and 21 in. in diameter respectively, with a stroke of 14 ft.

The brass-finishing shop — illustrated on Plate XXXIII.—forms the upper floor of a two-storey building, the ground floor of which is devoted to water-tube boiler work. In this shop are lathes, milling machines, and screwing and grinding machines ; a most interesting feature being a number of small English and American machines of ingenious design, for the machining of duplicate parts. In both of these shops small longitudinal and transverse overhead travellers are arranged, as well as a powerful hydraulic hoist for the transport of material to and from the brass-finishing department.

The main boiler works are divided into four bays, being 410 ft. long, with a total width of 190 ft. In the two largest bays the cylindrical boilers are constructed, and there are several very powerful tools, notably plate-edge planers for dealing with plates 38 ft. long, and a vertical machine for cutting ovals for manholes on cylindrical boilers. In the main bay there is a plate furnace 20 ft. long by 10 ft. wide, with a powerful steam-hammer, the whole set being commanded by an hydraulic crane. There are several powerful flanging machines, multiple boring and drilling machines, vertical cold-plate rolls, taking 12-ft. plates, and many punching, shearing, drilling, and tapping machines, besides several large riveting machines. The third bay is largely utilised for the construction and erection of water-tube boilers.

The electric generating plant for shipbuilding and engineering departments has a total capacity of 3000 kilowatts, and the consumption of current for lighting and power reaches about 50,000 units per week : a fact which suggests the extent of the application.

There are also hydraulic and compressed-air plants.

PLATE I.

TURBINE-DRIVEN QUADRUPLE-SCREW CUNARD LINER "LUSITANIA."

CONSTRUCTED AND ENGINED BY MESSRS. JOHN BROWN AND CO., LIMITED, SHEFFIELD AND CLYDEBANK.

FIG. 14. KEEL-PLATE.

FIG. 15. DOUBLE BOTTOM AFT, LOOKING FORWARD.

PLATE II.

TURBINE-DRIVEN QUADRUPLE-SCREW CUNARD LINER "LUSITANIA."

CONSTRUCTED AND ENGINED BY MESSRS. JOHN BROWN AND CO., LIMITED, SHEFFIELD AND CLYDEBANK.

FIG. 16. DOUBLE-BOTTOM FRAMING, LOOKING FORWARD.

FIG. 17. PLATING OF THE SHIP AT THE STERN.

PLATE III.

TURBINE-DRIVEN QUADRUPLE-SCREW CUNARD LINER "LUSITANIA."

CONSTRUCTED AND ENGINED BY MESSRS. JOHN BROWN AND CO., LIMITED, SHEFFIELD AND CLYDEBANK.

FIG. 18. BOSSED FRAMES FOR WING PROPELLER SHAFTS.

FIG. 19. BOTTOM FRAMING AND HEEL OF SHIP.

PLATE IV.

TURBINE-DRIVEN QUADRUPLE-SCREW CUNARD LINER "LUSITANIA."

CONSTRUCTED AND ENGINED BY MESSRS. JOHN BROWN AND CO., LIMITED, SHEFFIELD AND CLYDEBANK.

FIG. 20. THE AFTER FRAMING, FOR INNER PROPELLERS, AND HEEL OF SHIP.

FIG. 21. THE SPECTACLE FRAMES FOR INNER PROPELLERS.

PLATE V.

TURBINE-DRIVEN QUADRUPLE-SCREW CUNARD LINER "LUSITANIA."

CONSTRUCTED AND ENGINED BY MESSRS. JOHN BROWN AND CO., LIMITED, SHEFFIELD AND CLYDEBANK.

FIG. 22. STERN POST AND BRACKETS.

FIG. 23. SHIP READY FOR LAUNCHING.

PLATE VI.

TURBINE-DRIVEN QUADRUPLE-SCREW CUNARD LINER "LUSITANIA."

CONSTRUCTED AND ENGINED BY MESSRS. JOHN BROWN AND CO., LIMITED, SHEFFIELD AND CLYDEBANK.

FIG. 24. DOUBLE BOTTOM AMIDSHIPS.

FIG. 25. PLATING FORWARD.

PLATE VII.

TURBINE-DRIVEN QUADRUPLE-SCREW CUNARD LINER "LUSITANIA."

CONSTRUCTED AND ENGINED BY MESSRS. JOHN BROWN AND CO., LIMITED, SHEFFIELD AND CLYDEBANK.

FIG. 26. MIDSHIP FRAMES.

FIG. 27. ENGINE SEATING.

PLATE VIII.

TURBINE-DRIVEN QUADRUPLE-SCREW CUNARD LINER "LUSITANIA."

CONSTRUCTED AND ENGINED BY MESSRS. JOHN BROWN AND CO., LIMITED, SHEFFIELD AND CLYDEBANK.

FIG. 28. VIEW 'TWEEN DECKS.

FIG. 29. VIEW ON PROMENADE DECK, LOOKING AFT.

PLATE IX.

TURBINE-DRIVEN QUADRUPLE-SCREW CUNARD LINER "LUSITANIA."

CONSTRUCTED AND ENGINED BY MESSRS. JOHN BROWN AND CO., LIMITED, SHEFFIELD AND CLYDEBANK.

FIG. 38.   VIEW OF SHIP IN DOCK FROM TOP OF 150-TON CRANE, LOOKING FORWARD.

FIG. 39.   VIEW OF SHIP IN DOCK FROM TOP OF 150-TON CRANE, LOOKING AFT.

PLATE X.

TURBINE-DRIVEN QUADRUPLE-SCREW CUNARD LINER "LUSITANIA."

CONSTRUCTED AND ENGINED BY MESSRS. JOHN BROWN AND CO., LIMITED, SHEFFIELD AND CLYDEBANK.

FIG. 40. VIEW OF PROMENADE DECK.

FIG. 41. VIEW OF BRIDGE FROM FORECASTLE.

PLATE XI.

REFRIGERATING MACHINES ON THE CUNARD LINER "LUSITANIA."

CONSTRUCTED BY THE LIVERPOOL REFRIGERATION COMPANY, LIMITED, LIVERPOOL.

FIG. 73.

FIG. 74.

PLATE XII.

THE TURBINE MACHINERY OF THE CUNARD LINER "LUSITANIA."

CONSTRUCTED BY MESSRS. JOHN BROWN AND CO., LIMITED, SHEFFIELD AND CLYDEBANK.

FIG. 114. ROTOR COMPLETED IN THE CLYDEBANK ENGINEERING WORKS.

FIG. 115. ERECTING-SHOP AT THE CLYDEBANK WORKS.

PLATE XIII.

THE TURBINE MACHINERY OF THE CUNARD LINER "LUSITANIA."

CONSTRUCTED BY MESSRS. JOHN BROWN AND CO., LIMITED, SHEFFIELD AND CLYDEBANK.

Fig. 124. View in One of the Shaft-Tunnels.

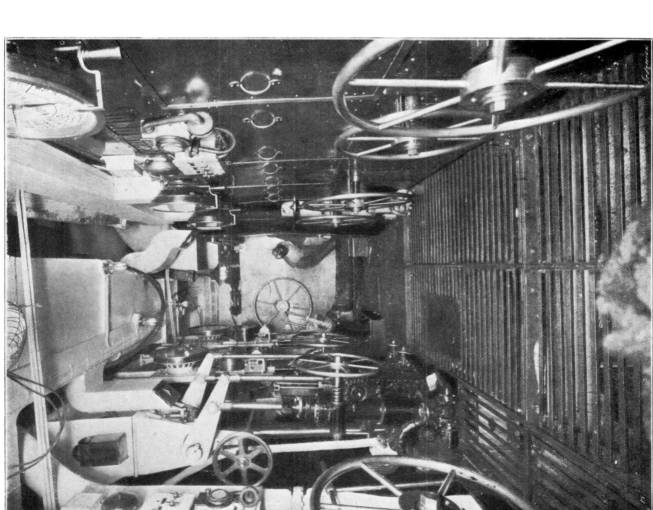

Fig. 123. View of Starting Platform in Engine-Room.

PLATE XIV.

THE TURBINE MACHINERY OF THE CUNARD LINER "LUSITANIA."

CONSTRUCTED BY MESSRS. JOHN BROWN AND CO., LIMITED, SHEFFIELD AND CLYDEBANK.

Fig. 125.   View above Turbines, showing Lifting-Gear.

Fig. 126.   View of Low-Pressure Turbine Casing and Bearing.

PLATE XV.

THE CENTRIFUGAL PUMPS OF THE CUNARD LINER "LUSITANIA."

CONSTRUCTED BY MESSRS. W. H. ALLEN, SON, AND CO., LIMITED, ENGINEERS, BEDFORD.

FIG. 142. GENERAL VIEW OF ONE SET OF CENTRIFUGAL PUMPS.

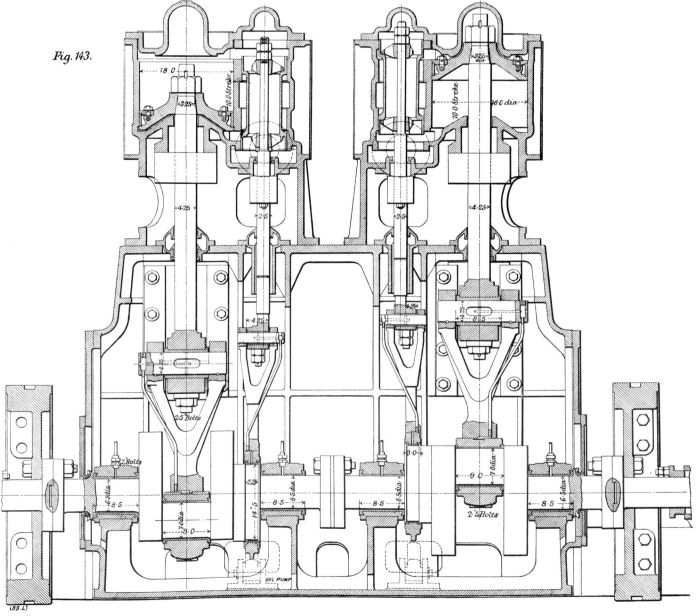

Fig. 143.

FIG. 143. SECTION THROUGH CYLINDERS AND VALVES OF ENGINES DRIVING CENTRIFUGAL PUMPS.

PLATE XVI.

WET AND DRY AIR PUMPS FOR CONDENSERS OF CUNARD LINER "LUSITANIA."

CONSTRUCTED BY MESSRS. G. AND J. WEIR, LIMITED, ENGINEERS, CATHCART, N.B.

FIG. 146. DRY AIR PUMPS.

FIG. 145. WET AIR PUMPS.

PLATE XVII.

TURBINE-DRIVEN QUADRUPLE-SCREW CUNARD LINER "LUSITANIA."

CONSTRUCTED AND ENGINED BY MESSRS. JOHN BROWN AND CO., LIMITED, SHEFFIELD AND CLYDEBANK.

FIG. 188. THE "LUSITANIA" ON THE WAYS.

PLATE XVIII.

TURBINE-DRIVEN QUADRUPLE-SCREW CUNARD LINER "LUSITANIA."

CONSTRUCTED AND ENGINED BY MESSRS. JOHN BROWN AND CO., LIMITED, SHEFFIELD AND CLYDEBANK.

FIG. 189. VIEW SHOWING THE FOUR PROPELLERS.

PLATE XIX.

TURBINE-DRIVEN QUADRUPLE-SCREW CUNARD LINER "LUSITANIA."

CONSTRUCTED AND ENGINED BY MESSRS. JOHN BROWN AND CO., LIMITED, SHEFFIELD AND CLYDEBANK.

FIG. 190. VIEW OF BOW AND LAUNCHING-CRADLE.

FIG. 191. VIEW OF STERN AND LAUNCHING-CRADLE.

PLATE XX.

TURBINE-DRIVEN QUADRUPLE-SCREW CUNARD LINER "LUSITANIA."

CONSTRUCTED AND ENGINED BY MESSRS. JOHN BROWN AND CO., LIMITED, SHEFFIELD AND CLYDEBANK.

FIG. 192. THE LAUNCH OF THE "LUSITANIA."

FIG. 193. THE "LUSITANIA" LEAVING THE WAYS.

PLATE XXI.

TURBINE-DRIVEN QUADRUPLE-SCREW CUNARD LINER "LUSITANIA."

CONSTRUCTED AND ENGINED BY MESSRS. JOHN BROWN AND CO., LIMITED, SHEFFIELD AND CLYDEBANK.

FIG. 194. FIRST-CLASS DINING-SALOONS, SHOWING WELL AND DOME.

PLATE XXII.

TURBINE-DRIVEN QUADRUPLE-SCREW CUNARD LINER "LUSITANIA."

CONSTRUCTED AND ENGINED BY MESSRS. JOHN BROWN AND CO., LIMITED, SHEFFIELD AND CLYDEBANK.

FIG. 195.   FIRST-CLASS DINING-SALOONS; VIEW FROM SHELTER-DECK.

FIG. 196.   A CORNER OF THE FIRST-CLASS DINING-SALOON ON UPPER DECK.

PLATE XXIII.

TURBINE-DRIVEN QUADRUPLE-SCREW CUNARD LINER "LUSITANIA."

CONSTRUCTED AND ENGINED BY MESSRS. JOHN BROWN AND CO., LIMITED, SHEFFIELD AND CLYDEBANK.

FIG. 197. FIRST-CLASS SMOKING-ROOM.

FIG. 198. FORWARD PORTION OF FIRST-CLASS SMOKING-ROOM.

PLATE XXIV.

TURBINE-DRIVEN QUADRUPLE-SCREW CUNARD LINER "LUSITANIA."

CONSTRUCTED AND ENGINED BY MESSRS. JOHN BROWN AND CO., LIMITED, SHEFFIELD AND CLYDEBANK.

FIG. 199. FIRST-CLASS WRITING-ROOM AND LIBRARY.

FIG. 200. FIRST-CLASS LOUNGE.

PLATE XXV.

TURBINE-DRIVEN QUADRUPLE-SCREW CUNARD LINER "LUSITANIA."

CONSTRUCTED AND ENGINED BY MESSRS. JOHN BROWN AND CO., LIMITED, SHEFFIELD AND CLYDEBANK.

FIG. 202. ONE OF THE *En Suite* BED-ROOMS.

FIG. 201. FIREPLACE IN FIRST-CLASS LOUNGE.

PLATE XXVI.

TURBINE-DRIVEN QUADRUPLE-SCREW CUNARD LINER "LUSITANIA."

CONSTRUCTED AND ENGINED BY MESSRS. JOHN BROWN AND CO., LIMITED, SHEFFIELD AND CLYDEBANK.

FIG. 203. THE ENTRANCE HALL ON THE BOAT-DECK, WITH HOISTS.

FIG. 204. THE ENTRANCE HALL ON THE PROMENADE DECK, AND BUREAU.

PLATE XXVII.

TURBINE-DRIVEN QUADRUPLE-SCREW CUNARD LINER "LUSITANIA."

CONSTRUCTED AND ENGINED BY MESSRS. JOHN BROWN AND CO., LIMITED, SHEFFIELD AND CLYDEBANK.

FIG. 205. THE SECOND-CLASS LOUNGE.

FIG. 206. THE SECOND-CLASS SMOKING-ROOM.

PLATE XXVIII.

TURBINE-DRIVEN QUADRUPLE-SCREW CUNARD LINER "LUSITANIA."

CONSTRUCTED AND ENGINED BY MESSRS. JOHN BROWN AND CO., LIMITED, SHEFFIELD AND CLYDEBANK.

FIG. 207. ONE OF THE ALLEYWAYS.

FIG. 208. THE THIRD-CLASS DINING-SALOON.

PLATE XXIX.

THE WORKS OF THE BUILDERS OF THE "LUSITANIA."

MESSRS. JOHN BROWN AND CO., LIMITED, SHEFFIELD AND CLYDEBANK.

FIG. 212. THE PRESS WHICH FORGED THE "LUSITANIA'S" SHAFTS AT THE SHEFFIELD WORKS.

FIG. 213. ENGINE-SHAFT, WITH STRAIGHT SHAFT FOR ELECTRIC GENERATOR (22 TONS).

FIG. 214. MACHINE SIMULTANEOUSLY BORING THE HOLE FOR THE PINS OF TWO DISC CRANKS (82-TON SHAFTS).

PLATE XXX.

THE WORKS OF THE BUILDERS OF THE "LUSITANIA."

MESSRS. JOHN BROWN AND CO., LIMITED, SHEFFIELD AND CLYDEBANK.

FIG. 215.   ONE OF THE MACHINE SHOPS AT THE SHEFFIELD WORKS.

FIG. 216.   EDGE-PLANING, SLOTTING AND SURFACE-PLANING MACHINES AT THE SHEFFIELD WORKS.

PLATE XXXI.

THE WORKS OF THE BUILDERS OF THE "LUSITANIA."

MESSRS. JOHN BROWN AND CO., LIMITED, SHEFFIELD AND CLYDEBANK.

FIG. 217. ONE OF THE MACHINE SHOPS AT THE SHEFFIELD WORKS.

FIG. 218. THE "ROBERTS" STEEL FOUNDRY AT THE SHEFFIELD WORKS.

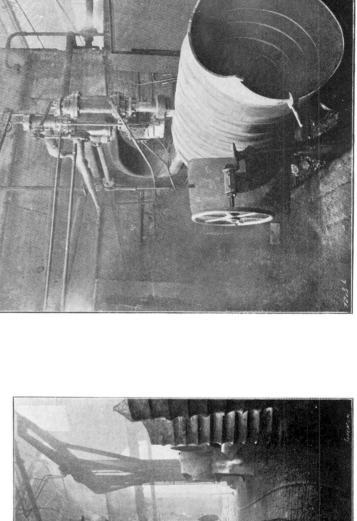

FIG. 220. WELDING BOILER FLUES AT THE SHEFFIELD WORKS.

FIG. 219. IN THE BOILER FLUE DEPARTMENT AT THE SHEFFIELD WORKS.

PLATE XXXII.

THE WORKS OF THE BUILDERS OF THE "LUSITANIA."

Fig. 222. Hydraulic Presses for Making Shells at Norfolk Works.

Fig. 221. Steam Hammer for Forging Projectiles at Norfolk Works.

Fig. 223. Machining Projectiles at Norfolk Works.

Fig. 224. Finishing Projectiles at Norfolk Works.

PLATE XXXIII.

THE WORKS OF THE BUILDERS OF THE "LUSITANIA."

MESSRS. JOHN BROWN AND CO., LIMITED, SHEFFIELD AND CLYDEBANK.

FIG. 228. BRASS FOUNDRY AT CLYDEBANK WORKS.

FIG. 229. BRASS FINISHING SHOP AT CLYDEBANK WORKS.

PLATE XXXIV.

THE WORKS OF THE BUILDERS OF THE "LUSITANIA."

MESSRS. JOHN BROWN AND CO., LIMITED, SHEFFIELD AND CLYDEBANK.

FIG. 230. BALANCING A TURBINE ROTOR AT CLYDEBANK WORKS.

FIG. 231. TURBINE CASING IN BORING MACHINE AT CLYDEBANK WORKS.

PLATE XXXV.

THE WORKS OF THE BUILDERS OF THE "LUSITANIA."

FIG. 232. IN THE TURBINE-ERECTING SHOP AT CLYDEBANK WORKS.

PLATE XXXVI.

THE TURBINE-DRIVEN QUADRUPLE-SCREW CUNARD LINER "LUSITANIA."

CONSTRUCTED AND ENGINED BY MESSRS. JOHN BROWN AND CO., LIMITED, SHEFFIELD AND CLYDEBANK.

FIG. 233. THE "LUSITANIA" STEAMING AT FULL SPEED.

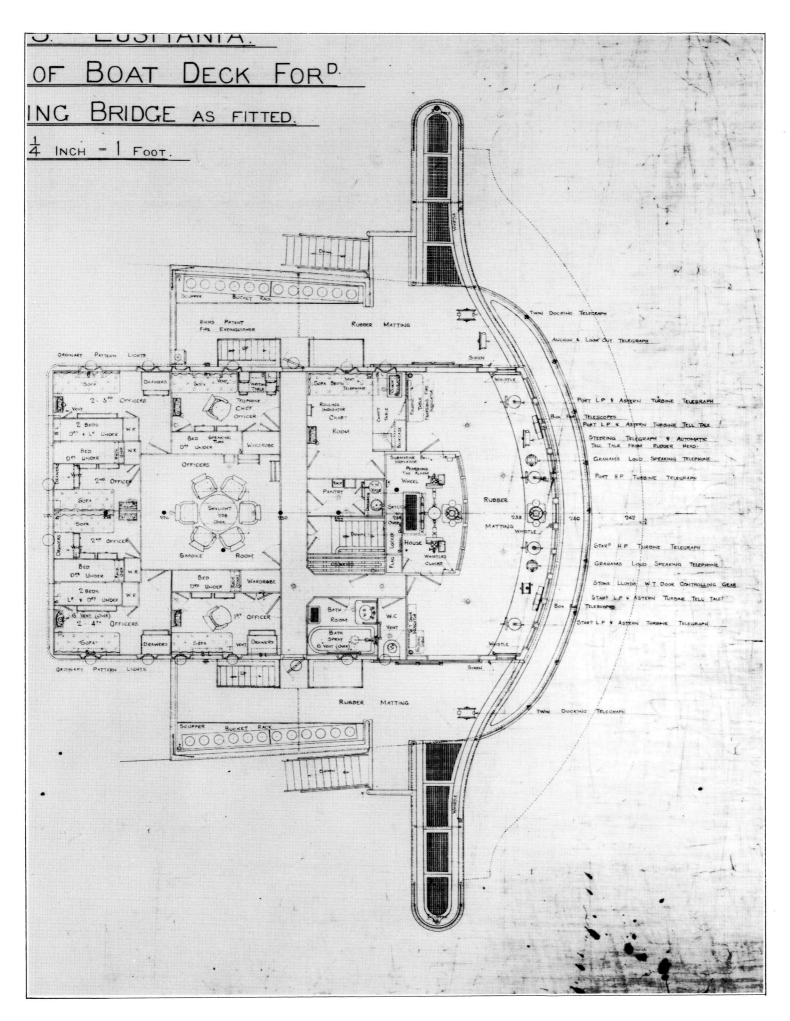

PLATE XXXVII.

THE TURBINE-DRIVEN QUADRUPLE-SCREW CUNARD LINER "LUSITANIA;" PROFILE AND DECK PLANS.

CONSTRUCTED AND ENGINED BY MESSRS. JOHN BROWN AND CO., LIMITED, SHEFFIELD AND CLYDEBANK.

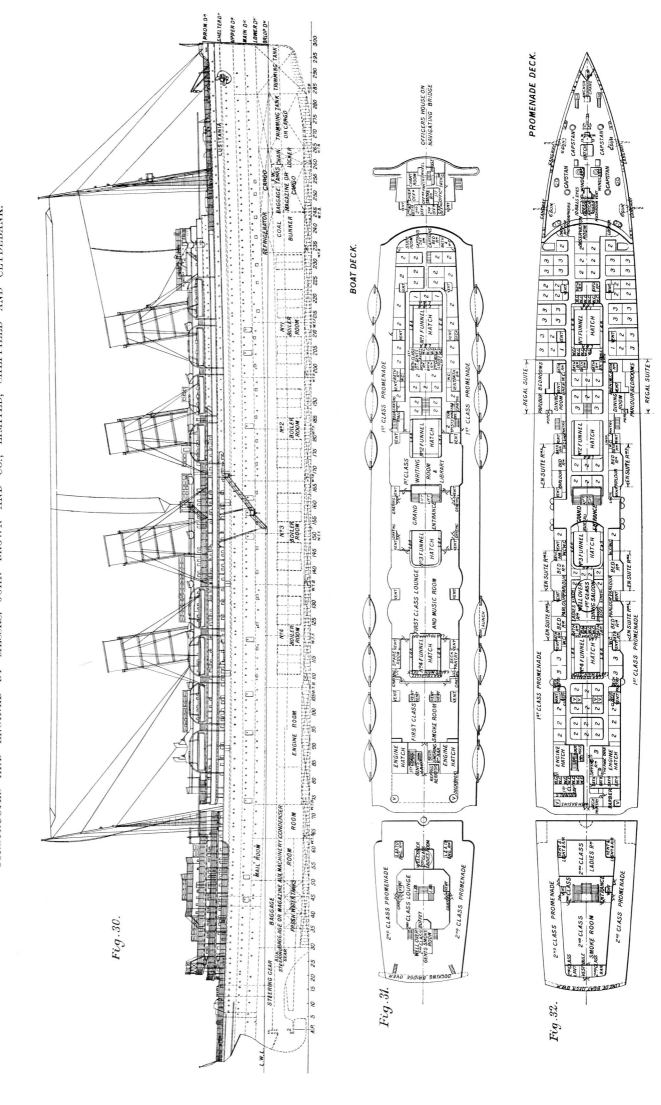

Fig. 30.

Fig. 31.

Fig. 32.

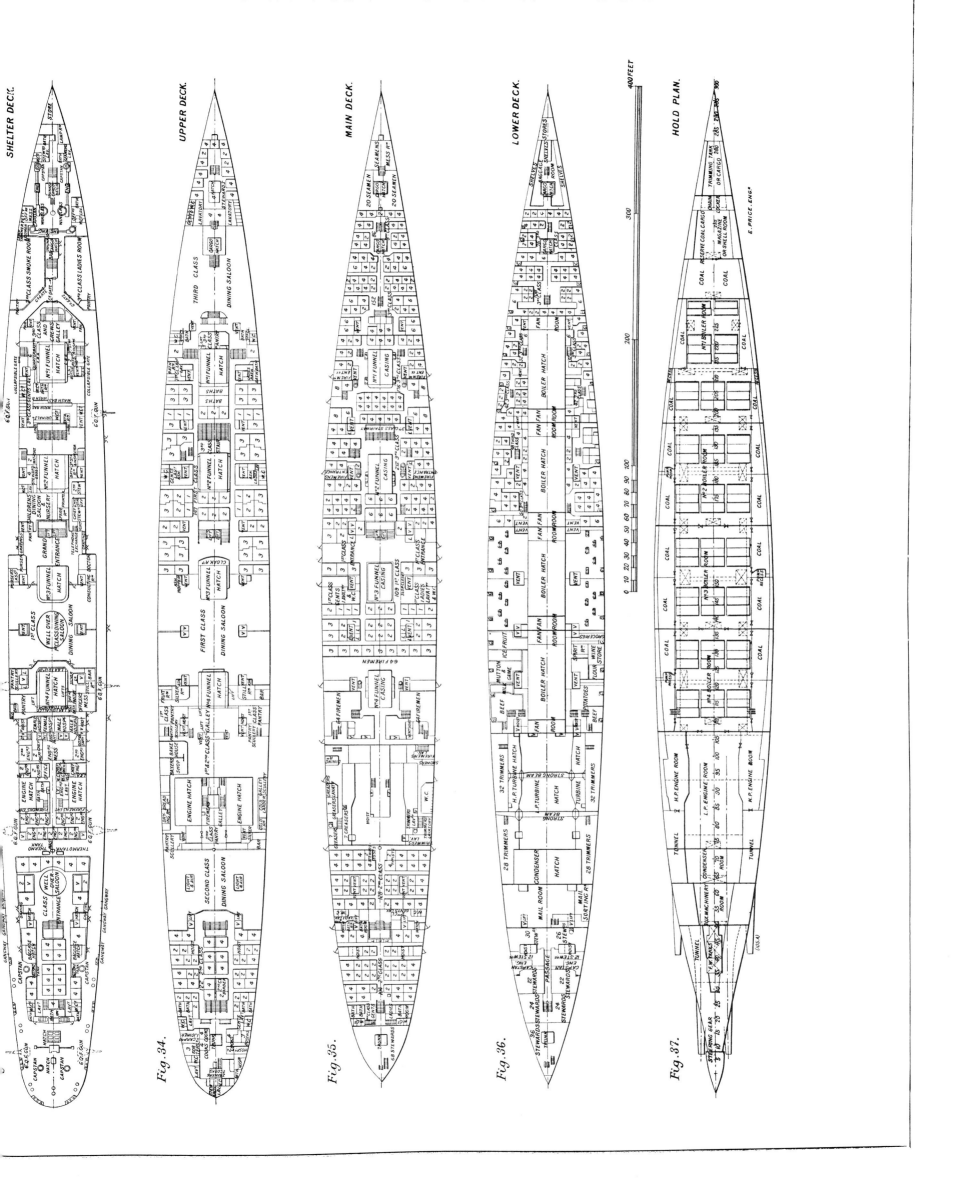

SHELTER DECK.

Fig. 34. UPPER DECK.

Fig. 35. MAIN DECK.

Fig. 36. LOWER DECK.

Fig. 37. HOLD PLAN.

E. PRICE. ENG.ᴿ

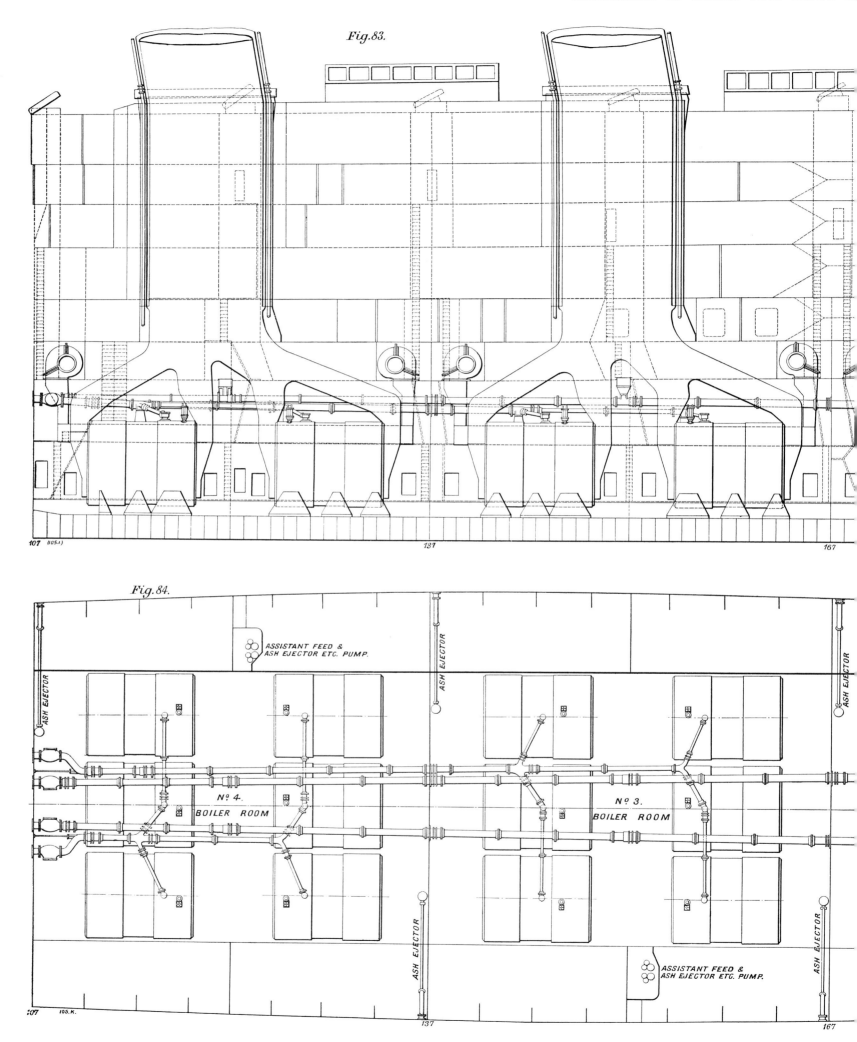

Fig.83.

Fig.84.

PLATE XXXVIII.

R "LUSITANIA;" GENERAL ARRANGEMENT OF BOILERS.

O., LIMITED, SHEFFIELD AND CLYDEBANK.

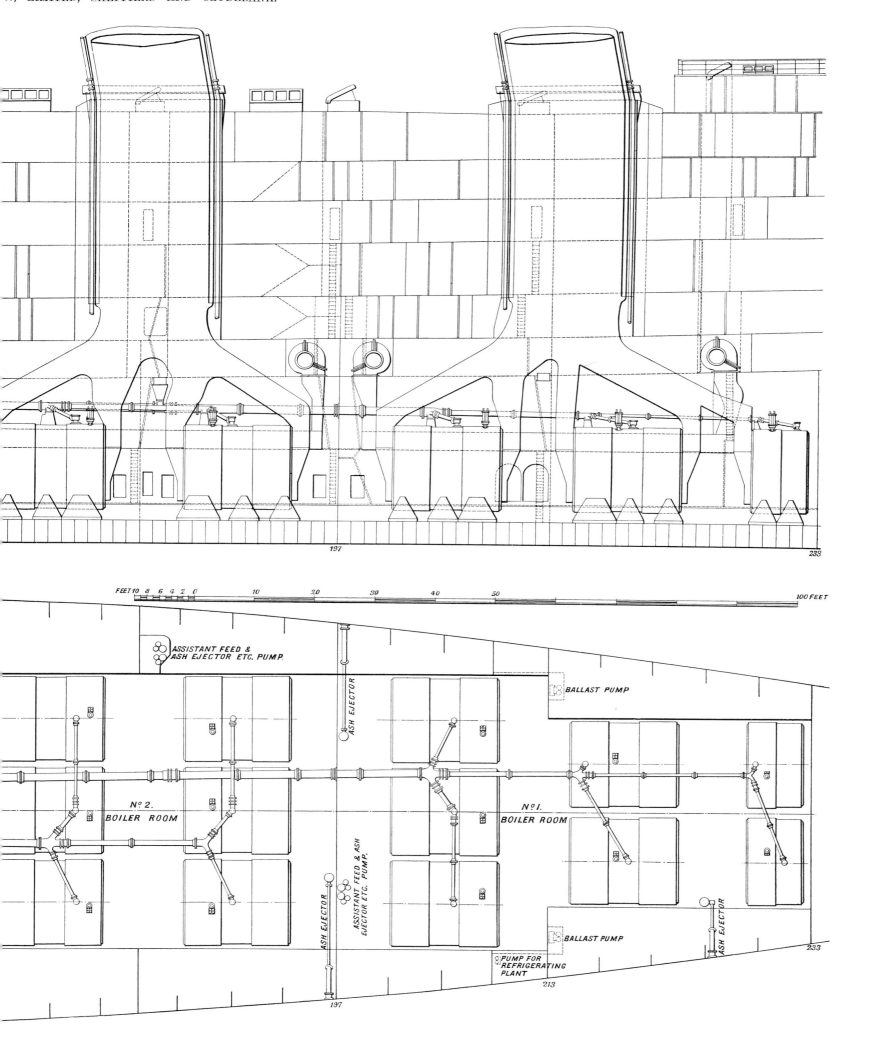

FEET 10 8 6 4 2 0   10   20   30   40   50   100 FEET

ASSISTANT FEED & ASH EJECTOR ETC. PUMP.

ASH EJECTOR

BALLAST PUMP

Nº 2. BOILER ROOM

Nº 1. BOILER ROOM

ASH EJECTOR

ASSISTANT FEED & ASH EJECTOR ETC. PUMP.

ASH EJECTOR

BALLAST PUMP

PUMP FOR REFRIGERATING PLANT

ASH EJECTOR

197   213   233

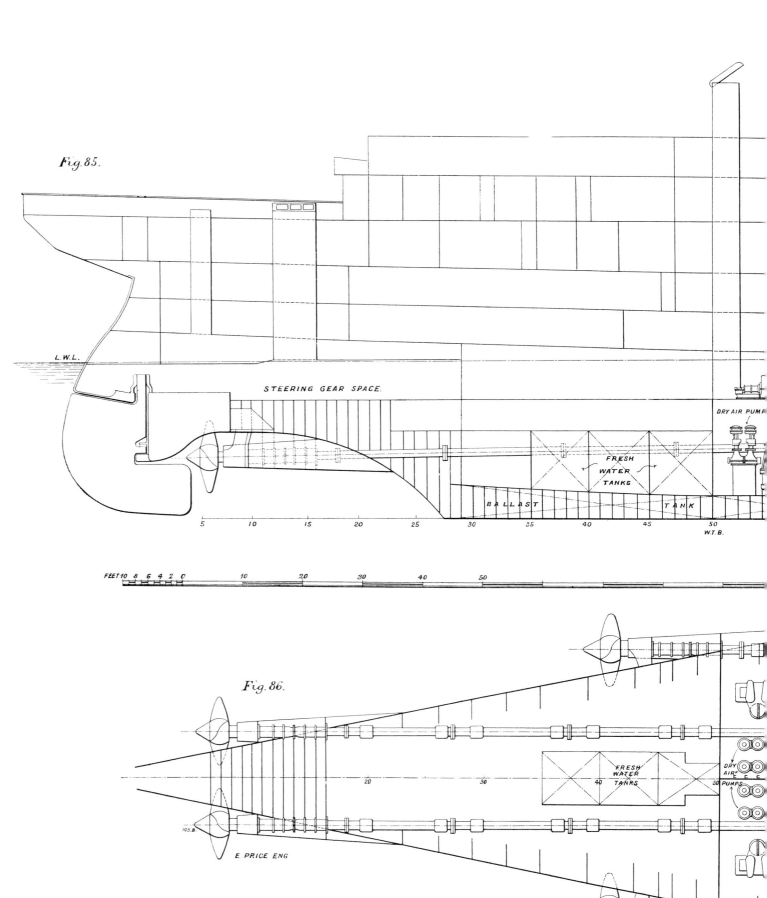

Fig. 85.

L.W.L.

STEERING GEAR SPACE.

DRY AIR PUMP

FRESH
WATER
TANKS

BALLAST   TANK

5   10   15   20   25   30   35   40   45   50
W.T.B.

FEET 10 8 6 4 2 0   10   20   30   40   50

Fig. 86.

FRESH
WATER
TANKS

DRY
AIR
PUMPS

20   30   40   50

105.B
E. PRICE ENG

PLATE XXXIX.

"LUSITANIA"; GENERAL ARRANGEMENT OF TURBINES.

O., LIMITED, SHEFFIELD AND CLYDEBANK.

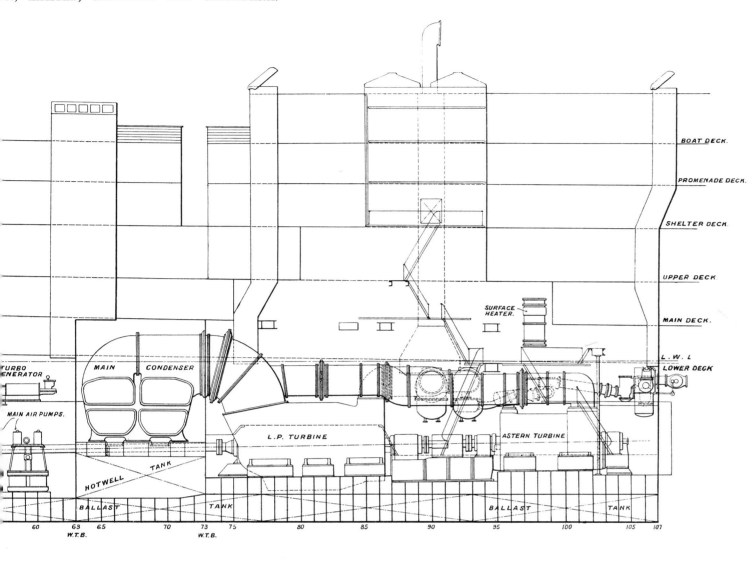

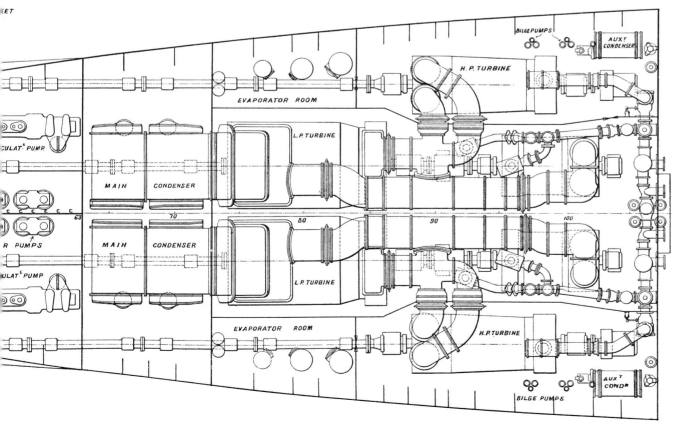

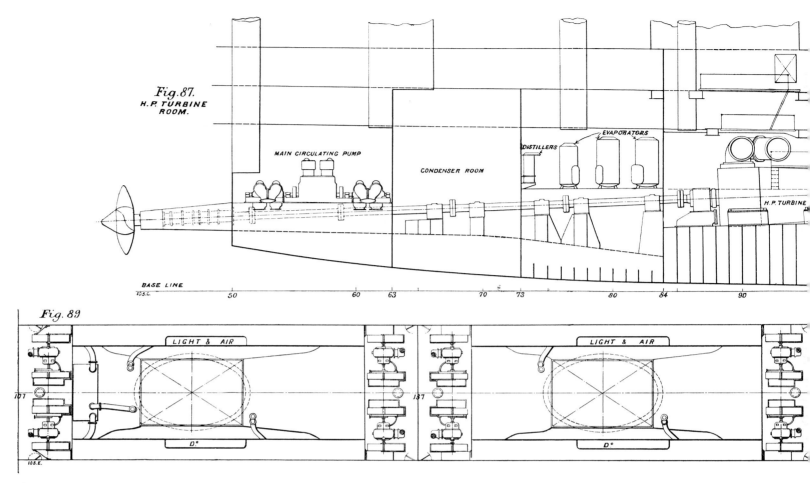

Fig. 87.
H.P. TURBINE ROOM.

MAIN CIRCULATING PUMP

CONDENSER ROOM

DISTILLERS   EVAPORATORS

H.P. TURBINE

BASE LINE
105.C.

50   60   63   70   73   80   84   90

Fig. 89

LIGHT & AIR

LIGHT & AIR

107

137

D°

D°

105.E.

FEET 10 8 6 4 2 0   10

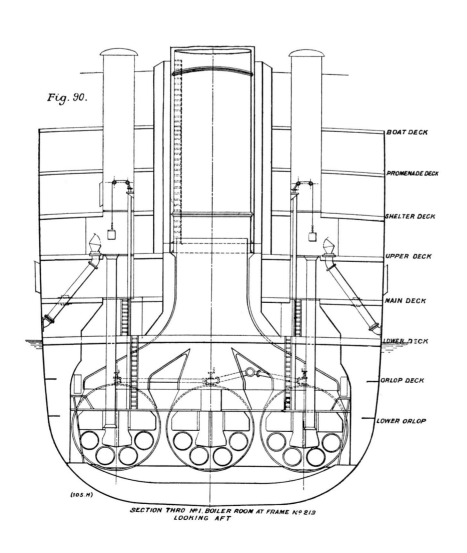

Fig. 90.

BOAT DECK

PROMENADE DECK

SHELTER DECK

UPPER DECK

MAIN DECK

LOWER DECK

ORLOP DECK

LOWER ORLOP

(105.H)

SECTION THRO N°1. BOILER ROOM AT FRAME N° 213
LOOKING AFT

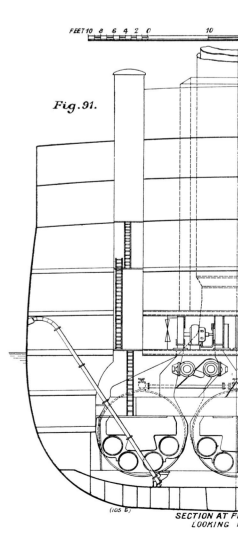

Fig. 91.

(105.B)

SECTION AT FR
LOOKING F

PLATE XL.

'LUSITANIA;" GENERAL ARRANGEMENT OF MACHINERY.

AND CO., LIMITED, SHEFFIELD AND CLYDEBANK.

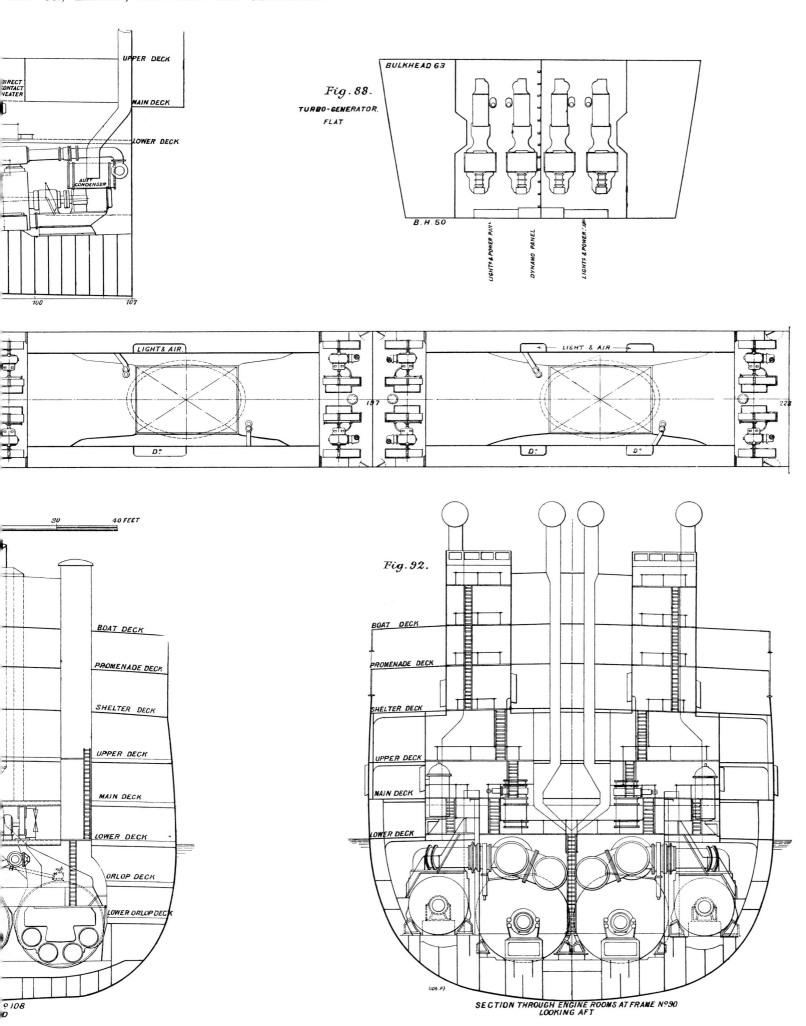

Fig. 88.
TURBO-GENERATOR.
FLAT

BULKHEAD 63

B.H. 50

Fig. 92.

SECTION THROUGH ENGINE ROOMS AT FRAME N°90
LOOKING AFT

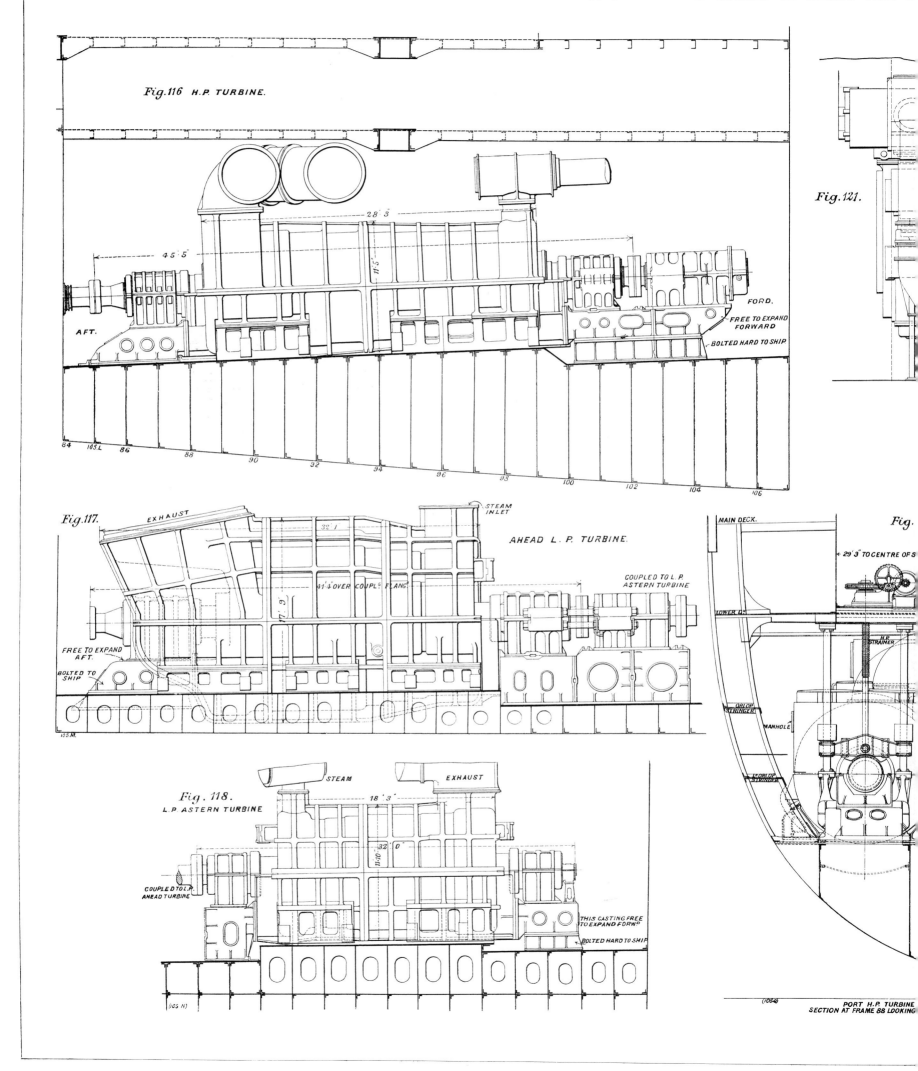

Fig.116 H.P. TURBINE.

28 3

45 5

11 5

FORD.

FREE TO EXPAND
FORWARD

BOLTED HARD TO SHIP

AFT.

Fig.121.

84 105.L 86 88 90 92 94 96 98 100 102 104 106

Fig.117.

EXHAUST

STEAM
INLET

AHEAD L.P. TURBINE.

32 1

41 4 OVER COUPLᵍ FLANG.

17 9

COUPLED TO L.P.
ASTERN TURBINE

FREE TO EXPAND
AFT.

BOLTED TO
SHIP

105.M.

MAIN DECK.

Fig.

29 3 TO CENTRE OF S

LOWER D.

H.P.
STRAINER

ORLOP
STRINGER

MANHOLE

ORLOP
STRINGER

Fig.118.
L.P. ASTERN TURBINE

STEAM

EXHAUST

18 3

32 0

11 10 0

COUPLED TO L.P.
AHEAD TURBINE

THIS CASTING FREE
TO EXPAND FORWᵈ

BOLTED HARD TO SHIP

(105 N)

(105)

PORT H.P. TURBINE
SECTION AT FRAME 88 LOOKING

PLATE XLI.

LINER "LUSITANIA;" DETAILS OF TURBINES.

AND CO., LIMITED, SHEFFIELD AND CLYDEBANK.

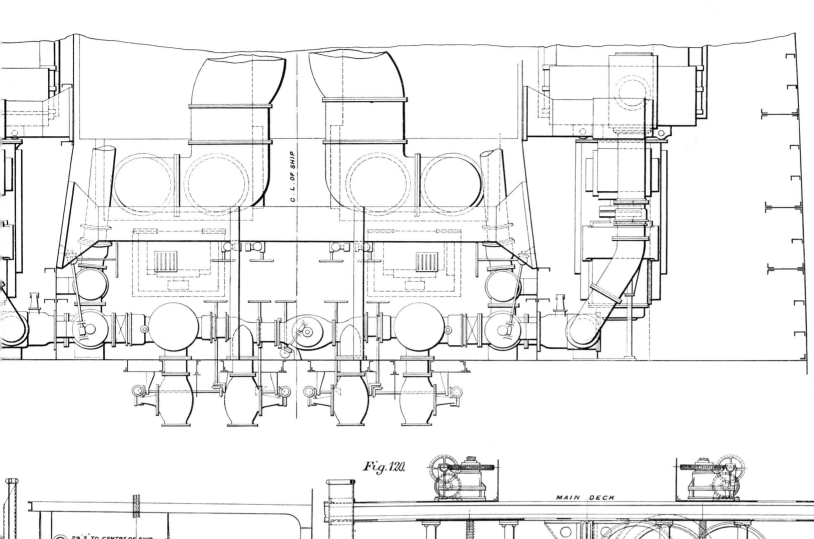

C. L. OF SHIP

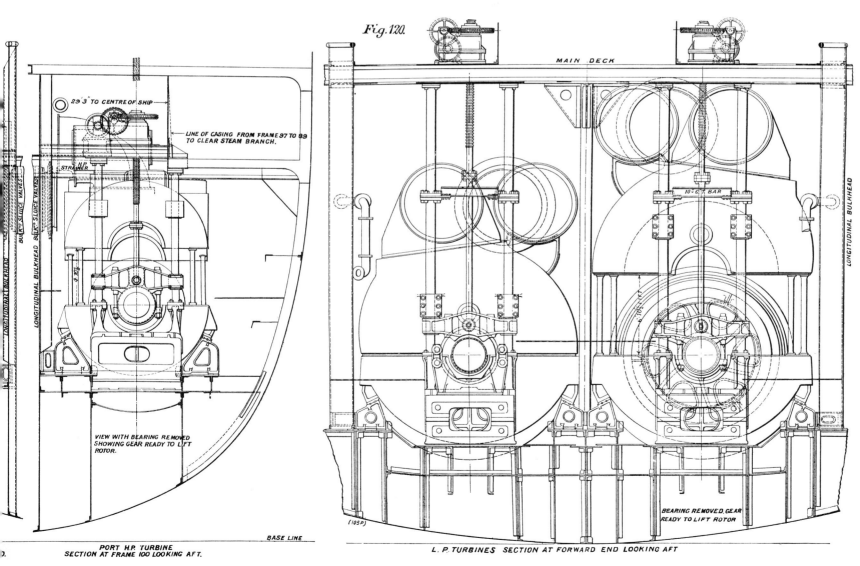

Fig. 120.

29' 3" TO CENTRE OF SHIP

LINE OF CASING FROM FRAME 97 TO 99
TO CLEAR STEAM BRANCH.

H.P. STRAINER

BILGE SLUICE VALVES

BILGE SLUICE VALVES

LONGITUDINAL BULKHEAD

LONGITUDINAL BULKHEAD

MAIN DECK

10'-6" BAR

LONGITUDINAL BULKHEAD

VIEW WITH BEARING REMOVED
SHOWING GEAR READY TO LIFT
ROTOR.

(105 P)

BEARING REMOVED, GEAR
READY TO LIFT ROTOR

BASE LINE

PORT H.P. TURBINE
SECTION AT FRAME 100 LOOKING AFT.

L. P. TURBINES SECTION AT FORWARD END LOOKING AFT.

PLATE XLII.

TURBINE-DRIVEN QUADRUPLE-SCREW CUNARD LINER "LUSITANIA."

CONSTRUCTED AND ENGINED BY MESSRS. JOHN BROWN AND CO., LIMITED, SHEFFIELD AND CLYDEBANK.

FIG. 235. FIRST-CLASS WRITING-ROOM AND LIBRARY.

FIG. 234. FIREPLACE IN FIRST-CLASS SMOKING-ROOM.

PLATE XLIII.

TURBINE-DRIVEN QUADRUPLE-SCREW CUNARD LINER "LUSITANIA."

CONSTRUCTED AND ENGINED BY MESSRS. JOHN BROWN AND CO., LIMITED, SHEFFIELD AND CLYDEBANK.

FIGS. 236 AND 237. FIRST-CLASS WRITING-ROOM AND LIBRARY.

TURBINE-DRIVEN QUADRUPLE-SCREW CUNARD LINER "LUSITANIA."

CONSTRUCTED AND ENGINED BY MESSRS. JOHN BROWN AND CO., LIMITED, SHEFFIELD AND CLYDEBANK.

PLATE XLIV.

TURBINE-DRIVEN QUADRUPLE-SCREW CUNARD LINER "LUSITANIA."

CONSTRUCTED AND ENGINED BY MESSRS. JOHN BROWN AND CO., LIMITED, SHEFFIELD AND CLYDEBANK.

FIG. 238. FIRST-CLASS ELEVATOR, BOAT DECK.

FIG. 239. A CORNER OF THE FIRST-CLASS DINING-SALOON ON SHELTER DECK.

PLATE XLV.

TURBINE-DRIVEN QUADRUPLE-SCREW CUNARD LINER "LUSITANIA."

CONSTRUCTED AND ENGINED BY MESSRS. JOHN BROWN AND CO., LIMITED, SHEFFIELD AND CLYDEBANK.

FIG. 240. VIEW OF BRIDGE.

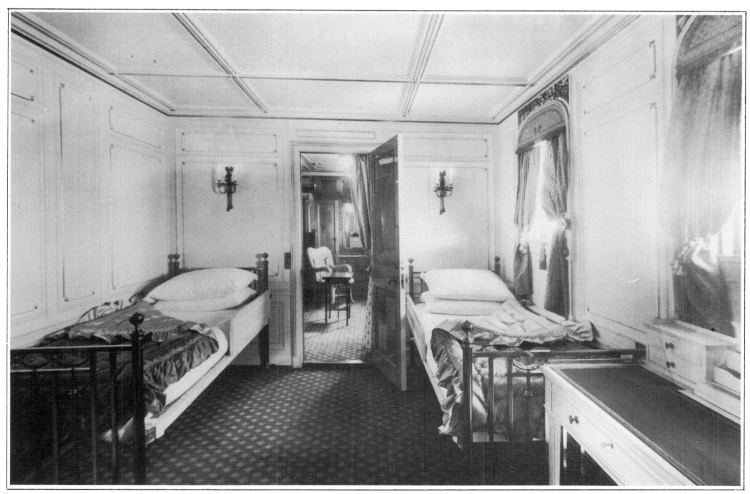

FIG. 241 ONE OF THE *EN SUITE* BEDROOMS.

PLATE XLVI.

TURBINE-DRIVEN QUADRUPLE-SCREW CUNARD LINER "LUSITANIA."

CONSTRUCTED AND ENGINED BY MESSRS. JOHN BROWN AND CO., LIMITED, SHEFFIELD AND CLYDEBANK.

FIG. 242. REGAL SUITE DINING ROOM.

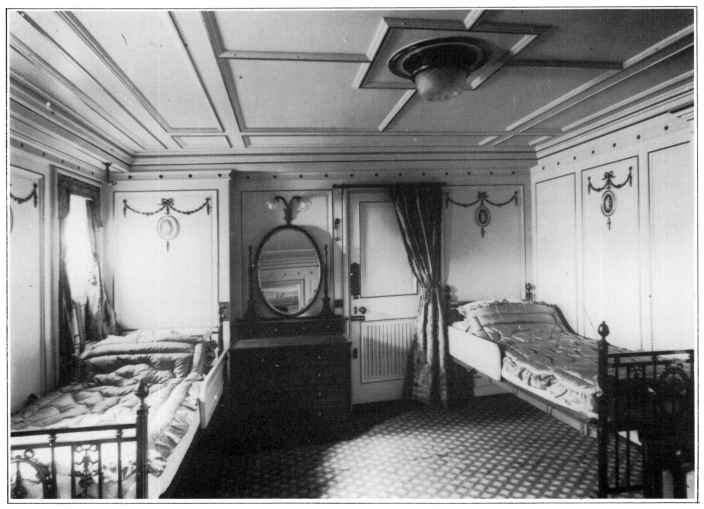

FIG. 243. REGAL SUITE BEDROOM.

PLATE XLVII.

TURBINE-DRIVEN QUADRUPLE-SCREW CUNARD LINER "LUSITANIA."

CONSTRUCTED AND ENGINED BY MESSRS. JOHN BROWN AND CO., LIMITED, SHEFFIELD AND CLYDEBANK.

FIG. 244. REGAL SUITE BEDROOM.

FIG. 245. *EN SUITE* BEDROOM.

PLATE XLVIII.

TURBINE-DRIVEN QUADRUPLE-SCREW CUNARD LINER "LUSITANIA."

CONSTRUCTED AND ENGINED BY MESSRS. JOHN BROWN AND CO., LIMITED, SHEFFIELD AND CLYDEBANK.

FIG. 247. FIRST-CLASS THREE-BERTH STATEROOM.

FIG. 246. CORNER OF FIRST-CLASS DINING SALOON.

PLATE XLIX.

TURBINE-DRIVEN QUADRUPLE-SCREW CUNARD LINER "LUSITANIA."

CONSTRUCTED AND ENGINED BY MESSRS. JOHN BROWN AND CO., LIMITED, SHEFFIELD AND CLYDEBANK.

FIG. 248. FIRST-CLASS VERANDAH CAFÉ.

FIG. 249. FIRST-CLASS BARBER'S SHOP.

PLATE L.

TURBINE-DRIVEN QUADRUPLE-SCREW CUNARD LINER "LUSITANIA."

CONSTRUCTED AND ENGINED BY MESSRS. JOHN BROWN AND CO., LIMITED, SHEFFIELD AND CLYDEBANK.

FIG. 250. THE SECOND-CLASS LOUNGE.

FIG. 251. THE SECOND-CLASS SMOKING-ROOM.

PLATE LI.

TURBINE-DRIVEN QUADRUPLE-SCREW CUNARD LINER "LUSITANIA."

CONSTRUCTED AND ENGINED BY MESSRS. JOHN BROWN AND CO., LIMITED, SHEFFIELD AND CLYDEBANK.

Fig. 252. The Second-Class Ladies' Drawing Room.

Fig. 253. The Second-Class Dining-Saloon.

PLATE LII.

TURBINE-DRIVEN QUADRUPLE-SCREW CUNARD LINER "LUSITANIA."

CONSTRUCTED AND ENGINED BY MESSRS. JOHN BROWN AND CO., LIMITED, SHEFFIELD AND CLYDEBANK.

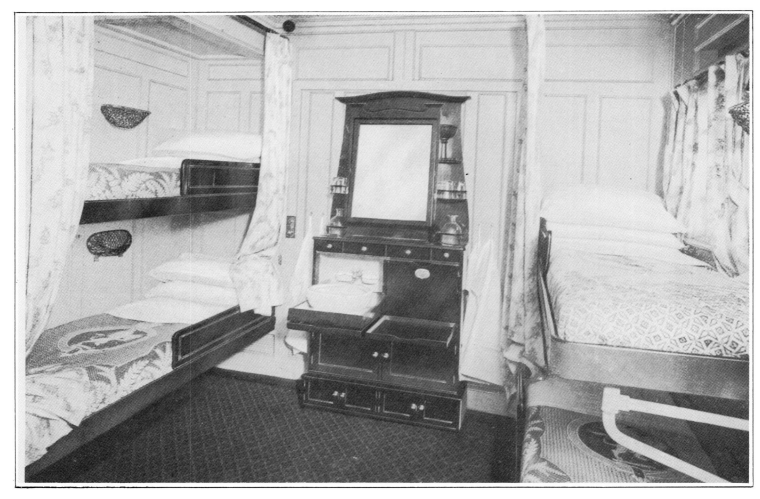

FIG. 254. SECOND-CLASS FOUR-BERTH STATEROOM.

FIG. 255. THE THIRD-CLASS GENERAL ROOM, SET FOR DINING.

PLATE LIII.

TURBINE-DRIVEN QUADRUPLE-SCREW CUNARD LINER "LUSITANIA."

CONSTRUCTED AND ENGINED BY MESSRS. JOHN BROWN AND CO., LIMITED, SHEFFIELD AND CLYDEBANK.

Fig. 257. Third-Class Four-Berth Cabin.

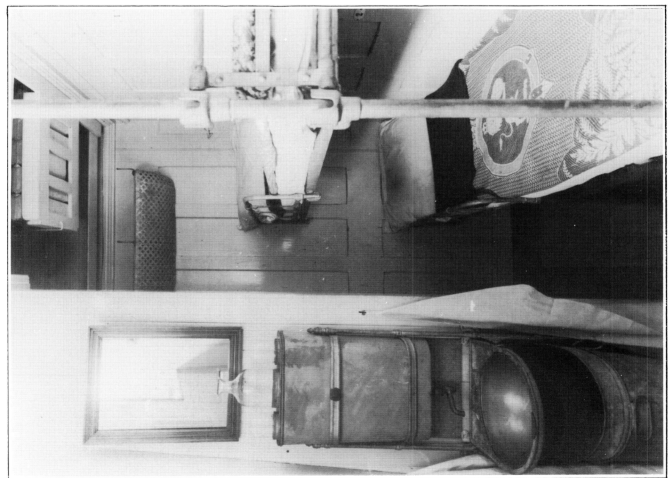

Fig. 256. Third-Class Two-Berth Cabin.

PLATE LIV.

TURBINE-DRIVEN QUADRUPLE-SCREW CUNARD LINER "LUSITANIA."

CONSTRUCTED AND ENGINED BY MESSRS. JOHN BROWN AND CO., LIMITED, SHEFFIELD AND CLYDEBANK.

FIG. 258. SECOND-CLASS PROMENADE, BOAT DECK (PORT SIDE).

FIG. 259. SECOND-CLASS PROMENADE, BOAT DECK (STARBOARD SIDE).

PLATE LV.

TURBINE-DRIVEN QUADRUPLE-SCREW CUNARD LINER "LUSITANIA."

CONSTRUCTED AND ENGINED BY MESSRS. JOHN BROWN AND CO., LIMITED, SHEFFIELD AND CLYDEBANK.

FIGS. 260 and 261. MAIDEN VOYAGE. ARRIVAL NEW YORK. 13 SEPT. 1907.

PLATE LVI.

THE TURBINE-DRIVEN QUADRUPLE-SCREW CUNARD LINER "LUSITANIA;" CUTAWAY OF SECOND-CLASS DINING SALOON

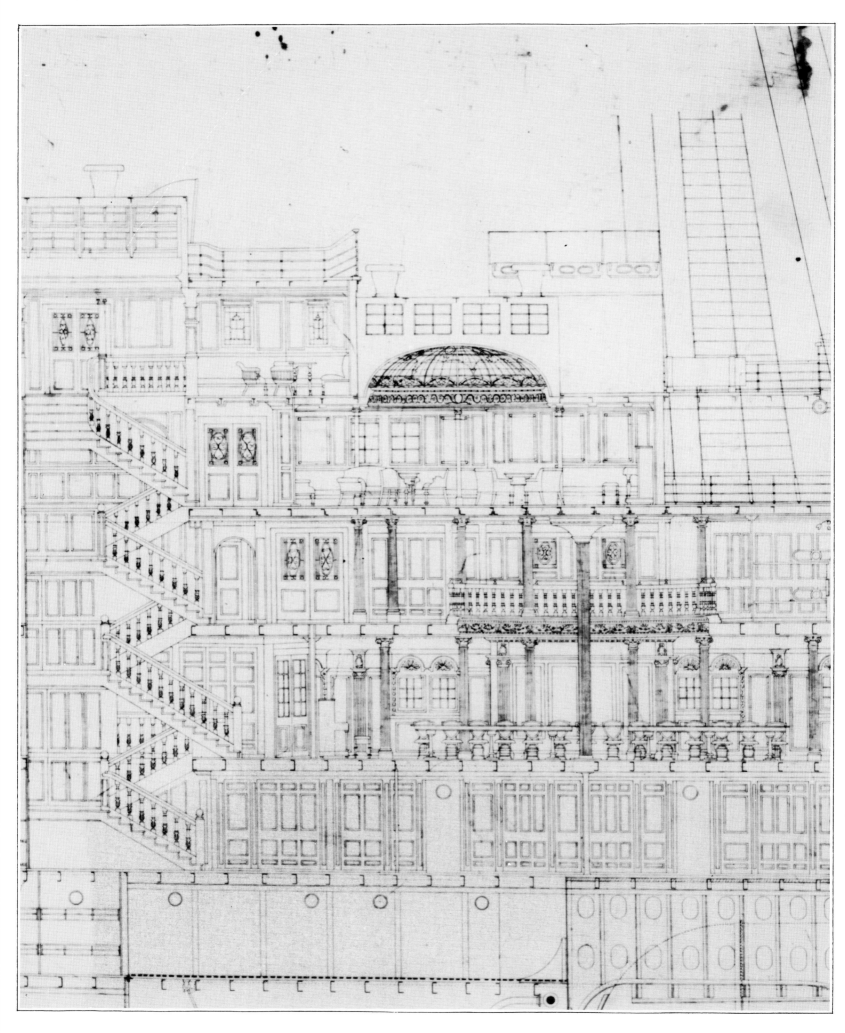

FIG. 262. CUTAWAY OF SECOND-CLASS DINING SALOON.   (CROWN COPYRIGHT)

PLATE LVII.

THE TURBINE-DRIVEN QUADRUPLE-SCREW CUNARD LINER "LUSITANIA;" CUTAWAY OF FIRST-CLASS DINING SALOON

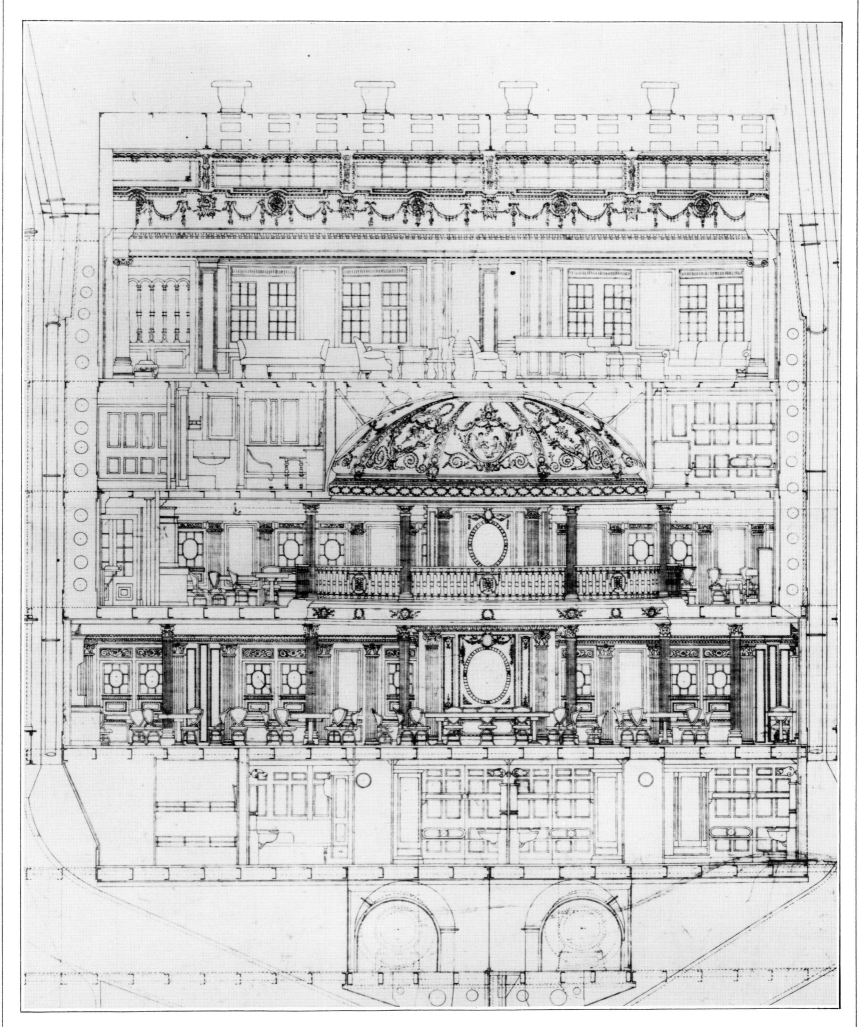

FIG. 263. CUTAWAY OF FIRST-CLASS DINING SALOON. (CROWN COPYRIGHT)

PLATE LVIII.

THE TURBINE-DRIVEN QUADRUPLE-SCREW CUNARD
LINER "LUSITANIA;" CUTAWAY OF ELEVATORS

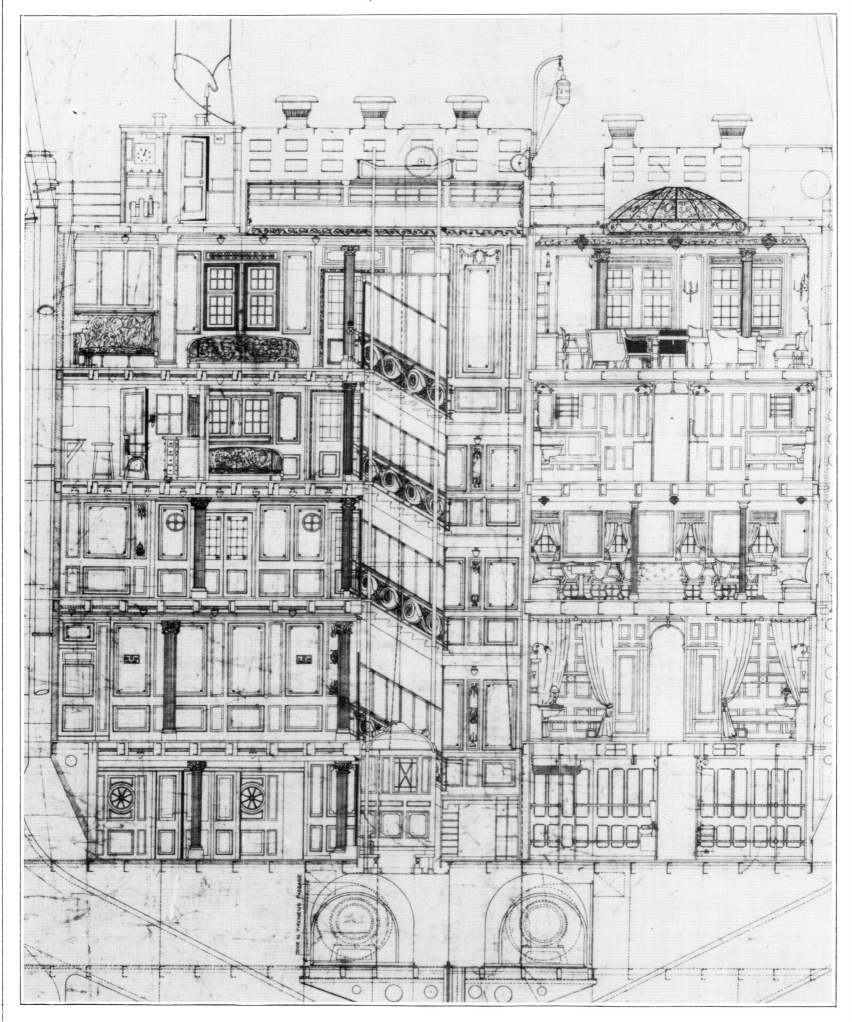

FIG. 264. CUTAWAY OF ELEVATORS.   (CROWN COPYRIGHT)